Matters of Death

(Volume Two of *Matters of Life and Death*)

Matters of Death

Meanings of the End of Life

by

Norman Weeks

Matters of Death

ISBN: 979-8-5962-8983-1

Copyright © 2021 Norman Weeks

Cover photo: The dove of the Holy Spirit, apse window, St. Peter's Basilica, the Vatican, Rome.

Matters of Death

Table of Contents
(by section numbers)

"A Prelude in Sentences" (section 101)

"Death Interpreted" (sections 102 to 133)

(Wayside:) **"The Morbidity of Authors"** (sections 134 to 165)

"Incidents of Death" (sections 166 to 200)

"A Prelude in Sentences"

i.

Death is no more like sleep than blindness is like a blink.

Death is the hemorrhagic evacuation of the accumulated contents of personal consciousness.

Death is no loss to the one who dies. For how can we possibly believe that Life is something we possess? And how can one who is no more suffer any loss? You will not lose your life; Life will lose you.

Birth isn't a pretty process. Dying isn't pretty, either. So, how about a little refined aesthetic in between?

How much appreciation, how much love can a human live out? Never enough, always wants more... Then death cuts off the yearning.

ii.

The one who asks "Why must I die?" may be the same one who once asked, "Why was I ever born?".

How can I believe in my own death? I've never known such a thing.

When others die, we may wish we had known them better. When we ourselves are to die, we wish we never came to know ourselves so well.

Those who die gradually have leisure to conduct a final evaluation of their own lives, an opportunity those who die abruptly do not have. Blessed are those who miss that opportunity!

To live in obscurity, to die soon forgotten... Could any autobiography know such bliss?

iii.

Reading obituaries is the taking-the-pulse of one's own mortality.

The sorrow at the news of a friend's death is tempered by the thought, "Well, he's dead, but I'm not."

The dead do not feel they have left, even if the survivors feel they have been left behind.

The loss of one friend or loved one may be the loss of friendship itself, of love itself. When a certain body dies, the embodiment may die.

The dead remain in memory…until memory too dies.

iv.

The tragedy of death is not the loss of living, but the loss of loving.

The human grief of Adam and Eve was not for the eternal loss of Paradise for both, but the eternal loss to one by the death of the other.

Have you heard of the widow whose new romance began at the funeral of her husband? Life goes on…and love may be resurrected from the dead.

The one whose death I would regret most would be the one whose love I could never prove worthy of.

If only we could devour ourselves before we died! If only we could totally devour our beloved before she died!

v.

As life is moralized, so too is death. And so, there can be no animal innocence in either.

Death is bad…only in the sense that empty nothingness is worse than something. Death is good… Well, at least it is good-bye.

The good death is one that is accomplished without thoroughly demoralizing the bystanders.

But: No one who has died has to endure any criticism about how he did it.

Protracted dying is tedious. Protracted living no less so.

vi.

I once had a dread: "My funeral. What if nobody comes?" Today I think: "My funeral. Now all these people show up and finally show me some attention."

Those who think that death is the end of vanity have not read the deceased's instructions for the funeral arrangements.

Every priest's most fervent fantasy is to preside at his own funeral.

To attend a divorced spouse's funeral: "Well now, this love, this connection, is truly done for, at last."

A child conducts a funeral for a dead pet:—An expression and show of mock sorrow, precedent and practice for many another funeral the child will attend through life.

vii.

The human is the only animal that can think about death... But then, the intellect can also contemplate the Void.

Life must have meaning, we believe. Well then, so too death must have meaning... See where all that semantic craving leads?

Who can know the instant of one's own conception? Who can know the instant of one's own death? One's own beginning and end are unknowable.

Death is like life, in that it carries us along, we hardly perceiving what it's all about, what's happening to us.

Those who write about death are ignorant. Those who write about life may be ignorant too, but they believe they have some little experience to back them.

viii.

"The physical dies. The spiritual lives forever."— Now, isn't that the most decisive trump you've ever heard?

"Dying is the means to eternal life."—the most absurd paradox ever conceived by the mind of the human animal... Oh, I meant to say, "the most comforting revealed truth".

To the religious person, death is the beginning of the mystery. To us naturalists, death is the end of the mystery.

It is better to live with philosophy than die with religion.

But: At death, religion reads some last words over the corpse of philosophy.

ix.

Death is lights-out...unless there is a metaphysical sunrise.

"Last Judgment"...What is God, a spiritual autopsist?

Earth...Heaven...Limbo...Purgatory...Hell:—What a lot of vast real estate in all our living and dying!

Heaven is the dream the dead one wants to have. Hell is the subject of death's only possible nightmare.

The fantasy of Heaven
Is one Hell of a distraction
From the reality
Of Earth.

x.

"Here today, gone tomorrow." How many more to-days will there be? Which tomorrow will be the dreaded one?

Death-anxiety, "Death, what then?", the sequel to life-anxiety, "Life, what next?".

Even God must be afraid of death. He tried it once, but only by surrogate proxy.

It is not death that we fear, but dying... Have we spent all our lives fearing living too?

We are not undone by our dying (at the end). We are undone by the *idea* of death (long, long before):— —

"Death Interpreted"

102

"Faulty Grammar"

It is a curiosity of our English language that we *are born* but we *die*, the former verb in the passive voice, the latter in the active.

True, being born is nothing we do. Rather, birth is done unto us. We are thrust into the world, passive objects, not active doers.

Yet, we say, "He died", as if he did something, performed some act. But that does not correctly describe the reality of it.

Death is not something we do. Like birth, death is done unto us. We are wrenched out of the world.

Our grammar misrepresents. Neither being born nor dying is any of our doing. We are processed into Life and processed out of Life. At both birth and death our bodies are passive.

In the two great events of our personal existence, we are *done unto*.

103

"The Dimensions of Death"

Considered from the perspective of Nature, death is the cessation of the life-sustaining processes of the body and the gradual breakdown of the whole corporal complex into constituent elements. Death is the end of individual life and the decomposition, dissolution, and recycling of the physical remains.

Human death is biological, but it is psychological too. What dies with the human is not only the physical-corporal, but the personal individuality. Human death is the sudden termination of unique identity, temperament, personality, intelligence, and character. When the body becomes inert, the person of its occupant is extinguished.

Animals have their individuality too, of course, but theirs is rudimentary compared to the rich personal individuality of the human, an individuality that emerges, develops, and attains mature idiosyncratic culmination. The distinction of human death from animal is that what is lost is not only an organism, but a person, a uniqueness of a complexity and sophistication unknown in the rest of Nature.

The human dead may have anticipated, but they cannot themselves experience the social consequences of their own death. Because the human is a social animal, loss-by-death is suffered by others; it ripples out through all the concentric circles of social relatedness.

The most personal loss is the sharp, deep grief felt by another human who had a one-to-one relationship of intimate love with the deceased. Death severs the bond of love, abruptly, completely, irrevocably. Feelings do continue, but love for the dead is a futile self-spending fantasy, because the dead can neither accept, nor respond to, nor reciprocate love. Death ends real relatedness, inter-relatedness. With the beloved gone, there remains only the grief vented in memories. Death leaves the mate bereft.

Death is the cessation of individuality and the severing of the bond of the individual with the one special other. Death is also a tear in the web of wider relatedness, that of the family, the basic unit of social belonging.

The rending of the web of family caused by a death gapes until it is filled by a still-living family member or until some other compensation can be made for the loss. The loss to the family is not only that of an indi-vidual, but of a filled role of responsibility, as mother, father, son, daughter, grandparent. Some losses, those of key members, or of several family members in a short time, might even cause an unraveling of the family web, leaving survivors feeling abandoned, insecure, and anxious about their future relatedness. Death orphans adults, as well as children.

A less devastating but still significant dimension of the death of a human being is the subtraction of that person from the grid of community and society. A particular death is felt personally by few in the wider society, but a void opens in the social structure as it does in the family. A death means the loss of a teacher or doctor or job-creating entrepreneur or the charismatic leader violently removed by assassination. An animal herd, after a death, suffers a slight reduction in strength-in-numbers and perhaps a brief struggle for leadership. For us humans, with our specialized roles, some among us are so indispensable that one death may be a social catastrophe.

The death of a single animal has little significance in Nature. The death of a human being, however, has great significance, significance psychological, social, and cultural too:

The human is the significating animal. The human assigns significance to death. Death is meaningful. A human death, especially that of a prominent person, in its situation of occurrence or manner of happening or untimeliness or association with a shared belief or conviction, may take on a significance seemingly out of all proportion to the commonness of the event. The Crucifixion, after all, was just a single death. The deaths of martyrs and heroes are as significant as their lives, in some cases even more so. Such deaths are taken as didactic and exemplary; and they are symbolic. That one crucifixion was invested with profound meaning.

The human feels a need to interpret deaths,—and to interpret death itself. Death, ordinary, common, universal, really quite trivial in the grand scheme of Nature. Yet, the human does not accept it so. We elaborate our interpretations of deaths and of death itself even to the level of ideology.

Memory keeps the dead alive long after their bodies have become the proverbial dust. Fond memories serve to reconcile the living to loss, to death, and to their own inevitable death-and-loss. Memory is also subjective and tendentious; it is an interpretation.

For us humans, death is not just a happening; it is also an idea. The emotionality of coping reactions to death eventually subsides, further feelings kept to oneself. Our ideas about death, on the other hand, are kept in mind, propagated among us, and forced as interpretation upon the next death we have to deal with. In the human, death as a natural phenomenon has been pre-empted by the intellect and has become fully enculturated.

104

"Inhumation/Cremation"

The manner of the disposition of the dead has its psychological consequences upon the survivors.

Burial is thought to be the oldest method of disposition. The dead no longer belong to the community of the living. They cannot just be laid aside, for then the living would still encounter them. If the dead are buried, they are removed. Interment is effective physical separation of the dead from the living.

However, out-of-sight is not out-of-mind. Interment may not necessarily be effective psychological separation, for if the grave is in a place known to relatives, it may be visited; psychological connection with the deceased may be continued. Such continuing proximity to the dead and ongoing connection may be psychologically unwholesome.

(—My mother told me that, when she was a girl, her father would force her and her sister to go to the grave of her mother, who had died of tuberculosis when my mother was thirteen; go to the grave every Sunday. That protracted mourning was a blight on a young girl's life.—)

Among the ancient Greeks and Romans, it was considered a terrible accursed fate for the dead to remain unburied. To be killed was terrible; to have one's burial neglected or prevented was even worse. To the pagans, burying the dead was a moral obligation; failure to fulfill that obligation or obstructing burial constituted sacrilege.

The Jews and Christians were most dutiful in their carrying-out of their obligation to bury the dead, accompanying the simple act of disposition with solemn requiem rites and ceremonies.

The Christians went beyond individual burial. In the Roman catacombs, they constructed vast complexes for the inhumation of their co-religionists, the community of those to be saved. The catacombs were the mustering station from which *the resurrection of the dead* would proceed.

Burial of the intact body suited the Christian ideology regarding the resurrection of the dead. The catacombs were also a place of frequent resort for the living, who sought in continuing contact with the holy martyrs an assurance that they would eventually join the resurrected *elect*.

The psychological consequences of Christian inhumation as practiced in the catacomb cult were chronic obsession with death, idolatry of corpses, a descent into macabre magic and superstition (the fetishism of relics), in all, that most unholy and unwholesome full-blown necrophilia that I have indicted elsewhere.

Against burial itself I make no psychological objection, provided the burial be in an unknown place, so that the living are distanced from the dead and from the morbid infiltration of death into life that protracted contact induces. But, you might object, anonymous burial goes against most cultural practice. So it does, but who thinks that culture is always psychologically wholesome?

Among the ancient Roman pagans, anonymous burial, as in the *puticuli*, the dumping pits on the Esquiline Hill, was considered a disgrace almost as bad as being left unburied. Only the destitute or pariahs suffered such impersonal mass disposition.

Shouldn't we show a respect and reverence for the dead? Yes, we should, but only insofar as that respect and reverence are for the living one that the deceased used to be. Veneration of corpses is nothing but a fetishism that verges upon pathological obsession. Let us venerate the dead, yes, but not prostrate ourselves regularly over their physical remains. The person of the person we remember was in the vital principle—call it *identity*, *personality*, *character*, or even *spirit* or *soul—*, not in the carcass left behind. Burial of loved ones at a known accessible place poses psychological risk to the bereaved.

The *puticuli* of ancient Rome were shameful, but the most primitive law of the city was enlightened. The Law of the Twelve Tables prohibited burial within the boundaries of the municipality. That taboo showed a wisdom psychological as well as hygienic. The dead must be separated from the living, by physical distance as by healthy forgetfulness. Grieving should have an end. Chronic grieving, exacerbated by the proximity of the

remains of the deceased, is unwholesome and subversive to living.

The pagan Greeks and Romans generally practiced
cremation, which was more conducive to the healing of
grief than inhumation was. The fires of the pyre ac-
celerated the dissolution that follows death. The soul of
the deceased, the person, ascended in the rising smoke
out of the world of the living. Healthy forgetfulness
could begin among those left behind.

Cremation should be followed by a scattering of the
ashes, for the dead can be outlived only if the remains of
the dead are gone. If the ashes of cremation are kept in
an urn and deposited in a mausoleum—as in the pagan
columbaria of ancient Rome—, there is the same sus-
ceptibility to necrophilic fetishism as there is in burial
in a known place. Worst of all is the urn of ashes on the
mantelpiece of the hearth of the home.

In Roman archaeology, we find both inhumation
graves and buried ash-urns, sometimes in promiscuous
mix in the same plot of ground, the necropolis of the
Roman Forum itself, for example. Roman tolerance of
cultic and religious differences was admirable.

When Christianity took Rome, the Church prescribed disposition by burial, in accord both with Jewish
precedent and with the doctrine of the resurrection of
the dead. During the Enlightenment and after, anti-
clerical atheists had themselves cremated to spite that
doctrine and the Church that espoused it. Cremation
then came under the ban of the Church, not as objectionable in itself, but for its ideological association
with atheism and spiteful heresy. In our own time, the
Catholic Church has eased its ban on cremation. The
Christians are now somewhat accommodating to pagan
ash-urns.

Disposition of the deceased is seemingly a hygienic
matter. Either inhumation or cremation is hygienically

adequate. Psychologically speaking, keeping of the corpse and keeping of the ashes are unhealthy, because they tend toward keeping close to the corpse and the ashes. But the person of the deceased, the living loved one, is gone; there is nothing of that person in the corpse or the ashes.

Whichever the manner of disposition, it should be followed by complete removal or irrecoverable scattering and by the gradual healing forgetfulness that comes from them. We must not let the dead seduce us away from wholesome living-on.

105

"Grave Goods"

"You can't take it with you" are words of wisdom that the human race has never really believed in. For, although we come naked and propertyless into the world, we have not gone out that way.

From the earliest known burials, 50,000 or so years ago, we know that material things for the deceased to take with were placed in the grave. The deceased would be clothed—(whether in everyday attire or in new duds, we cannot tell)—, natural nakedness furnished with at least a loincloth or other rudimentary animal skin. Upon the body or within reach would be placed implements and tools, weapons (the tools of the hunter), domestic utensils, and other material things from daily life. Besides such utilitarian items, the deceased would be further provisioned with artifacts to please vanity,—bracelets, necklaces, rings, beads and baubles. (Perhaps primordial man had not yet conceived the words of wisdom.)

The placing of material goods in the grave with the deceased did not confess that materialistic acquisitiveness we have been warned against, nor was it mere funereal ostentation. Rather, the practice indicates belief in an afterdeath continuity. If the deceased somehow continued, they would need the useful things of this world. The afterdeath was an afterlife. Human survival depending upon tools, grave goods were the means to postmortem survival.

Archaeologists are interested in grave goods for the evidence they provide for the developing technosphere, the tools of Neanderthal, Cro-Magnon and subsequent following a material evolution from chipped stone to copper to bronze to iron, from hunter-gatherer tool stage to agriculturalist to urban artisan, from crude to well-crafted. Grave goods are the most important remnant artifacts of the economy of early man.

From the material we infer the psychological or spiritual; from the things to the ideas:

Some Cro-Magnon graves of 30,000 or so years ago contain a quantity of red ochre. Was there a rite of sprinkling the corpse with a symbolic blood-of-life?

We have clues that primordial humans shared our tenderest feelings. Evidence for that is the poignance of pollen. How could pollen have been found buried with the deceased, unless a mourning loved one had cast flowers upon the body?

If primordial humans were to survive in a dangerous world, they had to look out for, and care for, one another. That care extended beyond death. Even as far back as the Neanderthals, food in the form of game meat was put into the grave for the nourishment of the deceased.

Grave goods are evidence that the primitive mind conceived of death in terms of extension and continuation of familiar daily life. (What do we *really* know, even today, except our own life as we human beings live it?) The deceased hunters were furnished with weapons, the agriculturalists with farm implements, the warriors with their spears (and perhaps their horse buried with them), and so on, unto the domestic day-to-day of highly civilized life, the pharaohs of Egypt provided with suites of furniture and even toilet facilities.

We have always come into the world with nothing, but few are destitute at their death-and-departure. The materials of our material life accompany us out.

That the dead should need tools or want jewels means that even early man believed in postmortem continuity. Afterdeath existence was pretty much like the life we knew. The body and the needs of the body went on, and it was up to the living to meet those needs. And so the bestowal of grave goods.

In attempting to infer psychological characteristics or spiritual beliefs of early man, our own metaphysical and religious imagination might impute to primitives too much of our own sophistication. Thus it has been thought that the Neanderthals buried their dead in a crouch to replicate the fetal position—(in which case we *would* go out of the world in the same way as before we came into it)—and practiced inhumation because burial was a return to Mother Earth, out of which we all come. I doubt whether the Neanderthals were embryologists or dogmatic about metaphors. More likely they interred the deceased in a crouched position just to economize on the labor of digging. And "Mother Earth" is an anachronism in relation to the Neanderthals.

Burial as a method of disposition would frustrate the hyenas and vultures, preventing the dismemberment and desecration they would commit upon loved ones, with whom there were strong lingering emotional bonds. Burial had its protective aspect.

Death has always been a grave matter, and a good grave required its grave goods. As we love life, or, at least, as life is all that we know, we interpret death as continuity of the familiar. What is more familiar than the tools by which we live?

If there is continuity beyond death, there should be a continuity of labor and vocation, for which we need the tools. I wouldn't think it unseemly if my ashes were intermingled with what I would like to take with me,—a pen and a pad of paper.

106

"Home Bodies"

At one Neanderthal burial, the grave was found surrounded by an outline arrangement of ibex skulls. The place of the dead was demarcated and delimited, taboo against trespass.

The body of the deceased may have been buried out of sight, concealed, but a visual marker may reveal where the body is. An enclosure sets off the space that had been chosen as the exclusive piece of Earth that belonged forever to the deceased.

Grave markers and enclosures identify and memorialize, as well as fend off profane encroachment.

In some cultures, earth is heaped up over the grave to form a barrow; in Italy, there were the Etruscan *tumuli*. A burial mound prevents careless trampling over the deceased and distinguishes the grave from what might otherwise be considered empty terrain. Whenever you excavate, deposit something in the hole, then fill up the hole, there is always soil left over, so even the very first graves must have had their mound of earth, if slight. With the barrows and *tumuli*, the mortuary landscape took on the topography of mounded abodes.

Abode is an appropriate word, for, as the instrumentality of grave goods indicates a belief that death is a continuity of daily work, so any markers at, enclosures around, or a structure over, a grave means that the state of the deceased within the grave is a continuity of abode. The pagan Romans used to place roof tiles over a grave, a clear analogy. The grave is a homey place, although you couldn't say that the occupant *lives* there.

Earliest humankind were nomadic, without fixed house-and-home, but, once dead and buried, even a nomad acquired property rights.

The Neanderthals surrounded their graves with ibex skulls, in order that the spirit of the deceased might have game to hunt—(ibex, a spirit-game)—nearby. The hunter, wanderer though he was, wouldn't have to go far to get the meat to sustain him. The ibex were corralled with him.

In later times, when humans became fully settled and residential, they thought that their dead would want to continue in a shelter. Graves then took on a residential appearance.

In the eastern Mediterranean, there are rock-cut tombs, the facades of some of which are house fronts. In various cultures, where there was family wealth to bear the expense, a stand-alone house might be built as the abode of the dead, a house that mimicked the domestic architecture of that particular culture. Even in our modern cemeteries you find family mausoleums in the form of a house, domesticity continuing on into eternity. Some grand mausoleums take the form of a temple or church, in order for the deceased to dwell with the god.

Like the utilitarian grave goods, house tombs are a homely conception of what the afterlife is like. Even dead, we go on with our work, and we continue in the enjoyment of domestic life, too. The deceased should not be left either empty-handed or homeless. They deserve to be furnished with all the familiars of Earthly existence. Death is to be understood, first of all, by analogy to life. The unknown might be very much like the known.

Our modern religions are much more sophisticated in their conceptions, of course. We smile indulgently at the primitive notions of provisioning and sheltering the dead body. What lives on, we say, is the *soul*; the soul needs neither tools nor shelter. We are not bound to the material; our nature and destiny are spiritual.

Christianity tells us that our true home is in Heaven; our body, as well as our soul, will one day take up residence there. Even so, we remain attached to the known domestic happiness of having a house to live in. While alive, our heart is where our body is, that is, *at home*. The soul will have some convincing to do to get our heart to abandon our home on Earth.

107

"Memory and Memorialization"

I don't know what memory of a deceased mate an animal might retain. Despite the Nature lore about the Canada goose, which will reputedly pine and waste away at the side of the corpse of the gander, animals live in the present ongoing. Of the passing of time, as of death, one of the events of the passing of time, animals are oblivious. They may witness death but not much re-member it.

Not so we human animals. We live in the past and the future, as well as in the present. Regarding the past, our memories are vivid and lifelong. Memory attaches us to the past and to those who have passed away. Memory motivates us to memorialize the dead; memorialization then revivifies memory, the two processes back-and-forth.

The flimsy grave markers of primordial peoples have long since crumbled back to the elements, but, with the working of stone, memorialization of the deceased could endure long past the lives (and so the memories) of those who created the memorial artifact. When living in Rome, I read funereal epigraphs in Latin words incised upon stone two millennia ago. Memory, both personal and collective, is also communicable and transmissible, even unto perpetuity.

The buried dead are planted, one might say, and they (or at least their bodies) are forever rooted in a particular plot of soil. Accordingly, the first human memorialization of the deceased must have been on the grave itself,—a marker, enclosure, or, later, structure. Return visits to the site, whether daily in fresh grief or annually as an anniversary-of-death remembrance, kept memory mindful. When graves came to be located in a designated necropolis, as in the catacombs, memorialization of the dead could take on a community aspect.

There was a physical proximity between identifying markers and the remains of the deceased. The first memorialization was *in situ.*

However, unless the remains were kept in or about the house—(the unwholesome practice of some cultures)—, the place of interment might have been of little significance in the life of the deceased or in the lives of their loved ones.

In the next stage of the process of memorialization, there came about a dissociation of the memorial from the site of the grave. And so we have the *cenotaph,* a memorial to the dead at some place other than at the grave, some place of significance in the life of the deceased.

The cenotaph simulates the grave memorial in its form and architecture; sometimes you are unsure whether you are at a grave or at a cenotaph. Cenotaphs could be erected in abundance, multiplying in proportion to the association of various places with the life of the illustrious deceased or according to the needs of those who want to affiliate themselves and their community with the great one. The body is confined within the grave, but the significance of a person's life is not.

There was to be some muddling of grave and cenotaph, out of a materialistic doubt whether a cenotaph could really contain the identity and spirit of the deceased, if there was no physical part of the body there. The cult of Christian relics is an example. A saint's intact body could be buried in only one place (and thereby possessed by the locals), but what if other communities revered the saint, claimed some association with him or her, and wanted their share, not only of memorialization, but of powerful salvific magic?

The solution to the problem was dismemberment of the corpse and a distribution of the parts all over Christendom, that scattering of saints so notorious in the Middle Ages. Every church named after a saint was a memorialization of that saint, a cenotaph, but, because it held some part of the body (the relic within the altar), it was a mausoleum too.

In the fetishistic materialism of relic trafficking, some body parts were more of the essence than others. A bone from the little finger of the left hand is very little of the essence of St. James of Campostella. A skull would be much better, as would be blood, the life fluid, even when it was only a desiccate stain on clothing.

All of the churches dedicated to Jesus Christ are, by dogma, pure cenotaphs.

With the discovery of a certain heap of bones of an old man under the high altar of St. Peter's in the Vatican during the excavations undertaken in 1939, it was hoped that that church was not just mere cenotaph memorial to the great saint, but his very grave itself.

Archaeology would make St. Peter's all the more deserving of pilgrimage, if Peter himself was there.

Peter's successors, the popes, have suffered competing claims to their eternal presence. Although the popes have presided at St. Peter's, they have often resided elsewhere, for example, in the Quirinal Palace. Many bodies of the popes are interred in St. Peter's, but the hearts and viscera of several dozen of those from recent centuries are preserved in a church near the Quirinal. (Their bodies were in the workplace, but their hearts stayed close to home.)

Actually, relics were not tied to any place at all. If you could obtain one—(and, in the Middle Ages, the trade in relics was Rome's principal enterprise)—, you could carry it about with you as talisman, the saint your very own personal travelling companion and powerful protector, (maybe not just a medal of St. Christopher, but a piece of St. Christopher himself).

I have dealt with relics extensively elsewhere, so let me return to the subject of memorials:—

Monuments to the dead started out simple, but they eventually became elaborated into imposing mortuary architecture,—the Pyramids of Egypt, the Mausoleum of Halicarnassus, the Taj Mahal, and on to our modern Tomb of the Unknown Soldier. The builders of such colossi went beyond simple heartfelt memorial. Such monstrous monuments were out of a hypertrophy of mourning and memory (as in the case of the Taj Mahal) or out of a calculated campaign to indoctrinate ideologies of religion and politics (the other three cases). As well as done as tribute, memorialization may be propagandistic.

It is intriguing to wander through cemeteries and muse over the memorials there, attempting to decipher from them the significances, both personal and generally human. There is always the name of the deceased, of course, the individualizing identification, and the dates of the life-span, the extent of time during which the life was lived. There might be an effigy or picture of the deceased to provoke visual memory. Or, lacking that, some symbol of the person, the significance of which is not always apparent to strangers. And there may be a motto or sentiment, whether a traditional formula or something especially composed, which may tell more about the survivors' feelings than about the deceased. Flowers or jewelry or toys or other poignant tokens may have been left by recent visitors. There is the symbolical architecture of the monuments, too, and the cemetery context itself, a necrocityscape.

If memorialization of the dead could be dissociated from the physical remains, why couldn't it be dissociated from the physical itself? After all, memory is psychological. Memorialization too could be purely psychological. Feelings could be expressed in refined form, like the elegiac poems written by Walt Whitman about Abraham Lincoln. Some would hold those poems a memorialization more suitable than the monstrous cold stone pile of the Lincoln Monument. Imperishable words could make the memory of the great man imperishable. And ideas idealize.

Literary memorialization, like the other forms, sometimes has its morbid pathological aspects, as in the case of Edgar Allen Poe's poems to his deceased child bride. Anyway, even a poor person can compose a grand literary memorial to a loved one; even an obscure person may become immortal by being memorialized in words.

Stone monuments have too much of the inert geologic to affect us deeply; rock has little to do with flesh or spirit. Fine elegiac words, like Lincoln's own Gettysburg Address, convey the spiritual substance and significance of lives and deaths, and so are more satisfying to us.

Memorializing words are the finest of all homages to the dead.

108

"Duties to the Dead"

We are all responsible for one another, our duties depending upon our particular roles in a family and community, as, for example, spouse, parent, friend, relative, partner, employee, citizen. Others demand their due from us.

We owe one another nurturance and sustenance, emotional support, cooperation and collaboration, labor and services. As we discovered in considering grave goods—the provisioning of clothing, tools, and jewels—and grave shelters, human economic duties extend even beyond death.

Seemingly, the deceased would have left behind any need for the services of the living. Yet, for their part, the living feel a necessity to continue in responsible relatedness despite the interposition of death.

Consider now the matter of emotional support. We usually think of the survivors as bereft, suffering the pangs of grief and the lingering ache of mourning. Despite the self-involvement of the survivors, they can feel empathy and sympathy for the dead person. Perhaps the dead might be suffering, too, in a terror at what happened to them. They may need the living to rally to their aid.

Emotional outreaching to the dead is expressed in various ways in different cultures.

The loving touch is the simplest way that human beings provide emotional support to one another. The tender loving treatment of the body of the deceased, besides showing respect, is reassuring and comforting to the dead one. At a wake, the mourners will approach a body and give it a loving touch.

Not only a touch, but words. It makes no sense to speak to a corpse, but that is what the mourners do, addressing to it words of gratitude, love, blessings, fervent wishes for peace and rest.

It is simplistic to be reductionist by asserting that what the mourners do is for themselves alone. Their emotional outreaching is an attempt to comfort the deceased too. Death does not mean the abrupt detachment of perceived human relatedness and responsibility.

The handling of the corpse is the same tender treatment we give to the living body of the beloved. The kind words are like those we speak to the living. In some cultures, there are offerings of food and drink—a further instance of continuing nurturance—or memorial family meals at the tomb, carrying on the deceased's belonging to the family. Family gatherings on the anniversaries of the death prolong the felt relatedness indefinitely.

—-(In the various aspects of the human reactions to death, the idea of continuation keeps recurring.)—-

Whether among the primitives, who might actually believe that the dead can consume the food they bring, or among modern sophisticates who are fully aware that what they are doing is merely symbolical, the sense of dutiful responsibility toward the deceased is the same.

Some services to the dead are peculiar. Where the needs of the dead are different from those of the living, there must be different means to meet and satisfy those needs. The dead need more than material and emotional support; they need spiritual succor. One example is the Catholic doctrine of ransoming souls from Purgatory by means of Masses and prayers.

Prayers are offered for the benefit of the deceased, and it is firmly believed that those prayers are efficacious,—for the deceased, not for the mourner. We wish our loved ones well; death does not stop our love-wishing. For the beloved deceased we wish the ultimate of good; we wish them Heaven. (It is also believed that, once in Heaven, the deceased may reciprocate, interceding with God on behalf of the living, thereby continuing to discharge their own human duties.)

Among the Jews, one responsibility toward the deceased is keeping the memory of that person alive, by, for example, naming a newborn after a deceased grandparent. In memory there is immortalization, just as there is in the genetics of the physical bodies of linear descendants. One duty to the dead is to never forget them.

The memory must be a benign and benevolent one. Whatever the failings or meanness of the deceased during life, it must be forgiven and forgotten upon death. Slander of the dead is a taboo; *de mortuis nil nisi bonum.* The dead cannot defend themselves and certainly cannot take rebuke to heart and reform. So, the living must speak good words about them, good words only. Kindly thoughts, eulogistic words; in all, the respect that is due.

Every life may be inspirational or cautionary to every other life. In remembering the dead, we can take the appropriate lesson, in the privacy of our own mind if that estimation of the deceased contradicts the *nil nisi bonum* we practice in society. There may be some hypocrisy in our show of respect for the dead, yes. In some cases, the discharge of duties to a certain deceased might be distasteful, because of the bitterness of bad memories. Then we do our duty not out of love, but out of social expectation.

All mortuary practices and funeral rites and ceremonies are responsibilities carried out on behalf of the deceased. We may consider them mere stereotyped procedures or even as tiresome obligations; no one enjoys attending wakes and funerals, because they force upon us a demoralizing reminder of our own eventual demise. Nonetheless, such practices provide pre-existent ways to discharge our duties to the dead. If it were up to the individual or family, distraught by grief as they are, to come up with a suitable ceremonial, the dead might not receive their full due.

Duties to the dead may go to extremes, as in ancient Egyptian mummification or in the ancestor cult of old China. Such scrupulosity and retrospective drag upon the living is too much of death-in-life.

You might insist that the dead are beyond help, have no real needs that can be met by the living, and so all funeral practices and rites are futile exercises, except insofar as they assist the survivors through their ordeal of mourning. But what is important in this matter of duties to the dead is not whether or not there is any effectiveness in what is done; what is significant is the dutifulness-in-itself.

Feeling and showing responsible dutifulness is one of the finest traits of the human. We feel, we care, we try to support and aid and do right by one another. By such does the human become humane. By such, toward the dead as well as toward the living.

109

"Heroism against Death"

Of all the works of world literature, one that I have admired most is the *Epic of Gilgamesh*, a Sumerian-Babylonian story-cycle of third-millennium B.C. Mesopotamia, reconstructed from the portions of it found on cuneiform tablets. It is the most honest work dealing with death that I know.

Gilgamesh, the hero, was king of Uruk, a great ruler and builder. Part god, part man, he was formidable in mind and body.

Out of the wilderness there came Enkidu, part man, part beast, to challenge Gilgamesh. The struggle between them ended, however, in coming-to-terms, mutual appreciation, and advancing to deep friendship. The human part in each must have been what they found in common, whereas the divine in Gilgamesh and the beast in Enkidu made for a mutually fascinating difference. (Friendship is the in-common of the otherwise different.)

The two heroes joined forces to battle monsters. After several seeming triumphs, Enkidu was stricken, languished in despair, and died. Enkidu had always dreaded death, and now he succumbed to what he dreaded. Gilgamesh, by contrast, had never feared, or even thought about, death, until he witnessed it in Enkidu.

Gilgamesh suffered over the death of his bosom friend, sitting by the corpse day after day, until the stench and visible decay forced upon him an undeniable recognition of the reality of death.

Couldn't the hero who had slain monsters also overcome death? Gilgamesh set off on a quest to find the secret of eternal life,—not for himself, but to restore to life his beloved Enkidu. After some wandering, he heard about Utnapishtim, the grand old man who had survived the Great Flood and, so, had to know something of the mystery of death and the secret of Life.

Gilgamesh sought out and found Utnapishtim. Yielding to pleading, Utnapishtim directed Gilgamesh to a magic plant that contained the essence of Life.

Gilgamesh found the plant, but, as he dozed in weariness after a cleansing swim in a pond, a serpent consumed the plant, sloughed off its skin (a little symbolic immortality), and stole away. Gilgamesh awoke to find himself robbed of the magic secret of immortality.

Discouraged and disconsolate, Gilgamesh returned to Uruk, but then, under the advice of a goddess and by his own realization, he came to accept death as the lot of man. We must all enjoy the simple pleasures of life while we can and find whatever satisfaction may be in our relatedness to other people and in our personal achievements.

The *Epic of Gilgamesh* is generally interpreted as expressing Mesopotamian pessimism and the pessimistic view of death. "Nothing to hope for" seems to be its lesson on the subject of the meaning of death.

I do not find the story so much pessimistic as realistic, depressing only insofar as destruction of illusion, true recognition, and honest acceptance of the inevitable are so. Gilgamesh's excursion into death eventually led him back into Life; if only all the subsequent philosophical and religious explorations of death had followed a similar course.

It is significant that Gilgamesh did not seek immortality for himself. (Although part-divine, his human component made him as mortal as any common man.) It was, rather, for the revival of his friend that he sought immortality. It was not the ego that craved to live forever; it was love that wanted the beloved to live forever. That is a high and noble motivation, a heroism of the heart, if not of feats. If Gilgamesh failed in his quest, he succeeded by his realization.

Gilgamesh was told by the goddess that immortality belongs exclusively to the divine, and, even though he himself was godlike, the humanness of him linked him to the animals and to their mortality. Whatever one may wish, however much one may love those who are deceased, it is necessary to see and to accept "That's the way things are". Instead of vain aspirations and futile longings for immortality, it is wiser and better to appreciate and live out the life that humans are privileged to enjoy.

The real lesson of the *Epic of Gilgamesh* is a sound counsel of recognition, acceptance, and making-the-best-of-it. Truth is therapeutic.

Most early peoples expected little of death. (The Egyptians were the conspicuous exception.) Death was a grim unknown. Death could be speculated about, but such speculation tended toward the morbid and demoralizing.

How much better the moral of the *Epic of Gilgamesh*: Forget about death and devote your attention to living.

We do know life. As we live it, we are fully capable of crafting an enjoyable life for ourselves, never mind our ignorance and helplessness regarding the after-death-come-what-may.

Unlike Odysseus, Hercules, and other such brawny boys of myth, whose feats are mindless curiosities, Gilgamesh is a hero of the human mind. The most terrible monster he slayed was the fear of death. The ordeal he underwent led to his enlightenment.

110

"Dreams, Origin of Afterlife"

That human beings believe in an afterlife for themselves is due to the phenomenon of dreams. Belief in the afterlife has a physiological and psychological explanation.

What we believe comes from our sense impressions and experiences. There is little in our waking world that would evoke belief in an afterlife. When the proto-hominid perceived death with his senses, he must have interpreted it as an end and dissolution. No animal he killed ever revived, no deceased elder ever returned. Like Gilgamesh, he could have stared at the corpse for days, touched it repeatedly to attempt to arouse, waited and waited, but there would never be any revival. If his sense of smell could stand it, he could apply that sense too. And so he would come to a most certain sense-knowledge that death is dissolution. (But a timely burial of the deceased could conceal the evidence and avoid a facing-of-facts).

Not even a near-death phenomenon would have led the primitive mind to belief in afterlife. If early man observed coma, perhaps, he could still perceive the breathing in the stillness, and so his mind would associate coma with sleep, not with death.

The ill and injured would lie down, eventually getting up again, but the dead never did so. We use sleep as an inapt and inept metaphor for death, but even the protohominid knew the difference.

All intellection is rooted in sense experience. The senses presenting no evidence or indications of afterlife, the conscious mind could never have conceived of such a thing.

But the awake mind is not the all of mind, nor is perception of the outside world the only sense experience. Every night the human dreams, and in those dreams are other sense experiences.

One modern scientific hypothesis about learning holds that all experience and learning, however fleeting and intangible it may seem, however evanescent, produces a chemical, material change in the brain, becomes a sort of permanent file. We never really forget what we have learned; we just have trouble finding the file. If you have ever tried and tried to remember some fact you knew, then gave it up as forgotten, only to have that fact rise to consciousness spontaneously—(the file found)—, you will admit the plausibility of the hypothesis.

Now, when we know a person, we receive and accumulate many sense impressions of that person, impressions that are, according to the hypothesis, stored permanently in the brain. We retain an image of a known person, which is why we recognize even someone we have not seen for a long time (thirty-two years in the case of a reunion I recently experienced). We recognize the person not only in a live encounter, but also in a dream. In a dream, we see, we hear, we may touch, and so we recognize, not in real life but in a chemical experience in the brain during the dream.

What if we dream of a reunion with a deceased parent? That would not lead to belief in afterlife, if it weren't for a particular characteristic of dreams, that is, that we can remember a dream when we awake. If we never remembered our dreams, we would never have developed belief in an afterlife.

Someone deceased, a loved one toward whom we had a strong emotional attachment and yearnings of love, reappears in a dream that is remembered the day after. The inner sense impressions—the image of the person, the sound of her voice, her mannerisms—even though just a chemical file—tell the mind that that person lives and speaks and still loves us.

Humans testify to one another that we all have dreams, so the dream phenomenon is not easily disposed of as a private hallucination or individual derangement. The universality of the dream experience not to be denied, neither, then, is the content of dreams. But what does that content mean?

Now the conscious mind gets to work on the significance of the dream. Intellection enters in.

The thought process goes something like this: "I saw my mother in a dream. But my mother is dead...She died, yes, but last night she came back to me in my dream. So she must not be really dead. She must be still living. Not here but someplace else, that place she came from to be with me in my dream. When I buried her, I must have buried only her body. Somehow she lives on. Others of our tribe have told me that they too dream of their dead relatives. Their dead, all the dead, must be still alive somewhere. Maybe all of us, after we die, will be still alive somewhere. My dreams are real. They tell me this is true."

Subsequent philosophy and religion are out of such interpretation of dreams. The *soul*, actually only a dream-image, and the afterlife, actually only the dream world, become engrossing subjects of speculation, imagination, and reasoning, embellished unto the utmost sophistication of metaphysics and eschatology. The motivation for it all was the deep emotional yearning for, and attachment to, loved ones whom we want to go on living. As in the *Epic of Gilgamesh,* it is human love-longing that refuses to accept the finality of death.

That belief in an afterlife is almost universal in human culture is due to the fact that all human beings dream and remember their dreams. Common psychology produces common ideology.

If animals that dream remembered their dreams, they too might incline toward belief in their own immortality; but they lack the intellection to carry their dream-images to such a conclusion, or at least they lack the communicative powers to tell us that they believe so. (Animals don't believe they will live forever; but they don't believe they will die, either. Animals are short on belief.)

The primitives and ancients endeavored to find premonitory meaning in dreams; belief in an afterlife is the ultimate premonitory meaning of dreams. So fascinated and awed were the ancients by their own dreams but so lacking in science, we can excuse them letting their excited logic run heedless to the most fantastic of inference. We ourselves ought to know better.

If we are now skeptical about our dreams, we should also be skeptical about that most fantastic inference from dreams, belief in an afterlife. Yet, on that belief, most of us still want our dream to come true, never mind skepticism, psychology, and science. We deal with the problem of death by dreaming it away.

It is in the dream, our *other life*, that the human found our belief in afterlife. Afterlife is all a dream, really.

The primitives and ancients reported their dreams to one another and marveled over them. Today, we inculcate belief in the afterlife upon our children, pre-empting any skeptical interpretations they might have of inferences from their own dreams. The intellect has taken hold of the dream, as it has taken hold of death, and it doesn't want to let go.

Nature would tell us that the dreaming mind dies in the death of the dreamer. If there is afterlife, it would have to be dreaming dreaming itself.

The long night of death follows the long day of life. In that particular night, Nature would further tell us, there are no dreams dreamt.

111

"Pagan Afterlife"

Among the Mediterranean pagans, the Greeks and Romans, imagination did not venture very far from the psychological origin of the notion of afterlife, that is, dreams.

The pagans imagined the deceased as *shades*, insubstantial wraiths, spectral figures. In short, the form of the deceased was very much like a dream-image.

Where was the place that the *shades* carried on their lifeless, lingering existence? (In practicing cremation, the Greeks and Romans liberated the spirits of the dead from home confinement in their graves.) What someplace-else could pagan imagination find that would be a suitable realm for the dead?

The canopy of the heavens seemed to belong to the gods, who there made display of their powers by awesome astronomical and meteorological phenomena. The above was claimed by the divine immortals.

Where the gods dwelt upon the Earth, it would be where the Earth touched the heavens, as at Mt. Olympus, aetherial terrestrial abode of the gods.

Land and sea belonged to the human race, although the gods claimed rights there too. Gods and goddesses enjoyed a promiscuous mixing with mortals on the Earth, the divine lusting after human sexual experience. But for neither gods nor men should there be any promiscuity with the dead. The spirits of the deceased could not be permitted to roam the Earth amidst the theophanies and the living mortal bodies. Death had to be banished from the world of life-and-sex.

Modern science postulates alter-universes, but the ancient Greeks were very much this-world, real-world. (You might consider Plato's Realm of Ideas an alter-universe, but the philosophers were a somewhat aberrant Greek type.)

To the Greeks, the unknown realm was the subterranean, whatever lay under the perceptible tiers,—the celestial, the terrestrial, and the maritime. That realm was an underworld.

The underworld was unknown because imperceptible, removed from human experience. However, there were certain places where the underworld provided indications of itself, as it were. The Mediterranean basin is volcanic. Groaning rumblings could be heard from the bowels of the Earth. The underworld seemed to vent itself, as at Etna and Vesuvius, a flatus of gas and fire. The underworld expelled water too, from springs. Caves and caverns, somewhat accessible but unlivable, seemed like portals or *atria* to what must be a vast netherworld.

In the milieu of the Mediterranean, the only vacancy available as the realm of the dead was the underworld. That was the someplace-else to which the dead went.

What was that realm like?

First of all, as it was conceived as a physical place removed from the world of the living, there had to be a crossing-over to get there. The Greeks were seafarers, so the metaphor of fluvial passage came readily to them. Crossing a river, Acheron or Styx, was the ideological analogy to the streams of lava or springs flowing from underground, or, more broadly, the Mediterranean itself. Only those who had been duly buried or cremated, who had received the prescribed rites, could secure passage. All others were stranded upon the near shore.

The name *Styx* means hatred-of-death. Beyond Styx was the realm of the dead. A featureless place, devoid of the wonders of Nature and the works of man. An uninteresting emptiness. And it was dim or dark, like the night, the night in which dreams are dreamt. To the pagan Greeks or Romans, the afterworld was very much like the aura of any dream of the dead they may have had.

What did the dead do in the realm of the dead? Enfeebled, the dead could do little; they just drifted aimlessly. Even the heroes were rendered impotent,—a terrible fate for those dynamic doers, the Greeks and Romans. The dead might sigh or moan, so little of the faculty of speech could they muster. A Greek bereft of speech, another dreaded fate. Uncommunicative, the spirits of the dead were as isolated from one another as from the living,—yet another terrible prospect to a Greek, that most sociable of all peoples.

In the pagan conception of afterlife, there was the loss not only of the person who died, lost to this world, but of many of that person's most valued human faculties. It was like one of those dreams where we struggle to speak or move but cannot. Death was an incapacitation.

To the Greeks, life was vitality, appreciation of our bright, beautiful world, dynamic activity, and social interaction. Death was a stripping-away of all that. When a Greek died and went to the afterlife, it was not only the body that died, but much of cultural identity too.

Greek intellection, philosophy, would later venture beyond traditional myth to the most sophisticated abstractions of metaphysics. But, as far as death and afterlife were concerned, most Greeks kept their belief in their dreams. That is, until Epicurus came along.

112

"Nothing, Nothingness"

Death isn't something. Death is nothing.

We use the word *death* to designate an event, but that event is the cessation of life, a termination of what had been going on. When a process ceases, when it stops, it does not thereby become something else. Life does not become death. Death is the moment after the last moment of life. As an event, it is empty.

Death is an experience, we believe, but, if it is so, it is only the experience of the deaths of others. We may experience our own dying, but not our death itself. How could we? Death is an empty event; therefore, it cannot be experienced.

We think of death as an event, we experience the deaths of others, then we infer that death is a something. But it is not. An empty event, an unexperienceable experience, is nothing.

Whether or not *Nature abhors a vacuum*, the human mind certainly does. There is no room in our mind for the nothingness of death. We have to think of it as a something.

When the process of mind operates, it must think of something, it cannot think of nothing. (When I said in a prelude sentence that the mind may contemplate the Void, I meant that it may do so only by conceiving the Void as a something.) Something is of the essence of the mind thinking. The mind abhors nothingness.

We cannot accept that our end might be nothingness. Instead, we interpret death as transition,—to afterlife, to rebirth, or to some afterbeing, afterstate, or afterprocess. We abhor a vacuum, especially the vacuum created by the extinction of our own personal ego-existence. We want to be persistent somethings going on and on, just as the thoughts in our mind go on and on.

The notion of afterlife is a something-out-of-nothing, an *ex nihilo*; life out of death is life out of nothing.

Gone from the world, where would our afterself reside? The answer to that question is another something-out-of-nothing, metaphysical real estate,—Hades or Tartarus to the pagans, Sheol or Gehenna to the Jews, Paradise and Jahannam to the Moslems, Heaven and

Hell to the Christians. The dead live on, we aver, in places no living persons have seen or been to. But there is a destination the afterself is headed to.

Naturalists deny afterlife, but few can be naturalists, because, although we may recover from love-longing for the deceased, it is more difficult to disengage from egotism. Disinterested natural understanding cannot avail against the imagination of the craving ego: I want to live forever, so I believe I will.

And yet, a powerful argument for the nothingness of death is from Nature. Before we came to life, weren't we nothing? Except for the Hindus and their fanciful reincarnations, most would agree that conception is a coming-into-being of something that had not been before. (Not *ex nihilo*, of course, but *ex altero*.) If coming-into-being, why not, then, a going-out-of-being? That would seem the natural order of things.

Nature does not share the abhorrence of nothingness felt by the human mind. Extinction is essential in the evolution of Life; Life must make way for newly generated life. Death is Nature's mechanism and process for removing defective or old worn-out living for the new and fresh and vital. Nature's interest is in generation, not in resurrection. Nature is the Nature of the living, not of the dead. Death, extinction, clears the way. Nothingness is a necessity of Nature.

If death is transition to afterlife, naturalists may argue, why don't all other living beings, all plants and animals that have ever lived, die into their own afterlives? A crowded metaphysical realm, then. Immortal bacteria! That proposition, logical by simple analogy, is, to our human egotism, absurd. After all, unlike the other living creatures, we have a *soul*. And so the mind concocts yet another fantasy, one to distinguish the human from the animal, never mind that animals and humans share the breath-of-life, the breath that one day must cease in death. The human ego is selfish and exclusionary.

The fact of nothingness is the big bugaboo of the human mind, especially in so far as it involves ego. We argue against the nothingness of personal extinction. Instead of an animal body that lives, then dies, then ceases to be, we consider our real self to be a soul that, once born, is immortal. The body on Earth is only a temporary carrier of a soul on its way to Heaven. And so, the mind confutes Nature,—at least in its own mind.

What is death? Nothing. Where are the dead after death? Nowhere. What is after death? Nothingness. Do the dead exist? No, except in the memory of the living.

The previous paragraph is all negation. To save ourselves (forever) we negate negation.

Contrary-to-Nature affirmations are not true just because we want to believe and we find that most of our fellows too want to believe. (We are all dreamers, as I said before.) What we are affirming is not the truth about death, but only the utmost of egotistic ambition out of the illusion of human cosmic specialness.

The Greek Epicurus and Lucretius, his Roman advocate, were philosophically lonesome characters, but at least they could see the *Rerum Natura*, the nature-of-things, accept it, and submit themselves to reality-as-it-is. Nothingness was one way of Nature, nothing terrible to them.

We want to get a mental grasp upon death, to understand it, both in itself and in its aftermath, if any. In understanding, we hope, there is alleviation of anxiety about death. We'll get a hold on death, before it gets its hold on us. Yet, our intellectual dealing with death—in fantasies of Hell and such—serve only to exacerbate anxiety.

Epicurus was the healer of that anxiety.

The only *wise* philosophers are those who are good psychologists. As the wise Epicurus recognized, our vain attempt to contradict Nature and deal with whatever fears might be natural have only resulted in the perverse conjuring of worse and more terrible monsters-of-the-mind. The mind may become a self-torturer. I can scare myself to death about death.

Against free-floating anxiety about death the truth of nothingness is effective antidote. "After death you will be what you were before you were conceived," is the Epicurean therapeutic truth.

If I were to speak about death, I would say nothing, because nothing can be said about nothing. If I were to write about death, I would write nothing, because nothing can be written about nothing. (Like Nature, a writer is incapable of generating *ex nihilo*.) This book is not about death. It is about *matters* of death, that is, death interpretations, ideas and ideologies, longings and fantasies, situations and reactions, instances and incidents. This is a book about the delusions of the living regarding death. Any something-of-death is delusion.

113

"Fear, Natural and Unnatural"

Fear is a natural emotion of our animal nature.

When an animal perceives a danger to its life, it reacts physiologically. The senses lock on to the danger, heartbeat and blood pressure increase, muscles tighten up, bowels or bladder might discharge, the whole body becomes wound tight, a tension to be broken by *fight or flight*. Fear is stressful, but it is self-preserving.

We humans experience that selfsame fear when danger threatens, and we show many of the same physiological reactions. Fear is natural to us.

Natural fear is a reaction to the immediate and imminent; it is a here-and-now fear. Further, it is a reaction to a real danger, or, at least, a danger that is perceived to be real. (Like the animals, we are sometimes deceived by errors of sense.) Natural fear has nothing to do with past or future or with any conjured fantasies.

As the human is a step-up in complexity from the animal, so is our human fear. Beyond the physiological, we endure fears that are psychological. Danger may not be immediate and imminent, but we are afraid that it is lurking nearby and may attack soon.

Our psychological fear sometimes takes the form of free-floating anxiety, but psychological fear is by no means all pathological. We are able to judge situations revealed to us by our senses better than an animal can. Animal fear may come too late to be self-preserving; the lion has already sprung before the physiological reactions of the prey were triggered. The human knows to always beware of the lion when one is in lion country; the unseen lion poses a danger.

Animals are almost always on the alert. Their alertness may be collective, as in the flock or herd. Our human collective alertness involves the most sophisticated communication. For example, the National Weather Service can tell us with relative certainty that a hurricane is headed our way, warn us while the sky above us is still clear, a day or more before the event. The general warning stirs our apprehension and fear, even though our individual senses do not indicate anything amiss. Responding to the communicated warning, we take steps for self-preservation.

Some human psychological fear, however, is pathological, a derangement of the self-preserving function. One instance is the recurring posing of the apprehensive "What if...?" The mind conjures up all sorts of disasters that might befall a person, disasters plausible in themselves but more or less unlikely and certainly not immediate and imminent:—"What if I lose all my money?", "What if I get cancer?", "What if the plane should crash?", and so on. Some people may become so attuned to their psychological fears that they might be oblivious to real and present dangers; but our bodies are done in by real dangers, not by conjured fantasies.

Natural fear is appropriate and episodic, ending when the danger is dealt with. The stress upon the organism eases and healthy equilibrium is restored. Psychological fears, however, may be chronic, their low-level stress continual. Instead of preserving the body, psychological fear wears it down. To the health of the body the mind may be the greatest danger of all.

The most insidious type of psychological fear, of mind-against-body, is apprehension and anxiety induced by the conjuring of ideas that are wholly fanciful. If you live on the savannah, the lion is a real danger and lion country is a danger-in-itself; but does a Big Bogeyman Spook Ghost lurk in the high grass, ready to eat you up?

Human imagination is the conjurer of fears psychological. Even as children we frighten ourselves. Then, when intellection gets to work on what the imagination has conjured, imaginary fears become cogent, because they get incorporated into a seemingly rational thought-system, an ideology.

The generalized fear of death is an example of the human's escalation of fear over that of the animal. The animal feels fright at nearly being killed by a particular predator in a particular situation of the here-and-now, but the animal does not mull over the problem of death-at-any-time-inevitable; it does not fear death-itself, death-in-the-abstract, "Death, what then?". Only the human feels such ideological fear.

The animals experience physiological fear. Our own fear of death runs the entire gamut from physiological to psychological to ideological, from body to emotion to imagination to intellect. We *are* afraid of death-itself, in the abstract and general as in the real and specific.

Out of dreams, night-imagination, came our belief in afterlife. Out of nightmare, derangement of dream imagery, came our belief in afterlife in Hell, the eternal damnation of the soul. Once again, intellection took over. Nightmares were converted to doctrinal ideology.

The myths and, in their more sophisticated forms, the religions have taken as one province the fear of death. Against it they have elaborated explanations, rites, and doctrines ostensibly intended to ease our anxiety. The religions deny the real finality of death and make alternate explanation, as, for example, death-as-rebirth or death-as-passage-to-afterlife.

But then, just when religions would seem to be psychotherapeutic—assuring us, "Don't worry, you won't *really* die—, they concoct fanciful doctrines that, instead of relieving the anxiety of the fear of death, make it all the more intense. Now, not only do we fear the few minutes of physical suffering during the death ordeal; we have an eternity of torment in unquenchable fire to worry about. Dying is no longer a transient natural event; it may be the doorway to everlasting spiritual doom.

The religions have inculcated ideological fears to supplant the natural physiological and reasonable psychological ones. Ideological fear, the most incapacitating of all fear.

Ideological fear carries conviction; doctrines (even divinely revealed) are certain, the only certainties in an uncertain world. Conviction is not only intellectual; it is psychological, and, as such, may be pathological. The human being, the intellectual animal, suffers fears of such chronic intensity that the lower creatures never experience.

The wise Epicurus was the diagnostician of the problem of pathological psychological fear, the free-floating anxiety about death. His prescription for cure proved unpalatable to most. Anxiety is compulsive and addictive; it resists its cure. The human will not accept the peace of mind that comes from the acceptance of afterdeath nothingness.

We have turned fear of death into fear of afterdeath. We fear damnation. And, in the process, we have damned our living.

114

"The Mystery of Death"

You may have heard the expression, *the mystery of death,* as a complement to *the mystery of life.* If both life and death are a mystery, it would seem that we know very little about what is most important to us, those *Matters of Life and Death.*

Mystery means the unknown and probably un-knowable, whatever is (and shall remain) beyond the grasp of human reason. It is not a word that should be used lightly, because tagging that word upon a subject discourages empirical investigation and venturesome critical thinking.

Fortunately, science has not been deterred by *mystery*, nor is the word to be found in a philosopher's vocabulary. The word is most often heard on the lips of the ignorant and lazy or of poets.

Much of *the mystery of life* has been dispelled by the sciences of biology and medicine and their related disciplines. We know life analytically and microscopic-ally. We can snoop into the most hidden life-processes, tamper with them, replicate them, and one day soon even create some new forms of life. There is no operation or process that is a *mystery* to a knowledgeable and experienced technician. Life presents its problems, but those problems are solvable.

Some may be dismayed that the mystery has seemingly been taken out of life, but that presumes that there is more magic in ignorance than there is in knowledge. We may have solved the mystery of conception, but that has not made the miracle of conception any less wonderful.

The theologians fulminate that the scientists "play God" with Life; if so, God shouldn't have created humans as such capable problem solvers. The tree of *mystery* is gradually being reduced to sawdust.

The theologians are actually rallying not to God but to themselves and their tenuous futures, for they are the last in the line of mystery-men, from shamans to witch doctors to miracle-workers to sorcerers to necromancers and so on to themselves.

In science, Life has taken hold of itself, the living have taken charge of their living. If there were too much *mystery*, little would be attempted, little accomplished, no progress made, life wouldn't get better. Awe is incapacitating; as such it is inimical to science. Even so, as I said, the scientist, as he goes about his systematic and successful problem solving, may feel the wonder of it all.

So, science has pretty much put an end to *the mystery of life*, for good or ill. Not that Life is any different from what it has always been; rather, the human relation to it has been transformed. Mystery has yielded to mastery.

Now, what about the so-called mystery of death?

Considered naturalistically, as I have urged, death is a necessity of life, a consequence of the way things are.

Living beings are born, grow and develop, reach maturity, suffer injury and illness that attack the integrity of the body, begin to break down, age, deteriorate, and, at last, die. Death is just the last event in the whole natural process.

Life and death are not equals, by any means. Life is prime, death just secondary and subsidiary, an after-effect. We talk about LIFE-AND-DEATH, but it should be LIFE-and-death. The mystery men have hyper-trophied death out of all deserving proportion in the scheme-of-things. Really, death is just a natural consequence.

The conceiving of new life is wonderful and important, because it leads to so much, even, eventually and especially, to the generation of further life and to generations of new lives in a chronological chain that is a virtual eternality and immortality of Life. Life-coming-to-be is one of the most important phenomena of the natural world.

And death? What is it, what does it lead to? A decomposition, disintegration, and dissolution into basic chemicals, a regressive process. It does have a significance as a recycling of organic material, but any one death is of little impact on an Earth that already teems with the materials out of which life can be made. To naturalists, death, because it doesn't lead to anything much, is neither important nor interesting; to the otherworld mystery-men it is both.

Ah, *otherworld!*—That's where the importance of death is supposed to be, where the *mystery* lies. To the theologians and their proselytes, natural death is the entering into the afterlife in the otherworld, from which event death derives its *mystery*. (It is the soul, they say, that lives on, so, in that regard, the theologians would hold death of the body as insignificant as naturalists do, if it weren't for the doctrine of *the resurrection of the body*.)

Now, with these notions of *soul, afterlife,* and *other-world,* and all their associated metaphysical fancies, we are indeed in the Land of Mystery.

"Who has ever seen that land?", the scientist wants to know. "How can we investigate it?" "No one, and you can't," the mystery-men answer. "What sense, what plausibility, what reasonableness can I find there?", the philosopher asks. "There is neither human sense nor reasonableness there," the mystery-men answer. And so, scientists and philosophers are excluded from *the mystery of death.* It's all a matter of faith.

As Mark Twain's schoolboy defined it, "Faith is believing what you know ain't so."

The naturalists (to which association I belong) have something of the scientist, something of the philosopher. A bit of the poet, too, but just because we feel wonder doesn't mean we can't face facts and think straight.

The theologians have never been to their claimed domain, so their testimony, their competence is suspect, unlike the scientists, whose competence is proven, whose testimony is testable. The philosophers make their own sense, at times anyway; they are valuable, because they know how to ask good questions, even if they have no quick, sure dogmatic answers.

Now, to us naturalists, students and experts of Life, there is no *mystery of death* at all. Death is a fact, but not a fact to make a big to-do about, to become preoccupied with, to get all worked up over with anxieties and fanciful expectations. Such hypertrophied significance of death is absurd.

I don't generally like mechanistic analogies, but in this case one is apt. A mechanic would not scratch his head and call it a *mystery* when an old, worn-out machine breaks down for good. Neither would a naturalist regarding the organic body.

Whatever *mystery of death* there may be, it is metaphysical, not natural. The metaphysical is wholly in the mind. The *mystery of death*, then, is wholly in the mind.

There is no mystery about natural death. There is only the mystery of the human mind. Regarding that mystery, the scientists, the philosophers, and we naturalists too are all perplexed.

115

"Redemptive Death"

In the culture of the West, death in general has not been interpreted naturalistically, could not be interpreted so, because of one particular historical death that was invested with so much meaning and significance that it changed the ideology of death ever after.

The ancient Jews had developed a detailed moralism that was comprehensively applied to every aspect of life. At first, when the Jews were still the Hebrews or Israelites, rewards or punishments for moral or immoral behavior were confined to the duration of life; you would be rewarded by God with material prosperity and a large family of sons, for example, or you would be punished by God with horrible illness or destitution. Death was left out of the moral scheme-of-things, because death was the destiny of good and evil alike. Of any afterlife, the early Jews had as vague and dreamlike a notion as did the pagan Greeks and Romans, Sheol not much distinguishable from Hades.

But then the apocalyptic metaphysics of visionary prophets got mixed in with the morality, especially in the matter of retribution. Common experience of the good suffering and the wicked prospering on Earth contradicted the simplistic correlations of the get-what-you-deserve-in-life scheme. Perhaps God, Yahweh as Judge, would render ultimate correct justice after death. Morality, like law, finds its cogency and coercion in the threat of punishment. The legalistic and juridical Jews would not have been satisfied with the pagan Stoic doctrine that virtue is a reward in itself or the general Greek acceptance of the tragic as an inevitable part of life.

The Jews not only gave a moral significance to life, they made morality its prime significance. Death too would take on moral significance. Death would be the summons to the bench of judgment of the morality of one's lived life.

The problem of good-and-evil may have vexed the Jews more than any other people. The Book of Job is the classic in the world literature on the problem.

The Jews inclined toward a belief that evil was hereditary, an in-the-blood concupiscence traceable to the Original Sin of Adam. The sins of the father devolved upon the sons. In fact, the sins of the primordial grand-father did so.

What could break the grim chain? And where was ultimate justice?

A certain moralistic, heterodox prophet from Galilee, proving himself by miracles and powerful, inspired elo-quence, proclaimed his own vision of eschatological jus-tice. (Incidentally, he contradicted the doctrine of hered-itary guilt.) The prophet's career was cut short by his arrest, trial, conviction as a political subversive, and summary execution.

Then, among his erstwhile followers, an astounding reaction occurred. Believing their Master innocent, they became fixated upon the cruel death inflicted upon him. (The suffering of an innocent man was the problem of

Job all over again, but now in a real-life case, not a mere hypothetical literary one.) Their demoralization and despair were turned to hope and enthusiasm by rumors that their Master had been resurrected from the dead. If so—yes, so!—, he had triumphed not only over the injustice inflicted upon him, but over death itself.

Whoever was resurrected from the dead or resurrected himself—(the followers weren't sure which)—must have been a suprahuman being, somehow related to the one known suprahuman being, Yahweh the One God. An interpretation was then imposed upon what had happened:—

The Son of God—(although *son of man* was how he had characterized himself)—had come to Earth, in order to deliberately sacrifice himself in a death expiatory of the Original Sin. Then he was resurrected, not only by that miracle to prove his truth and his true identity, but to prefigure the destiny of all men. There would be afterlife after death, during which, the god-man himself said in his eschatological prophecies, all would undergo judgment of their moral or immoral life. Yes, there would be ultimate justice.

The ideology of the Jewish moral scheme-of-things was now culminated and complete. Human destiny was death, resurrection, judgment, reward-or-punishment. The problem of Job was solved by a divine intervention, a *deus ex machina*.

The Jews themselves, outraged at the blasphemous claims the followers made about their Master, repudiated that revelation. The apostate sect then drifted off to the Greco-Roman world and proselytized the pagans to their schismatic version of Jewish moralism.

Soter (savior) was one designation in Greek that the new sect used to characterize their founder-and-god. The *Soter* saved us from sin and death. He did so by dying himself (although he was sinless) and being resurrected. His Resurrection was the deathblow to death. Human ultimate destiny was eternal life.

What should have been of most significance in the Christian religion was the Resurrection, the miraculous conquest of death and the prefigurement of the salvation of eternal life awaiting all. The teachings of the *Soter* too should have been of prime importance, because they were the moral requisites to be tested at the Judgment; nonetheless, the moral teachings receded before the compelling idea (and later the imagery) of the *Soter's* redemptive death.

It was through that death, the willing, actually self-chosen, death of that one, that all men would be redeemed from sin and from the subjection to death that sin caused. Never mind the parables or even the Resurrection, it was that death that became the most significant event in the entire history of the human race. Out of love, an immortal god had died to save us.

The early Christians (especially the Pauline ones) seemed to show more enthusiasm for the death of their model than for his life and teachings. The craving to imitate that death, the cult of martyrdom, became a sectarian hysteria. One's own death could be redemptive, if it were imitative of, and in the spirit of, the model's death. The Christians zealously set about replicating the sacrificial redemptive death in their own persons. And the martyrs became the exemplary heroes of the new sect.

The Roman political Establishment, baffled by it all but worried for social order, accommodated Christian suicidalism, until a certain emperor co-opted the zeal of the true believers to serve his own political purposes. Even though martyrdoms thereby came to an end, the fixation upon martyrdom, in the image of the crucifix-idol, as well as in scriptural ideology, became entrenched. Never before, not even in the stereotypically necrophilic culture of ancient Egypt, had death-consciousness become so central to a culture.

For a millennium and more (until European culture repaganized, then secularized), the crucifix-idol, the image of redemptive death, was the icon of an entire civilization, Christendom.

(As I said, the Resurrection should have been the most important event in the redemption story, but, with the fall of the Roman Empire and the consequent anarchy and social collapse, morbid medievalism fixated upon the death instead. Happier times might have gloried in a Resurrection cult.)

Who could say that death had no meaning, or that death was just a natural process, when the Divinity himself had found death so significant as to make it the means by which the human race would be redeemed? God himself made death the access to eternal life.

Christianity proclaimed the problem of human death solved, the entire metaphysical scenario of post-death reality all explained and specific. There would be ultimate justice, and there would be eternal life, either salvation or damnation. Theology dogmatized it all with confident certainty.

Because of one particular death, we have not been able to take death lightly or naturalistically since, so fraught is death with eternal significance. One death was the climax of all human history, transforming all that had gone before, determining all that would come after. Not all the lives of all the human beings who had ever lived or would live added up together could approach the significance of the single redemptive death.

What happened two millennia ago in Palestine excited and astounded contemporaries. Even today our heads still haven't cleared.

When a naturalist hears the doctrine of the redemptive death he can only react with stupefaction.

116

"Seed Corpses"

I recall reading somewhere in the early Christian writings that the buried bodies of the faithful were like seeds planted in the ground, ready to sprout. Corpses were seeds, seemingly dead but with the germ of life hidden within them. From death would come new life, in a resurrection of the dead.

"I am the sower," said Jesus of Nazareth. What he sowed was his words. The disciples, eating those words, the words-of-life, would have themselves sown in the ground, seed-corpses, that, having eaten, and been nourished by, the words-of-life, would rise again and live forever.

The imagery was meant to be consoling. Consolation is what is desperately needed by survivors of the dead who anticipate and dread their own eventual demise. The Christian answer to "Death, what then?" was "Don't worry about it. Your corpse will be a seed; you will sprout and live again."

Did a typical Christian sinner, upon hearing the seed-corpse metaphor, wonder and worry whether his own corpse would prove a viable seed...or only a dead hull, chaff to be blown away by the great flurry of *the resurrection of the dead*? A moral life was some assurance of viability, although the doctrine said that all, the evil as well as the good, would rise, the former up only to be cast down to Hell—(where they would wish they had really died once-and-for-all)—, the latter raised to Heaven, the abode of eternal life, where the grip of death would be broken at last. The Christians believed in *karma* and also in reincarnation, but only once—(doctrinal shortsightedness, a Hindu would say).

Now, when you examine a seed, so dry and still, it does seem inert, but, when you plant it, it springs to life. All it needs is warmth and moisture.

If a seed is really dead, however, then the living plant engendered death, out of which, most paradoxically, life would sprout. *Vita ex morte*, life out of death! (It need not be stated that there were plenty of fantastic paradoxes in the Christian ideology.)

We naturalists have read too much in the scriptures of Nature to swallow any such seed-words as those about a resurrection of the dead. Death has never given birth to life. Life emerged out of an inorganic soup of compounds fused and frothed by the energy of the sun. No sunlight or rain ever reaches the depths of the catacombs, the burial plot in which the Christian seed-corpses were planted. No life will ever emerge out of those subterranean charnel houses.

Nature scatters her living seeds, some few to sprout to life, others to succumb to their own defects or to inadequacies or hostilities of environment. Nature is profligate, and she pursues variety, too. However much an offspring resembles its parents, no dead individual is ever reborn as itself. Being reborn as themselves is exactly what the Christians wanted, so egotistic were they in their shared humility. Nature refuted and flouted, the Christians would live forever.

Death is not the conduit that birth is. Death is the dissolution into minerals that seeds—living seeds I mean—of completely new life may take nourishment of. In that sense, in the recycling of organic matter, there *may be* eternal life. But it is not individual, like a single seed; it is a mass profusion, a seeding scattered to the winds. What is potentially immortal and eternal is the process, not the individual.

The identification of death with the germ of life, the corpse with the seed, is a perverse muddling of life and death.

The Christian doctrine of *the resurrection of the dead* was argued not only by the seed-corpse metaphor, but by reported gospel incidents of actual resurrections, that of the *Soter* most of all, but also those of mere humans, like Lazarus and the daughter of Jairus and the son of the widow of Nain. The stories of those typological resurrected ones prove the doctrine by instances of actual occurrences. Besides those individual resurrections there was a mass one following the Crucifixion (Matt. 27:52-53), the latter of clear prefigurement of the General Resurrection at the End of Time.

To the naturalist, the resurrected Lazarus was not a human but a zombie. A psychopathologist reacts similarly. Leonid Andreev wrote a short story about Lazarus, about how his resurrection caused such revulsion and terror in family and bystanders that they fled from him, abandoning Lazarus to his second life as a shunned pariah. And so the doctrine is carried to its psychological consequences. What reaction to one another will the arisen feel at the General Resurrection?

Religion and poetry both have their metaphorical fantasies. Strange that we should take the fancies of the former any more seriously than those of the latter. We ought to subject both to the standards of wholesome good taste, as well as to the criterion of Nature. The metaphor of the seed-corpse and the doctrine of *the resurrection of the dead* are in the worst possible taste.

When Paul proclaimed that doctrine in the *Agorá* of Athens, his auditors laughed in ridicule, as they should have. Their laugh was the last expression of pagan good taste. After that, it would be bad taste, Christian morbidity, medievalism, a millennium of death-in-life. The

Christians idolized the crucifix, a death-image icon, and yearned for death as the way to eternal life.

As it happened, the Christians perpetrated sacrilegious crimes against their own, looting the catacombs of their bones and selling them as relics of the martyrs. They dismembered the seed-corpses and then scattered them, making chaotic the re-assembling necessary for the doctrine to be proved at last.

Life-out-of-death, life dying, then living the same as itself, spiritual life, eternal life:—A lot of life-talk, but, really, anti-Life.

117

"The Christian Catacombs of Rome"

The first thing that must be done in treating the subject of the catacombs is dispelling the romantic myths. The catacombs were not hideouts, desperate refuges for escapees from persecution by the Roman imperial government. It was not police matters that built the catacombs. It was religion.

The catacombs followed Jewish precedent—(there are Jewish catacombs in Rome, too)—and monument-alized a basic Christian doctrine, *the resurrection of the dead*. The catacombs grew out of Christian values.

Nor were the catacombs mere quirks or curiosities of Christian practice. They were of the essence. That was the understanding I came to when I wandered the catacomb passages alone, my way lit by a single taper.

To understand Christianity, you must walk the catacomb labyrinths, as well as read your way through the labyrinthine lines of New Testament scriptures. The catacombs were intrinsic to the sect. They were faith in practice.

First, regarding their significance in the history of inhumation:—

Among primitive hunter-gatherers, as among nomads of any time period, inhumation must have been individual. When a member of a group died, he was buried where the group happened to be at the time. The body was then left behind by the wanderers, its location more or less remembered, any marker slight and flimsy.

When humans became settled and sedentary, living family life in a home, they began to establish family tombs, those related in life by blood continuing in that relatedness by the proximity of their burials. The family tombs of pagan Rome are prominent examples of that type, for the Romans developed a strong sense of family relatedness.

The Christians went beyond individual or family burial. For them sectarian belonging was even more important than family belonging; in fact, upon conversion of the family head, the entire family was inducted into membership. The Christians practiced inhumation by ideological affinity. The catacombs were the institutionalization of that practice.

Roman law was accommodating, because, although the Roman imperial government was suspicious of any association that might be subversive, it recognized burial associations as licit. Romans from families too poor to construct a family tomb could form a burial association and pool their meager resources to assure decent interment, escaping the shameful ending-up in the *puticuli* pits.

As the Christian sect recruited more and more members, drawing in more and more families, the subterranean ground space for the mass sectarian inhumation had to expand. It is estimated that a half-million Christians were interred in the dozens of catacombs around Rome; there were nearly 175,000 in one catacomb complex alone. Catacomb inhumation, established about A.D. 150, continued for two-and-a-half centuries.

The numbers of burials and the long span of catacomb usage required prodigious digging. The catacombs around Rome extend in tunnels of 150 miles (not in a straight line, of course, but in labyrinths).

We may think of the catacombs as dark, silent, and empty of living people, which is the way I found them when I ventured in alone. In their centuries of usage, however, they must have been teeming with activity. The digging itself must have been constant, not only the clawing out of new tunnels, but the lowering of floors of existing tunnels, several times, to expose more wall surface for burial niches. Then there were the probably daily activities of the cultists,—fresh sepulture ceremonial being conducted, gatherings for ritual meals and Requiem Masses on the anniversaries of the deaths of family members or the deaths of martyrs buried in the catacomb, in short, a constant coming-and-going:—

In this section, carloads of *tufa* rock fragments being drawn out through a tunnel and shaft to the surface; in another section, some deacons putting in clay tiles to wall up a niche newly occupied by a deceased; over there, a craftsman painting crude cultic symbols or penning a scriptural incantation; elsewhere, a funeral procession wending its way, the dark illuminated by smoky oil lamps, the silence broken by wailing women; in yet another area, a small chamber, a priest saying memorial Mass for a small group of those related to the deceased. The catacombs were bustling and crowded, like the streets of the Rome of the living. They were the central active institution of the Christian sect.

That institution was a death cult, one that violated traditional taboos. The Jews had considered the dead *unclean*; those who had to handle the dead were required to undergo purification afterwards. Yet, the

Christians repudiated Leviticus and its strictures, fondled their dead and mixed with them promiscuously, without scruple.

The Christians offended pagan taboo, too. For when Constantine, the emperor who co-opted the Christian cult, granted it legitimacy and leeway, the Christians broke the ancient provision of the Law of the Twelve Tables that interments had to be outside the city walls. The catacombs themselves, established under the old pagan regime, conformed, but, after Constantine, the Christians began to bury their dead in churches within the city of Rome. They even committed gross sacrilege by profaning the great sacred Pantheon itself; upon converting that pagan temple to Christian use, they carted in bones from the catacombs and installed them in the floors and walls, an outrage to pagan sensitivity.

The catacomb cult eventually faded into obsolescence and oblivion, first because Constantine had opened the city gates to, and had churches built for, the Christian dead, then, a century later, barbarian incursions to the very suburbs of Rome made the undefended catacombs dangerous to personal security. The barbarians, who themselves were Christians, took to looting the catacombs for their treasures of sacred relics of the martyrs. And so, the catacombs were abandoned, the whereabouts of some of them forgotten until rediscovered by archaeology and misinterpreted by Romantic imagination.

The values of the catacomb cult were these: Better afterlife than this life, better the otherworld than here, better dead than alive. That was the meaning of Christian *hope*.

The catacomb cult of the Christians was a ghoulish devotion and fetishism of death, all that nurturing of seed-corpses, the clinging to, and keeping close to, the dead. A more unwholesome and macabre cult it would be difficult to imagine.

It took Europe a long time to crawl out of those unholy holes. Even today we have not fully shaken off the chill of the catacomb claustrophobia of death.

There is nothing romantic—even gothic romantic—about the catacombs. They belong, rather, to the psychopathology of necrophilia.

118

"The Catholic Version"

I picked up a copy of the current *Catechism of the Catholic Church* to review and refresh my knowledge of dogmatic theology regarding death-and-thereafter.

First, the Catholic explanation of death itself:—

It seems that God the Creator had intended man to be as immortal as himself (*in the image of God*), but mankind, in the persons of the protopair Adam and Eve, frustrated God's generous intention by committing the so-called Original Sin. That sin was disobedience (human willfulness asserted against divine will); its hard punishment was to be mortality.

Well, let Adam and Eve take the consequences of their action, but why should what they did affect *me*? Because we are all children of Adam and Eve, Original Sin was their legacy to us. That sin is generic and genetic. ("In Adam's Fall/We sinned all.") It was through that sin that death entered into the world, and, even if humankind had never committed a second sin and subsequent sins, death would be with us, anyway. Catholic doctrine is the dogmatization of Jewish myth. Sin, guilt, and consequent death were all *ab origine*.

In the Catholic explanation, death is not a physiological phenomenon or a natural process; it is punishment for the Original Sin. Such a proposition inevitably leads out of the organic and earthly to the spiritual and metaphysical. Death, which the naturalist thinks of as matter-of-course dissolution, is to the theologian the consequence of offense against the Divinity. Now death has really become an important matter!

That all living creatures are born, live, and must die doesn't seem unfair or unjust to me personally. Why should I be resentful of the scheme-of-things? But that I should be culpable for what Adam did seems most unfair. My guilt is by association, and the most tenuous of associative relatedness at that.

According to the *Catechism,* God the Creator remains determined to carry out his intention of human immortality, despite the Original Sin. Each human life is to be a moral test, an opportunity to undo what Adam has done. I'm stuck with the Original Sin, true, but if I commit no sins of my own or (more realistically) if I repent of those I do commit—(Adam was unrepentant), I can overcome my congenital impairment (called *concupiscence*) and achieve blissful, divinely intended immortality. I can shake off collective guilt by a life of moral rectitude and personal blamelessness. There might be justice for me, after all.

Immediately after death, I will be summoned to particular judgment by Christ the Judge. (Jesus of Nazareth claimed that he had not come into the world to judge but to redeem; once back in Heaven, he reverted to the role of judgeship.) If I felt that it was unfair for me to bear the guilt of Adam's sin, I will eventually get my due of personal justice.

We are now back in thoroughly juridical thinking, in accord with the precedent culture of the Jews, the *people of the Law,* and, the Catholic Church being Roman, with the historical tradition of Roman law. The Christian version of the law code, however, is simplified and stripped to the essential. Those who have *loved* are adjudged innocent; those who have hated or failed to love are adjudged guilty. (Jesus the Lover recognizes and claims his own.)

The judgment is actually not so simple as that, because the Catholic Church has multiplied the Decalogue into long lists of sins venial and mortal, as well as accumulated tomes of doctrinal assertions, submission to all of which must be orthodoxy-tested at the divine inquisition. Still, Christ the Judge will cut through all that and render swift, fair justice.

Whether adjudged personally innocent or guilty, our spiritual destiny is *eternal life, everlasting life*. Almighty God's creative intention of human immortality will be fulfilled.

For those adjudged personally innocent, their reward is Heaven, which the *Catechism* describes most appealingly as "the state of supreme, definitive happiness". That happiness consists in induction into *the church triumphant* (the entire cast of characters of Christian heroism along with the more recent elect). All in Heaven share in a *beatific vision* of the Divine himself. (Whether Adam and Eve are among the company is unknown; my own grudge against them would hope not.)

For those adjudged personally guilty, their destination-and-doom is Hell, "immediate and everlasting damnation", as the *Catechism* succinctly characterizes it. Such eternal suffering was at first crudely conceived as the flames of fire—(the *Gehenna* of Jesus' rhetoric was a smoldering trash pile outside Jerusalem; throw the bad ones into the trash fire!); but a more refined theological conception interprets the misery of Hell as consisting in the awareness of eternal separation from God, a perpetual frustration of love-longing.

The love-or-hate, innocent-or-guilty, Heaven-or-Hell, be-saved or be-damned is part of the thoroughly dualistic dogmatics of Christianity. Dogmatic dualism can be terrible. "Depart from me, you cursed, into the eternal fire!", thundered the most judgmental Jesus of Nazareth the non-judge.

So, we have life-and-death in moral terms. Not all of us pure saints or degenerate sinners, however, there has to be an expansion of the metaphysical real estate to deal with less grave human imperfection. Hell is for moral felonies, but what about moral misdemeanors? In *Purgatory*, those guilty of venial sins have their little guiltiness purged away by fire, a fire cleansing and therapeutic, a cauterization, unlike the fire of Hell, which is torture pure-and-simple.

The souls in Purgatory may be ransomed by their still-living kin, their time of punishment and purging reduced or reprieved. The ransom may take the form of alms and indulgences and other such paying-in-cash, the abuses of which provoked the Reformation. Reformation notwithstanding, the Catholic Church has stubbornly kept to its notion of ransom through Masses for the dead, prayers to the Virgin Mary or the saints for intercession, and, yes, even those notorious indulgences.

A Dantesque medievalism clings to the imagery of Hell and Purgatory. (Dante proved a more influential Catholic theologian than Thomas Aquinas.)

As I checked through the index of the *Catechism*, I found no entry for *Limbo*, another parcel of metaphysical real estate, the one to deal with the souls of infants who died before being baptized against the Original Sin and had no opportunity to make moral choices, therefore neither meriting Heaven nor deserving consignment to Hell. The idea of Limbo must have been so vague that it has evaporated out of the corpus of dogma.

In postmortem trial and judgment, we have the old Jewish juridicalism. In Heaven-Hell-Purgatory, there are metaphysics and medievalism. Then, in the grand climax of the eschatological story, the General Resurrection and the Last Judgment, we encounter a scenario that outdoes Wagnerian opera. Jewish apocalyptic, that complex of ultimate retribution, reaches its cosmic crescendo:—

All the dead rise to life—God the Creator's intention completely realized—, the Earth and its lowlife destroyed—(Nature and her evidence against dogma done away with)—, the Judge returned to judge humankind—(although he has already judged each separately upon death)—, everyone who has ever lived now assigned to permanent residence in either Heaven or Hell—(Purgatory now closed down),—There, all finished!

Now, how does the human person, struggling through life and in apprehension of death, react to the Catholic version of death-and-the-thereafter?

Seemingly, the moral interpretation should motivate the person to a moral life, if only out of self-interest; "Be good and you'll get to Heaven". The promise of an afterlife should ennoble our earthly lives; everyone more loving, more moral, sin and crime shunned, a better life for us here. And so, a constructive dogma.

If there were only the incentive of Heaven, that might be the result. But Hell is the poisoner. Dualism takes away with one hand what it has given with the other. If there is a Heaven to aspire to, there is a Hell to dread. Dread is psychological. The Catholic version—never mind the legal moralism—is heavily psychological. And it is intimidating.

We should live in a "holy fear of God", the *Catechism* directs us. That we already fear the All-Powerful One is only simple prudence. But the Catholic version induces unnatural fear, nurtures it, exacerbates it. All moral dualism is ultimately terroristic. (They love the word *retribution*, but that word means, "You'll get yours!")

The Catholic Church claims a revelation regarding death, and not only death but all that is after death. That revelation eases the fear of death-as-extinction, but, at the same time, it inculcates the more terrible unnatural fear of afterdeath eternal damnation. The entire ideology is infected with intimidation, *fear of God,* as they put it. But what we fear we hate. How could we not secretly hate, as we fear, the Architect of Hell?

Fear of God is linked to submission to the Church, that authoritarian institutionalism that is so hypertrophied in the Roman Church. The dispenser of the power of God is powerful, too. Power involves the threat to punish; that threat induces unnatural fear.

Hell is a lot more terrifying than ever death was.

119

"Predestination"

The most cruel idea ever perpetrated by the perverse thinking of the human animal is the Christian doctrine of *predestination,* which holds that some are born to be saved, some to be damned. Not only to be damned, but born to be damned.

Christian theology is a heap of dilemmas and paradoxes, the logic out of which is bound to lead to bizarre and even revolting dogmatic conclusions.

In this case, the dilemma was this:—

If God is omniscient, He must have foreknowledge of the fate and destiny of all. Yet, if human beings have *free will*—(which they must have, in order to be culpable and therefore liable to judgment)—, there must be uncertainty about all their actions, including moral ones. Could God, the omniscient God, be in suspense about whether one might sin or not, deserve damnation or repent and be saved at the last minute? Could the human hold God on tenterhooks? Of course not.

Who will be saved, who will be damned?: The most vexing Christian problem.

The omniscient God already knows; He must not be susceptible to uncertainty and surprises. If He knows, then salvation and damnation are pre-determined (*foreordained*), never mind the idiosyncratic caprices of anyone's free will.

Predestination lies deep in the dogma, from Paul to Augustine to Thomas Aquinas to Luther, and, in its most notorious version, Calvin. Augustine coined the ominous Latin phrase, *massa damnata*, to identify the doom of the many. (It goes without saying that the holy divines secretly considered themselves members of the select *elect*. God must have bestowed upon them his saving *grace*. After all, they were the chosen bearers of his revelation.)

That God should have predestined the many to an eternity in Hell makes a devil out of the god. God becomes none other than the devil's accomplice and recruiting agent. How theology has demonized the very god it wants to worship!

What is most objectionable about the doctrine of predestination is not that God culls out the wicked from the good—(the goats from the sheep, as Jesus of Nazareth put it in pastoral metaphor)—, but that it is God himself who predetermines who the wicked shall be, who the good shall be, determines from conception. He then punishes his misbegotten and rewards his undeserving. The whole process of salvation seems a pre-rigged fraud.

Predestination means that some are cursed from conception. Imagine, life cursed at its outset! Oh well, it's all because of the Original Sin and all that, the theologians argue. So, we are back to our grudge against Adam and Eve. But even the Fall is suspect. Wasn't it too predetermined? The logic of determinism goes into infinite chronological regression and progression.

These are *mysteries of the faith*, of course. Perverse fantasies of the mind is more like it. A diabolical, sadistic God, an impotent free will, morality and responsibility mocked—(it doesn't matter really what you do)—, self-righteous glee in doom and damnation: *Mysteries of the faith*!

The moral consequence of belief in predestination might even be an immoral life, for, if God has predestined his elect, the verdict is immutable and you might as well live as you please. Such would be the reaction of logic.

The Calvinists insisted that no one knew just who were the elect, who the damned—(there was suspense to be endured, but by the human, not by God)—, but a moral life gave some indication, perhaps some assurance, that you *might* belong to the elect. Couldn't be sure, of course, but your moral life might be a sign that God has granted the grace of salvation to you. After all, how could God predestine a willfully wicked one to be saved? True, if God doesn't deign to bestow his grace upon you, a good life will not save you. You must use your free will to be moral, in any case... Fine paradoxes in a welter of doublethink and intimidation. And hypocrisy throughout.

Why should we humans, already living in a world of woe, deserve eternal damnation, such a heavy curse, after all? Well, it's back once again to that Original Sin and its hereditary taint. Not only hereditary taint, but innate wickedness in each and all from the moment of one's accursed birth. Now we have descended into the psychological perversity of Puritanism: Wicked, innately wicked, despise yourself and grovel before your Creator!

This whole outrage is the logic that follows from dilemmas and dogmatic paradoxes and from dualistic thinking in general. Conceptions about the nature of the divine can cause misconceptions about the nature of the human. When we turned psychology over to the theologians, we were done for. The theologians are the mystery-men, partisans of the soul and the afterlife, and, as such, hostile to the body and life in this our human Earthly world. There is plenty of misanthropy in the *love of God.*

And that love of God is actually a "cursing of God and enduring him forever," as Thoreau once indicted Puritanism.

120

"A Judgment upon Judgment"

It may have been the ancient Egyptians who first came up with the idea of a postmortem trial of the deceased during which one's entire life would be evaluated in moral terms. Out of that trial would come a verdict of eternal bliss or eternal damnation. The Jews and the Christians later developed that idea to an ultimate extreme of apocalyptic and eschatological Last Judgment.

If justice is commonly denied to us during our lives, it is only human nature that we should long for an ultimate righting of wrongs, such as a Last Judgment would provide. Presumably, a divine judge would be unerring in his verdict, and all would get their just deserts at last.

Once the Egyptians conceived of a judicial process as the inevitable ordeal of afterlife, however, some proceeded to corrupt that process. A way might be found to circumvent a guilty verdict. Spells and magic formulas and amulets and ritual texts and other such superstitious recourses might obtain salvation, even in despite of one's moral faults. Charlatans preyed upon anxiety by furnishing the paraphernalia of assured salvation,—(prototypes of rosaries and scapulars and holy medals and other such Christian talismans).

An ancient Egyptian faced Last Judgment on his own, alone against threatening demons. The Jews, by contrast, had a powerful corporate sense, one both ethnic and tribal. They conceived of their Last Judgment in collective, as well as in individual terms.

But what was the collective history of the Jews? The Old Testament and other ancient records chronicle it all for us. The story is one of frustration of tribal ambitions, oppression by the great empires, a gaping disparity between tribal self-estimate (the *chosen people*) and political reality, in all, a festering grudge against a world full of enemies. It should not be surprising that Yahweh, the god of the Jews, is characterized as an angry god, a god of wrath, a vengeful god, a god of retribution, a punishing god,—all projections of the craving for revenge against enemies.

The Jews felt that they had been wronged in life and during history, but they clung to the belief that their god would make it all right in the end, as we read in apocalyptic, a genre of religious writing invented by the Jews. Making it right meant vindication of the Jews as a people; it also meant punishing—smiting, striking down, casting into Hell, perdition, etc.—of the idolatrous tribal enemies of the Jews. The apocalyptic is a fevered delirium of righteous craving for revenge.

It should go without saying that if the judge is merely an agent for the aggrieved plaintiff, the entire judicial process is corrupted. (The Egyptians corrupted the evidence; the Jews got to the judge himself.)

Judgment must be fair, and, above all, dispassionate. You will find no dispassion in Jewish apocalyptic. Nor will you find any real justice. The *people of the Law* thought of divine law as effective weapon against their enemies.

The Christians took over the Jewish idea of Last Judgment, adding sectarian eschatology to apocalyptic. When the Christians began to proselytize *gentiles* (pagans), the ethnic and tribal nature of Jewish Last Judgment had to be dispensed with. In the cosmopolitan world of the Roman Empire, there couldn't be anything tribal or ethnic about attaining salvation. Yet, the Christians substituted another test-of-belonging, the sectarian test, to separate the saved from the damned, the sheep from the goats, as Jesus of Nazareth put it.

What severed the Christians from the Jews was exactly that person, Jesus of Nazareth, a Jew that the Christians claimed was none other than the son of Yahweh himself incarnate,—a blasphemy for which the Jews would condemn the Christian foul mouths to Hell.

Belief in the person Jesus as Son of God would be the new collective aspect of the Last Judgment. Sectarian belonging was now the criterion. Those who believed in Jesus would be saved, those who did not— (including the Jews, especially the Jews)—would be damned. Heaven would now go to the baptized, not the circumcised. The Christians turned Yahweh, the Jews' own vindicating judge, into the condemning judge of the Jews, a usurpation and dirty trick if ever there was one.

Christian Last Judgment became what it had never been among the Egyptians or among the Jews, that is, a test of orthodoxy. (The Egyptian was generally subservient to traditional belief, whereas a Jew was orthodox by fact of birth into the tribe.)

The Christians kept the moral test, certainly, the moral laws tested being the Ten Commandments of the Jewish code. (The Egyptians had considered as sins most of the same ones, but without a specific and mnemonic counting-to-ten.) But now an ideological test would be equal to the moral one. Wrong thinking was as sinful and damning as was criminal behavior.

The consequence of that was momentous, but by no means an advance into higher ethics and morality. Submission to orthodox belief, whether in its primitive Christian version belief in the person of Jesus or, in its later forms, belief in the corpus of dogmas elaborated by one of the various Churches claiming to represent that person, is a trial-by-ordeal of the mind. Out of that doctrine of Last Judgment as orthodoxy test came such instances of this-world enforcement as heresy trials, persecutions, autos-da-fé, Crusades, Inquisition, wars of religion, anti-Semitism, pogroms and the rest of the Christian intolerance that afflicted the history of the West.

The doctrine of Last Judgment inculcates unnatural fear. "You'll get yours someday!" If such induced apprehension deterred a single wicked one from a single crime, we might find some justification. But the wicked are not believers in eschatology. They are not deterred. The criminal may fear the police, but not Last Judgment. The threat is a crude method of behavior control, and a mostly unsuccessful one at that.

The doctrine of Last Judgment is more effective as intimidation of the human mind. Freethinking is more easily dissuaded than are criminal acts. That the heretics go to Hell along with the criminals is a deterrent all right, but to thinking, not to crime. When the Catholic Church had its monopoly upon thought, the threat of Last Judgment upon wayward thinkers was a powerful deterrent indeed. Any random thought in error could be one's damnation. (Thinkers are vulnerable to doubt.)

Don't risk your immortal soul by thinking! Just go along with what they tell you to believe.

To the ancient Egyptian, the Last Judgment was individual only. To the Jews, it was collective regarding ethnicity and tribe. To the Christians, it was individual and collective regarding sect, entitlement to which was acknowledgement of Jesus as Son of God and submission to the doctrines of his established Church. There are some who could pass the moral test but fail the test of orthodoxy. Derelict intellects are consigned to Hell.

Human psychology being the same, there has been the same temptation to corruption of the judicial process in the Christian scheme as there was in the Egyptian. Where an Egyptian might buy a magical text that would secure his acquittal, so a Christian who was a lifelong criminal might be saved by the timely deathbed intervention of a priest, some last-minute incantations, absolution, and Extreme Unction, a salvific lubrication. Cognizant of our own culpability, we dread facing the Last Judgment without countervailing magic, no matter how desperate.

What is objectionable about Last Judgment is not only some sneaky means to subvert it, but the very notion of Last Judgment itself. Regarding the Egyptian version, Last Judgment was just a superstitious terror. Regarding the Jewish ideology, retribution is not justice, if it is tainted by craving for revenge. Regarding the Christians, the Judge is not fair, if he is only the enforcing officer of orthodoxy; such Last Judgment is only Inquisition all over again. Even a guiltless man would want a jury trial of his peers under such circumstances. The Last Judgment sounds like a kangaroo court.

"Beware those in whom the urge to punish is strong," warned Nietzsche, that heretic. "Contempt of Court!", the Judge would thunder back at him. But oh those Christians do have such a strong urge to punish.

I have not ventured upon the humane objection to the Last Judgment, that is, that we ourselves are dispensing with capital punishment as an indefensible cruelty, and so an enlightened Judge should dispense with his Hell in emulation of us. We should not expect too much humane in the characterization of the divine that has been handed down to us.

Even without appealing to delicacy of feeling, to compassion, the Judge of the Last Judgment must be put under our own judgment. What is needed for reform is a sweeping-away of the whole Last Judgment legal system, especially in its orthodoxy tests, and a starting anew from fresh principles. For such a task we would want not another Moses but another Clarence Darrow.

121

"Person/Soul"

Universal Judge, which of the many persons that the one soul has been would you condemn to Hell?

Would it be infant or toddler, little boy or adolescent, young man or mature man, middle-aged man, elderly man, dotard?

The infant has an inchoate consciousness and no capacity for action, so certainly it is innocent in both thought and deed. If it were to die, I once heard, you would send it to Limbo, the holding area of your indecision. How would you then determine that soul's destination, whether Heaven or Hell?

If the infant lives and becomes a toddler, a housewrecker and general mischief maker, it still doesn't have a moral sense. The toddler blunders about, exasperating but not fully culpable for what it does. The toddler's behavior needs guidance and correction, but it is premature to talk about judgment.

The little boy then may be a naughty one, yes, and he knows that his naughtiness is wrong. He tells a lie, he takes something that isn't his, he strikes another child,—all sins, in fact. Such moral misdemeanors, venial sins, are all that the little boy is capable of, trivial harms all that the naughty boy can cause. You would not send him to Hell, because a heavy penalty should not be laid upon trivial offenses. A spanking by a parent is punishment enough.

And now the adolescent—(it is still the same individual soul I am talking about)—, so self-conscious, accuses himself of the worst sins, for he has discovered what sin is, he accuses himself of sin, just as he accuses himself of physical ugliness, intellectual inadequacy, and social ineptitude. The adolescent is the most severe judge of himself, all self-consciousness and conscience. He may even come to believe that he deserves Hell. Adolescence, miserable time of life, and miserable person the soul has become!

And if that adolescent's self-loathing should reach the extreme of suicide—how frequently that happens!—, do you, Universal Judge, dispatch that soul to Hell, suicide being called a mortal sin? The adolescent suicide, the wreckage of a life, stigma and sin. Is that distressed soul to be sent to Hell?

Now, if that same soul survives adolescence and proceeds to young manhood, that soul becomes yet another person. Perhaps one who succumbs to sexual dissipation. There can be no excuses now. The young man knows, has been inculcated with, the distinction between right and wrong. He knows the inventory of sins by heart, can distinguish the venial from the mortal. He is culpable for his actions, according to human law, and for both his thoughts and actions if he were to die and stand before the Universal Judge. Would you, Universal Judge, condemn the young man for falling before the instincts and impulses that ran roughshod over him?

When he becomes mature, he is yet a different man, another person. Instinct and wildness ebb. The mature man is more in control, more calculating. The sins he might commit are controlled, calculating ones. Embezzlement perhaps, white-collar theft, cheating in business, and other such calculating crimes. Thoughtful, deliberate culpable wickedness, you might judge. Or the mature man might revert to instinct and commit an adultery; but there would be calculation even in that.

There might be good actions to set against the sins and crimes. Do you, Universal Judge, follow a procedure like that of Egyptian myth, Anubis holding a balance and weighing the human heart against a feather, as Osiris the Judge looks on to give a verdict? Is the Last Judgment to be such a crude little mercantile act? If so, we should load up the scale-pan of good deeds to overbalance our sins and crimes.

The person in the middle-aged man seems to become less harmful to society, his passions evaporating. The middle-aged person does not usually commit a violence, but he may still have his private vices. Envy, avarice, hypocrisy. Generally, a middle-aged man muddles along. Whatever character he may have formed is now fixed, a solidification of the accumulated experiences and decisions of the earlier stages of his life. Middle age is a good time of life to try to attain sainthood, as Augustine discovered. The temptations are fewer, mind and body calmer, the motivation to get right with God intensifying the older one gets.

The elderly man barely remembers the person he was in his youth. When he comes to think of what he did then, he is at a loss for an explanation. His memory tells him that he committed this-or-that, but he would never do such things now. He is ashamed of the person he once was, regrets his lifetime of offenses. But what can he do about them now? He tries to forget, to spare his self-estimate.

Then, the dotard, reverting to toddler, morally speaking. He has no energy for evil thoughts, no capacity for evil acts. Invalids are incapable of sins, let alone crimes.

. . .This has been the biography-in-brief of a single soul. But that single soul has not been a single person. Many persons have come and gone over the lifetime of that soul. Strange that if that soul had been taken from life at one stage, in one person, that soul would have deserved Heaven, whereas if taken at a different stage, where there was a different person, that same soul would have deserved Hell. How important to our salvation it is to die at the right time, when one is one of the better persons that one is and becomes!

The theologians say that the only person that matters is the one who happens to be in the soul at the moment of death. Then, if innocent, one proceeds to Heaven. If guilty, there is still a chance for last-minute contrition and rescue, but woe to the bad person who dies unawares, bushwhacked by Death at an inopportune time. Meanwhile, the lifelong criminal and monster, contrite at the right moment, may be redeemed in an instant. Hitler in Heaven? It doesn't seem fair, it doesn't seem just.

Our faith is in the wisdom and justice of the Universal Judge. And so, Universal Judge, which of the many persons that the one soul has been through life would you promote to Heaven or condemn to Hell?

"The Wheel and the Line"

Despite the collectivity of *the communion of saints*, the Christian scheme of salvation is ultimately individualistic. You've got to save your own soul; that is your main task in life. Let all your family and loved ones and friends all be damned to Hell, if you have saved yourself you have succeeded.

The doctrine of the immortality of the soul is not only individualistic, but egotistic. Whatever I may do in life, whether good or evil, has significant consequence ultimately only for myself. My ego-soul will live forever; I must live on Earth in such a way as to secure my attainment of eternal bliss.

Because of ego involvement, the Christian prime virtue, charity, is hypocritical. Doing good to others is of most benefit to oneself as conducive to attaining salvation. So, the morality test is one of self-interest. The Christians use one another to save their own souls.

The immortal soul of the Christian follows a solitary straight line to its salvation or damnation. "Save yourself" is the goal.

It was the pagan Greeks who introduced, nurtured, and propagandized the *psyche*, the soul. The Christian theologians later made their contributions to the notion of the soul. The culture of the West became thoroughly individualistic, as it has remained, despite the retrograde collectivism of Communism and other such counter-currents. Our Western ideal is to be a free one, autonomous, a self-directed soul, the ego following a self-assertive straight-line course even into an afterlife.

The philosophies and religions of the East, however, have not got hung up on such extreme individualism. Instead, they place the individual into a larger scheme-of-things.

We roll our eyes at the outlandishness of the Hindu gods, all that colorful and egregious idolatry. The Buddhists go so far as to deny that there is even such a thing as a self. The human being is a transient, ever-changing consciousness, they say; that is antithesis to our own most basic belief in a solid unchanging ego. The Buddhists likewise disallow a God-Self. That was why Pope John Paul II, even while approving their morality, disparaged the Buddhists as heathens because of their putative atheism. (The Buddhists flunk the Western orthodoxy test.)

How could Asia have developed any cultures at all by denying or suppressing ego?, we wonder. After all, our own Western culture is the creation of our geniuses, our hyperinflated ego-types.

Yet, there is a sophistication in the Eastern doctrines on life-and-death that shames our own selfish scenarios of ego-soul salvation.

The Hindus conceive of a great interrelatedness of life and death, a comprehensive vision in which any individual life or individual death is just a tiny component. Your soul came from another and will be passed on to another; your birth was one event in that great process, your death will be another. The process was not invented for your personal salvation. You are on the wheel and ride along with it. You have no power to steer or direct.

Like the Christians, the Hindus and Buddhists see a moral consequence to individual lives, but instead of a personal Judgment as outcome, they trace a more general *karma*, a chain-of-consequence, whether good or bad, that affects, not just the individual, but all future life and all future living. Now, there's a moral significance of your life for you!

In the East, salvation is not so much an individual goal as a general human one. The critics make much of the pessimism and fatalism of Eastern thought—(as if Christian predestination is not susceptible to the same criticism). The wheel of *samsara* seems hopeless to us, the endless reincarnations absurd. What, will I be reborn as a mouse or a cockroach?

As with all religions, what is important is not the literal factuality of the doctrines, but the way to live promoted by the metaphors. Hinduism means: Live well, so that life will get better for all. Buddhism means: Disengage yourself from your illusionary ego and substitute human compassion for self-interest; you are saved only when you stop wishing for, and working for, your own little ego-soul salvation. Hinduism and Buddhism see the bigger picture, the Great Scheme-of-Things, of which any individual is a tiny part, no matter self-deceptive pretensions.

Death is the worst crisis of life to the egotist; it precipitates personal salvation or damnation. No wonder the Christians pray so fervently for a *good death.* In the Eastern view, however, death is the common necessary event in the turning of the wheel and the continuance of the great procession, nothing to get too excited about or worried over. Despite their divinely revealed doctrines and salvific methodology, the Christians die anxious. The Buddhist, however, knows death for what it is and faces it with equanimity. There is a great psychological advantage, a psychotherapeutic one, to be derived from the religions of the East.

The Hindu version of enlightenment is perceiving that the *atman* (the individual-soul-in-current-manifestation) is part of *Brahman,* the great All. (Reeks of pantheism, a Christian would say of that.)

The Buddhist attains enlightenment by being freed from craving, especially the craving of the ego, including that for egotistic personal salvation. Letting go of the self is the ultimate of liberation. The Christians want

Heaven; Buddhists find their *nirvana* in cessation of wanting itself.

During the Sixties, my contemporaries in the United States were seeking values to live by. Rejecting the Western values around them as unsatisfying and un-fulfilling, they discovered the philosophies and religions of the East. After a brief flirtation, however, they re-verted to the egotism of the West, so engrained had it been in them. We still want to save our personal souls. Toward that goal, we believe, our spiritual technology will be as effective for salvation as our material tech-nology is effective for our economic thriving.

We in the West are straight lines, or, rather vectors. We had an individual beginning in conception, and we follow a solitary course to salvation or damnation. The wheel of *samsara* of the East does not appeal to our ego-craving. We want to go it alone, after death, just as we have through life. Sure, dying is suspense, but we aspire to be heroes. The core doctrine of our Western belief is "*I* must live forever".

* * * * *

Which sequence is the <u>actual</u> course of human life, of an individual human life?:—

Pre-existence»»»»Existence»»»»Post-Existence, on and on, round-and-round in cycle?
(The Wheel: Hinduism, Buddhism)

or

Nonexistence»»»»Existence»»»»Post-Existence?
(The Line: Judaism, Christianity, Islam)

or

Nonexistence»»»»Existence»»»»Nonexistence?
(The Line to an end: Nature)

123

"Sin/Suffering"

The Christians say that the problem is sin.

The Buddha said that the problem is suffering.

I do not know what *sin* is.

I know what suffering is.

I want to be redeemed from...suffering.

124

"The Skeleton, the Ghost, and the Soul"

The various religions have elaborated their particular ideologies of death, dealing with the nature and significance of death, afterlife (if any), the duties of the living toward the dead, and so on. Ideologies abstract and generalize death. The experience of witnessing a death, however, is very concrete and specific. The ideology is imposed upon a specific death as its interpretation and meaning.

Besides the ideology of death, there is a symbolism of death; ideas are complemented by images. In so far as seeing is comprehending, we want to see death as a visual representation. Some of the iconography of death is peculiar to a particular culture, as Anubis and Osiris in ancient Egypt, Thanatos of the Greeks, Charun and Vanth of the Etruscans, the Grim Reaper of European peasantry. Other imagery of death is somewhat universal, because the symbolizing faculty may operate independently of culture, as it does in dreams.

One universal image of death is the skeleton. We never see the skeleton of the living person, but, when that person dies and decays, the skeleton, there all the time, reveals itself and persists as the only lasting physical remnant of the person. The skeleton is, as it were, the frame or rack upon which the living person was hung.

The skeleton has the recognizable form of a man, but stripped from it has been all that we associate with living,—corporal fleshiness, the warmth of the skin, the senses, movement, the expressions of the face, the ability to speak, the breath of life, and all those other perceptible evidences by which we distinguish a living person from, let's say, a manikin.

We know from biology that the skeletal system lives and grows, the bones full of blood. During life the skeleton is not an inert rack, but, rather, an animate component of the organism. Nonetheless, the image-making mind finds in the skeleton an analogy to the trunk of a dead tree, what remains long after the bark has fallen away, the branches and limbs and twigs barren of living leaves.

Primitive man had plenty of direct experience of skeletons, of the prey he killed, and of his fellows, whether or not the corpses of his kinsmen were buried out of sight before decay had too much advanced. When a creature died, the skeleton remained. The skeleton, then, is a simple imagery of a life that once was, and, therefore, of death itself.

The human shares skeletal structure with vertebrate animals, some of which, like the apes, have a skeleton similar to the human. In disassembled or scattered skeletons, it is not always easy to distinguish, for example, a human long bone from an animal one.

The most distinctively human part of the skeleton is the skull, that skull with face and forward-looking eyes and characteristic large-brained shape, distinguishable even from the skulls of apes. The skull, then, could serve, by synecdoche, for the entire skeleton. The skull, the container of human consciousness, is a concise representation of the death of a human being.

I don't think that even the most primitive of humans ever attempted to reassemble the bones of human skeletons in hope of resuscitating the life of the loved one out of the assemblage. No, life was not in the remnant bones, but in what had gone, evaporated or evanesced. The skeleton was proof of death, was death itself. Staring like Hamlet into the hollow, empty eye sockets of a skull is staring into death itself.

Another universal, or at least widespread, image of death is the ghost. The ghost is an image of the superficies of life, the silhouetted form of the body as it appeared when the person was living. Yet, as ghost, that body has a vague, insubstantial character to it. It lacks solid corporality (and so is invisible or barely visible), lacks delineated features, and it is feeble in the capabilities of the living, such as movement and speech; (recall the *shade* of pagan Hades).

The ghost is a sort of inverse of the skeleton, for the ghost seems to lack a supporting structure within. It is covering without a frame, as the skeleton is a frame without a covering.

Unlike the skeleton, the ghost is visualized as animate, if feebly so. The ghost floats around, haunts the precincts of the burial ground, may even intrude into the lives of the living. The ghost may have some power over physical objects; that power, if exercised by a malevolent ghost, might harm the living. Even so, the ghost is mostly an empty form like a shadow.

The skeleton as an image of death derives from the real experience of actual skeletons, whereas the ghost is an image out of dreams, where we encounter the dead as insubstantial versions of what they once were in life.

The most refined image of the ghost is the soul. The image of the deceased now becomes thoroughly decorporalized and intangible; it becomes spiritual. If the skeleton is what is discovered after death and the ghost is the remembered dream-image, the soul is the never-seen, impossible-to-see essence of individual life, which essence left the body behind at death and ascended to some otherworld realm.

How could such a notion as the soul be visualized? How could something we can't see or visually imagine be real? Well, the breath is something we can't see, and we know that not only is the breath real, it is of the essence of the life of the body. The soul, then, is like the breath-of-life. (In Latin, *anima*, soul, means breath.) The soul leaves the body with the last breath.

The skeleton is a concrete imagery. We find it in the iconography of death in many cultures and historical periods, even in our own. The meaning of the symbol is obvious and easily represented.

The ghost, however, presents a problem to iconography: How do you represent visually an image that verges upon invisibility? There are sculptures of hooded figures representing the ghost of the deceased, but they are too much like representations of the living. Painting, in its flatness and pale coloration, can represent ghosts better than sculpture, but the viewer may still doubt whether the intention was to represent a living person or a ghost; the clump of floating bed linen is a caricature.

With the soul, the iconographic challenge becomes almost insurmountable, except by arcane symbolism that must be explained, for example, the soul as the Platonic bird-in-a-cage or as a set of bird wings or as an ascending flame. (How could an artist depict a departing breath?) The elaboration of the notion of the soul, therefore, has belonged more to ideology than to iconography. Plato and the Christian theologians have made more out of the soul than any visual artist could.

Ideology is what we believe, iconography what we imagine. Death has its doctrines, but also—can I say it?—its aesthetic. Reasoned explanation satisfies one part of the human mind, symbolism and imagery another part. In the combination of words about death and images of death, in ideology and in art, we hope to fully grasp, come to terms with, and even, in the case of the soul, be reassured and consoled about death.

125

"The Malice and Menace of the Dead"

In some cultures, it is believed that the dead may pose a threat to the living. (Was that why early man went to the labor of burying the dead,—to remove the threat by smothering the deceased?)

The dead may not be truly gone, may linger to haunt their former premises, drawn back by some ill-will they bear toward the living, even attempting to do them harm.

The dead may be malevolent not only toward their enemies in life, as we would expect, but even toward family members and relatives, toward whom they ought to feel no malice.

The grudge that the dead bear may not necessarily be toward particular living individuals; it may be a general grudge against death itself and a consequent resentment against all who have outlived the dead one and continue in the enjoyment of life, of which the dead have been stripped.

That the dead should wish to do harm to the living, that they might even be capable of it, is no superstition limited to the primitive. Our own Hollywood horror movies play upon and pander to that very fear and apprehension.

Death would seem to be the ultimate incapacitation. Nonetheless, if the dead are able to exist on, they might have acquired some uncanny kind of power, a power of the spirit-world, that they can exercise in our own world of the living. What the power or powers might be the living do not know; the anxiety is free-floating.

To placate the malevolent dead or else to ward off and frustrate their intended harm, there must be rites and ceremonies and prayers and spells.

A Roman example of such *apotropaic rites* is the pagan festival of the Lemuria. *Lemures* was the name given to those supposedly hostile ghosts.

Against a household haunting and harm to the family from the Lemures, the *paterfamilias* would get out of his bed at the dark of midnight. He would make a *mano fico*, thumb inserted between two fingers, (a phallic obscenity still to be observed in Latin countries), as a life-against-death gesture. Then he would walk through the house spitting out or dispersing beans (insemination, further life-against-death symbolism). After some more hocus-pocus of words and deeds, the old man would go back to bed, the household now to be secure in its sleep.

Considered psychologically, it might be surmised that our idea of the hostile dead is a projection of our own hostility toward death. Death is out to get every one of us, we know. Dead individuals represent the idea of death itself. When we fear and try to ward off those individuals, we are personalizing our fear of death. Death is a kind of crime that the dead wish to perpetrate upon the living.

When a person dies, he goes over to death, the enemy. The us-versus-them formulation is really an us-against-it. The dead are guerillas of death's war against us. It's not the dead we want to ward off; it is death itself.

Strange that the personalization of the fear of death should be extended to fear of one's own deceased loved ones. Why should those we love in life want to do us harm after they are dead?

The explanation for that must be in ambivalence, that paradox of all human emotionality. Strong feeling toward those closest to us necessarily has its ambivalence. In our funeral rites and reverence for the dearly departed, we show our love for them. At the same time, we must secretly accuse ourselves of failures of that love, even of animosity at one time or another. Love is not pure-and-simple; in it there may be an admixture of hostility, even of hatred. Love-versus-Strife, even beyond death. Perhaps we fear that the dead are on to our hidden hostility and respond in kind. That might be why we believe they wish to inflict harm upon their former nearest and dearest.

Another, more common, aspect of ambivalence toward a deceased beloved is resentment at being abandoned, blame against the deceased, combined with a powerful yearning to join the deceased beloved: "Why did you die and leave me?" and "I want to die, too, and be with you." Death is an estrangement that aches for reconciliation and reunion. Survivors feel abandoned, blame and accuse in turn, then want to reconcile.

The Roman Lemuria was a ritual of hostility toward the hostile dead. As we would expect from human ambivalence, there should be an obverse, a respect ritual. Indeed, the Romans had their Parentalia, a festival of loving remembrance of the dead.

Our modern minds too practice an alternation of Lemuria and Parentalia. But we Christians are more likely to personalize death as the devil out to get us. Meanwhile, the dead in Heaven, still practicing Christians, attempt to intercede on our behalf with God to secure our welfare on earth and our ultimate salvation. In the Christian version of Parentalia, we pray for, and to, the dead.

In characterization of the dead, there is projection and ambivalence. In the idea that the dead might do something bad to us, we ourselves do something bad to them. We commit a slander.

The worst, most pathological complex of the human mind is the mixing-up and muddling of Life and death, of the living and the dead, whether it is obsession with afterlife or fantasies of malevolent haunting. Our superstitions and religions adulterate Life with death. Why can't we recognize and admit that death is innocent, the dead are innocent?

Much of human harm is self-inflicted. The mind conjures phantoms and imputes to them its own worst traits of character.

126

"Halloween"

The Lemuria and Parentalia are curiosities of ancient Roman superstition, seemingly as distant from us psychologically as they are chronologically. Yet, we moderns carry on an apotropaic tradition nowise advanced from the crude symbolic magic of the *paterfamilias* on the night of Lemuria. I am referring to Halloween, the pertinence of which to my current topics is driven home to me as I happen to be writing this on an October 31.

Halloween was originally a *hallowed evening* of Christian observance, the prelude to the honoring of the heroic martyrs on All Saints' Day and the family dead on All Souls' Day, the latter a clear analogy to the Roman Parentalia.

All hallowedness and holiness have been frightened out of the Halloween observance, however. Halloween has become, not only secular, but positively sacrilegious to Christian values. And I don't mean just the horrifics of Black Mass and devil-worship.

Some of Halloween is innocent, yes. Like Easter, with its eggs and bunnies, spring symbols, Halloween has taken on, in its apples and pumpkins of autumn harvest, the peasants' observance of rustic seasonality. The innocent extortion (or, in my own childhood, the not-so-innocent) of trick-or-treat is a curious aggression that has infiltrated Halloween observance, along with adolescent vandalism, but it has no dire significance for values. Nor does the costume-party aspect of the holiday, at least if those costumes do not personify and characterize fears.

But fear, that unnatural fear, is of the essence of Halloween. Behind our contemporary cultural aspects— Halloween costumes caricaturing current political figures, for example—, behind the extraneous secularizing customs introduced from the British Isles, behind the Christian origins of the date and observance, there is a medievalism of fear and ignorance and, further back yet, the most primitive of pagan rites,—not the laughing paganism of sophisticated Greeks and Romans, but the animism going all the way back to primordial humans huddled in a night-fright around the campfire.

On Halloween night, we deal with fear by feigning fear, trying to convince ourselves that our fears are as unreal and fraudulent as the costumed devils, witches, ghosts, ghouls, vampires, and other such fancies of pure imagination. Getting inside the costume is getting inside the fear; the costume itself is an empty, limp and lifeless rag. We confront our fears by mocking them.

Halloween is an orgy of death, when the mind immerses itself in the fear-of-death in an attempt to exorcise that fear. If we can play at death, death itself is only play. The feared unknown comes out of the night, but we know that the apparition is only a costume, a fraud. Our fear is fun; we laugh at it, or, by handing out a treat to a skeleton or ghost, we bribe death, we ransom ourselves from it for the meantime. Thus the apotropaic nature of Halloween.

On Halloween, the iconography of death is everywhere. Not only the personifications, the characters of imagination I mentioned above, but also the paraphernalia—the torture instruments, coffins, graveyard holes, tombstones, any other physical objects that may be associated with death; and the settings too,—haunted houses, cemeteries, caves, dungeons, and such locales suggestive of the claustrophobia of inhumation. The Halloween iconography of death is comprehensive of persons, places, and things.

When I was a child, adults did not participate in Halloween, except for handing out candy to the trick-or-treaters or conducting an apple-bobbing competition. Halloween was left to the children. In recent years, however, I have noticed increasing participation by adults. (I read in the newspaper that the purchase of costumes, decorations, and such has made Halloween the second-most important holiday for mercantile sales, more important than Easter, second only to Christmas.)

Halloween deliberately inculcates fear into children. Now it seems that the parents must accompany them on the trick-or-treat rounds, helping the children deal with the fear and, not incidentally, attempting to exorcise their own fear, never mind that their minds are supposedly educated and enlightened. There is in Halloween an aspect of child abuse, and of mental self-abuse as well.

Does Halloween work? Is it effective in exorcising fears of death and horrors of imagination?

How can any primitive superstition be effective in our modern rationalist world? We don't believe in the efficacy of apotropaic rites. Participating in Halloween will no more banish our fears than throwing salt over our shoulder will bring us luck. We are wise to our own superstitions. If superstition we have, it is that we want a priest to administer Extreme Unction when we find ourselves *in extremis.*

Halloween is an unwholesome observance, unsettling to the mind. It stimulates perverse imagination and thereby provokes the conjuring of unnatural fear, instead of easing fear that arises by itself. We may laugh at death, but we know that death will have the last laugh.

Halloween is not an exorcism, but a wallowing in death. Yet, just as the Christian Churches have not put a deserved ban on sacrilegious Halloween, neither have the psychologists made outcry against it. What sacrilege? What death-derangement? Why, it's just the kiddies having a little bit-o'-fun.

The hypertrophied significance with which we have invested death has all sorts of pernicious psychological consequences. Our perverse imaginations magnify death into a Medusa-monster, to the detriment of both our spiritual health and our emotional equanimity.

Halloween gives our entire culture the creeps. Wholesome spirituality and psychotherapeutics should both undertake a campaign to abolish it. Yet, that won't happen, because something in the human mind loves the fear-of-death, doesn't really want to give it up. As if death could be dealt with and won over by perverse love.

127

"The Pornography of Death"

One wouldn't think that death, correctly understood, could be an entertainment, yet the human mind has converted the end into a climax that could be exploited for its dramatic possibilities.

Pagan and peasant societies have had their myths and magic rituals of death-and-rebirth, as in the Greek cult of Demeter. In those, death was the symbol of winter, season of lifelessness, to be overcome by the renewed vitality of spring. Nature endures her seeming-death as a regularly recurrent ordeal, but then life always returns. The myth of Persephone was not about a woman who died, but about the fecundity of Nature held in abeyance by winter. The mystery-cult of Demeter and Persephone was, ultimately, a pageant of life.

In the Greek tragedies, deaths were human and personal and individual (significant but not symbolic). The tragic hero came to a bad end, a death inevitable but undeserved. The dramatic interest, however, was not in the death itself—(death, common, is banal)—, but in the traits of flawed character and sequence of ill-omened events that led up to it. The spectators all knew in advance that the tragic hero was doomed to die,—(as we all are; there is no suspense in that). The spectacle was not in the death; it was in the determining preliminaries, the plot.

Aristotle thought that tragic drama induced a *catharsis*, a purging of all the emotional states related to death,—anxiety, dread, fear, pity, grief, and so on. Viewing a tragic fictional death might be a prophylactic or anodyne to grief over an actual one.

In Christian lore, the death of the Christ was the grand climax, to which the gospel narrative of the life of the Christ was mere preliminary. The Crucifixion was the most spectacular climax in the history of tragic drama. Unlike other tragedy, in which the death may be a virtual anti-climax to the fine speechifying preceding it, the Crucifixion was a death-spectacle-in-itself, one of horrifying explicitness and gory detail. It was protracted (three hours) and anguishing. The physical suffering and emotional distress leading up to it were explicit, too, extending the death process over days; of Last Words, however, there were few.

It may seem irreverent to consider the Crucifixion in terms of tragic drama, and so, by implication, of entertainment, yet the Greek tragedies too were religious rituals. The two had in common the deliberate arousing of the cathartic experience by calculated pathos. (The Crucifixion was so supercharged with ideological meaning that the Greek tragic deaths offer no comparison there.)

I have called death an "empty event", but, if so, the dramatists have made a lot out of nothing. Death could be dramatized, just as life could; the death-related emotions could be evoked even where there was no real death that had occurred. The death was just fictional; that is, it was entertainment. Death could be a merely vicarious (voyeuristic) experience.

Death has become the principal entertainment of our contemporary culture (or, let's say, co-principal, because sex competes well with it). Our entertaining deaths, however, are devoid of any symbolic or mystical or ideological or even much human significance; they are just spectacles of death-in-itself.

There is not much stirring dramatic possibility in the death of a worn-out feeble old person in a bed, unless there may be some sentimental weeping of children at the bedside and gentle whispering counsel by the talking gray head on the pillow. No, the fullest dramatic possibilities are to be found in violent death. In violent death is the arousing of the death-related emotions,—anxiety, dread, fear, and pity (but not grief).

The dramatization of violent death has a generic aspect to it,—cowboys-and-Indians, the sheriff against the gunslingers, cops-and-criminals, monsters-killing-humans, our-soldiers-versus-their-soldiers, and so on. There must be a characterization of good-or-evil in the roles of the combatants, for, if they were morally equivalent, how would the death of one or the other be distinguished and so cheered or cried over? And there should be the preliminary of struggle, the plot of events that creates the suspense and arouses the emotions to be purged by the deaths. There has to be a story leading up to the climax of death.

Or deaths. Oftentimes, the story writing is a weak pretext, just a quick lead, to get to the vicarious excitement of witnessing violent deaths. Feathers fly and horses tumble, as the Indians are picked off by the pioneers in the circled wagons. In the big shootout at the corral, the bad guys take their bullets, clutch a part of their body, then fall left and right to litter the streets. The gangster with the submachine gun mows down a blockful of pedestrians. The gargantuan monster consumes busloads of shrieking humans. In the war movie, explosions scatter bodies over the landscape.

A single death does not seem sufficient. (Even in *Hamlet*, supposedly the most noble and cerebral of tragedies, Polonius and Rosencrantz and Guildenstern had to get it, too, not to mention Ophelia and Laertes and Gertrude and Claudius.) Dramatized death tends to proceed to surfeit.

The number of deaths can never be enough. (I don't remember the statistic of how many deaths a child has witnessed on television by the age of eight.) Nor can the explicitness of the depiction of death be intense enough. In the old small-screen, black-and-white days of my television childhood, the deaths depicted had a necessarily small scale, pale appearance, and ineffectual impact. Now, however, with *special effects* a developed cinematic science, the superscreen blood and butchery, decapitation and dismemberment are as horrifyingly real as the real thing. Satiety is fended off by ingenious variety in the mayhem.

We moralize over the ancient Roman gladiatorial games, not recognizing that our own entertainment is of like type. Our only advance over them is that we can get the same emotional effect without actually killing the actors.

We similarly moralize over the pornography of sex, without recognizing its pathological partner in our entertainment, namely, the pornography of death. The two are, indeed, sometimes combined in a powerful complex,—the explicit torture and rape and murder of a naked actress, for example, arousing both lust and horror. Sensuality and violence are fused into that "witches' brew" that Nietzsche warned us about over a century ago.

Another perverse combination of sex and death is the current popular genre of erotic vampires and zombies, a pornographic horror.

Unlike the pagan fertility rituals, in which death had to be endured for the sake of rebirth, in our entertainment we murder sex for the sake of death. The most primitive of the human mind is not the most remote in time.

Death, like sex, is now just show-biz, and that show-biz is a pandering pornography. Just as there is no human fulfillment in sexual pornography, so there is no anodyne therapeutic in death pornography. We are just rubbing our faces in death and subjecting ourselves to our fear of death over and over unto morbidity and addiction. It is not catharsis; it is self-abuse.

The pornography of death, I believe, is much more wicked than the pornography of sex. The latter is a playing with the generation of life; but violent death is not a toy to be played with. Even the pornographers of sex have come to recognize the inadequacy of lust for full arousal; they must amalgamate it with the further provocative simulations and stimulations of violence. The orgasm of sex is not enough. An orgasm of violent death must accompany it.

As simulated sex is disruptive to the spontaneous instinctual yearnings of the body, so the simulation of death is upsetting to the mind's equanimity. We exploit and corrupt both the mystery of the generation of life and the human significance of death. As if real love and sex were not enough. As if we are frantic in impatience for death to come.

Knowing the human mind as I do, how could I have expected that death would be accepted in its natural innocence and left alone? Death, like Life, is ravished by the perversity of the human mind.

128

"Anti-War"

In the days of my young manhood, I was an absolute pacifist, made so first by a misreading of the gospel, then by the rarest of experiences in Rome, a religious experience. Other inducements to pacifism I found in the Quakers and in Lao-tzu.

War was abhorrent to me, not only ideologically but personally. The ongoing Vietnam War confronted my commitment. At first, I was going to take the high road of conscientious objection, lead to what punishment it may, or else resort to the self-exile of expatriation; but a worldwise friend of mine found an expedient solution that enabled me to escape war without losing my freedom.

I vexed myself over the question, "How is war to be explained?". Other than humans, ants are the only creatures in all Nature to undertake the mass slaughter of their fellows in organized warfare. Soulless ants may be excused their wars, but it was difficult to make excuse for humankind, especially after we received the Sinai revelation on the subject.

Some said that the problem was in the nature of man, an innately evil creature inclined toward all manner of sin, crime, and cruelty. Others argued that it was in social institutions,—the politics of nation-states that enjoyed the sovereign power to declare and conduct wars.

Religion (not even the turn-the-cheek religion) proved no cure, the fifth commandment notwithstanding. (Anyway, Yahweh was a hypocrite with his own taste for war and slaughter and tribal genocide.)

According to the anthropological theorists of the Sixties, so influential at the time, the situation was hopeless. From his earliest origins as *the killer ape*, man was a killer of his own kind. Killing, including murder and war, was innate to the human. Social organization only enabled man to increase the efficiency and expand the scope of what came so natural to him. War was the ultimate cooperation to the gratification of every man's murderous drive.

One of my earliest boyhood history lessons, learned from the fathers of my playmates who had participated in it, was about World War II, which was nothing less than a universal slaughter. Such an event seemed to validate the view of the innate murderousness of the human being.

Animals kill, but only the human commits premeditated murder. (There is a huge moral difference between kill-to-eat and kill-to-kill.) War is organized, cooperative, premeditated mass-murder. What, if the individual did on his own initiative, would be a crime, becomes, when sanctioned by a government, a patriotic duty and source of honor, glory, heroism, and other such noble elations. That governments succeed in getting the masses to join in the war—(one would think that they would be able to recruit only criminals)—again seems to validate the every-man-a-killer hypothesis.

Murder, even premeditated murder, is considered an act of passion. Yet, it is remarkable how passionless the common soldier is. He has nothing personal against the man he sets out to kill. Far from being in a rage, he is detached, methodical, businesslike, a mere instrumental cog-in-the-wheel, just doing a job, as he did to earn a living before he was drafted. (Surprisingly, violent criminals are no good as soldiers.)

What characterizes a soldier is not an evil heart, but a convinced mind. Somehow he has been propagandized into participating in a dangerous venture that is actually against his self-interest (self-preservation, the most basic self-interest). He fights, not to gratify wicked bloodlust, but because he believes in some idea or cause and feels an obligation of loyalty to it.

How few of the wars fought by our own country involved any personal interest or gain by American soldiers. The Revolutionary War was purely out of ideas, ideas economic and political. The grievances against the British government were primarily pecuniary; to justify them, a political rationale was formulated. The colonial lived under no real terror that the British government was out to murder him in his bed, rape his wife, and sell his children to the slavers. Participation in the Revolutionary War was not out of the heart, but out of the pocketbook and its attached mind.

The Civil War, fought back and forth over the American landscape, through the homesteads and towns and cities, did involve real threats to the safety and security of family and home, which would arouse a passion of violent self-preservation. Yet, that war too was provoked by economics—the plantation economics of slavery—and subsidiary politics—the constitutional nature of the Union. (I do not overlook slavery as a moral issue; but mass murder is no solution to a moral issue.) Sectional animosity, the hatred of one regional American for an American from another region, was not a personal hatred. Rather, it was an ideological hatred out of economic and political differences.

What of our other wars,—the Mexican War, the Spanish-American War, World Wars I and II, the Korean War, Vietnam, the Gulf War, Afghanistan, as well as the military ventures in Panama, Grenada, Bosnia, Somalia, Libya, Iraq, and such? The individual American soldier can have felt no hatred for the citizens of such unknown, distant, unthreatening countries, nor could the soldier have derived any advantage to himself or his family. The soldier was just doing his patriotic duty, once again, working a job whose necessity he had somehow or other become convinced of. What was in his heart was not the lust to murder as many as possible, but to just get it over with and return to family and home. Hardly evidence of the pathological view of the human.

We shake our heads in lament over the horrors of war, then we go ahead with our recruiting for the next one. Evil hearts or not, young men can be convinced to war by some rationale or other. Convinced to it even against their own loving disposition and self-interest. The personal aspect of the problem of war is not the evil heart, but the mind lacking critical power and the will too weak to assert itself in one's own real interest.

We moralize over war, but, really, we should theorize. Instead of shaking our heads, we should exercise our minds.

Back in those days of my threatened induction to the war in Vietnam, I was not persuaded to the pathological view of the human; my own finer feelings and conscience argued against it.

It was in Rome, too, that I came across *The Anatomy of Peace* by Emery Reves. That reading was a revelation. It convinced me that the problem of war was a political one, with a political solution, namely, a world government that would disarm all the nations, making war as impossible as one state of the United States making war upon another. A world federal government, analogous to our own federal government, would abolish war by rendering it impossible. And so I became a universalist, a world-government man.

I still believe that world government is the answer. If the human heart is innately wicked, why, there is no cure for it, but political structures are most amenable to alteration.

I am not naïve or blind to the reality of evil in the human. (How could anyone who knows, who has lived through, the history of the twentieth century be so?) There are murderous people, and they must be stopped, especially when murderous people at the heads of governments can spread their own murderous tendencies to mass warfare. Within countries we deal with murder not as a psychological or moral problem, but as a police matter. Between countries it should be the same. War is a political police matter.

There are criminals among us, but most men, I believe, are lovers of peace-and-quiet. The human is capable of anything, yes. It is the duty and charge of government to render the criminals incapable of harming the lovers of peace-and-quiet.

The problem of war is not our passions, but our politics, not in our constitution, but in our constitutions.

129

"*Pro Deo et Patria*"

The phrase *Pro Deo et Patria* is one of those ideological formulations to which I react with an instinctive snarl. Any dedication or service to *Deus*, a metaphysical fiction, and to *Patria*, a political fiction, is energy squandered on behalf of delusion. As an idea, God-and-Fatherland is fantasy. And why make God a chauvinist warmonger?

The implications of the phrase are insidious. What do God-and-Country deserve (or, rather, demand)? Not merely dutiful service, but also sacrifice of oneself, of one's life. The context of the idea is always, "They *died* for God and their Country". Better if they had continued living for themselves and their families, I say.

Pro Deo et Patria is a pompous rationale for spent lives, the apologia for military murder and suicide. As I pronounce the phrase, an obscenity echoes back. If I sniff, the phrase raises a stench.

The military insists that the combination of religion and patriotism hallows any cause, makes happy any murder, and somehow renders war sweet and sublime. But do the dead share that smug conviction, as they lie in their coffins? Did they find their ultimate fulfillment in those little Latin catchwords justifying their deaths?

Organized religion was corrupt enough without becoming inseparable from, and incestuous with, the idolatry of nation-state patriotism. Yet, the fusion is intelligible, because both ideologies share certain concepts, like the primacy of patriarchal power (identified with a supreme male, *Deus* as person, *Patria* as personification), the insistence upon absolute obedience to the Father, unquestioning loyalty, and submission even unto martyrdom. The Cosmocrat became an Earthly politician. The Kingdom of Heaven was annexed and incorporated into the warring kingdoms of Earth.

God-and-Country? Far better to be an atheist cosmopolite breathing than a martyred hero moldering. Let our loyalties be directed to Life. God-and-Country's necrophilic prescriptions be damned!

130

"Death Fanatics"

Under such ideological formulations as *Pro Deo et Patria,* it is considered noble and heroic to die for one's beliefs and for a cause. Willful dying is the proof of one's conviction and commitment.

Death as an ideological statement must always be suspect. The only thing such a death proves is that the ideology was a life-and-death matter to the person who chose to die. It says nothing about the intrinsic worth of the ideology itself.

The Christian martyrs sometimes sought out prosecution, provoking arrest, confounding the judges who urged reasonableness, and blessing the executioners who gratified their wish. "They died for their faith." The Japanese kamikaze pilot took a more direct course to death, plunging his aerial steel against naval steel, the exploding fuel a fulfilling instant cremation. Our recent Muslim terrorists strap bombs to their bodies, detonate them in the midst of a crowd, thereby hoping to send many infidels to Hell, while the hero of *jihad* proceeds to a pat on the back from Allah and the eternal sensual pleasures of Islamic Paradise.

Such instances make one doubt the nobility of dying for one's beliefs. Those death fanatics were determined to die. "Something to die for" meant nothing to live for.

We believe that our creeds, our convictions, our ideological commitments are valid, but we can never be sure. There are as many martyrs to folly as there have been martyrs to truth. The former are dead dupes, as the latter may be considered heroes. It is sometimes difficult to tell which are which.

Regarding the Christian martyrs, the kamikaze pilots, and the suicide bombers, what is significant is not the Christianity, the cult of the Japanese emperor, or the Koran. Different ideologies, those three; and yet there is a commonality of psychology, or, rather of psychopathology. Some die willfully, not out of necessity or no-other-way, but out of compulsion, out of death fanaticism. It is not so much that they died for their beliefs, as that, alienated from Life, they simply wanted to die, found their fulfillment in death, and latched on to the ideology to ennoble or even glorify their suicidalism.

Life loves itself, and Life loves itself within us. Nature, as the biologists inform us, imbues each creature with an instinct for self-preservation, which is the controlling fundamental instinct. Yes, there are strange phenomena, like the mass suicide of the lemmings, but that is to be explained by nervous breakdown from the stress of overcrowding or some other kind of physiological mess-up. Obviously, if the lemmings killed themselves off too frequently and thoroughly, there would be nary a lemming left. Generally, animals do not kill themselves. Certainly, it is against their nature to premeditate to do so.

Our own human animal bodies want to go on living, but our bodies are subject to, and sometimes overridden by, our minds. We are susceptible to psychological mess-up. It is the most bizarre idiosyncrasy of the human that we can choose to flout Nature's prime instinct by willfully choosing our own death, not only impulsively—as one might jump ten stories to death to escape death by flames—, but also calculatedly, premeditatedly. We may choose to die for some *reason*, (a reason that may be more or less reasonable). The reason to kill oneself might be personal, or it might be ideological. In cases of mass fanaticism, we may even emulate the lemmings.

To want to die! Nature scowls at the human.

Never mind Nature, say the death fanatics. They imagine God's approval,—Jesus looking down upon the Christian martyrs or Allah upon his *jihad* warriors.

There are other cases where death is not wished for or provoked or effected by suicide; rather, death may be the undesired but necessary consequence of a moral stand.

Living is a wonderful thing, to be cherished as long as we can enjoy and experience it. Living is not an absolute value, however. There must be a quality to the living that makes it worthwhile, that deserves continuation. One aspect of that quality is the moral one. If my continued living were to depend upon my committing a moral outrage or becoming morally degraded, such continued living would not be worth it. Live-at-any-cost is a selfish desperation. If body, so if soul becomes pathological, it is better to die than to live a corrupted existence. If integrity and consequent self-respect are dead, the living body becomes a moral zombie.

Throughout human history, as there have been martyrs of ideology so there have been victims, those killed in persecutions and pogroms. Victims did not want to die; death was inflicted upon them as a consequence of what they were and what they believed, the Holocaust one such modern instance.

Very different from the cases of victimization is the fanaticism in which a suicidalist succeeds in glorifying his act of desperate death by seducing others to attach to it an ideological significance. Such a death is not noble but bizarre, not heroic but pathological, not edifying but corrupting, deserves not a eulogy but a curse.

The death fanatics run amok among us. Life must be defended against them; we must defend our own lives and liveliness against their pernicious example.

Martyrological death affects us emotionally, as all dramatic events do. Emotion yielding to valuation, such a drama is not a tragedy but a pornography. We should shun it, turn our eyes away, shudder off the influence, and return to the loving and cherishing of our own continued living.

"Private Suicide"

Even so, what is this righteous indignation against, this severe moral censure after-the-fact, laid upon the one who has committed suicide? We hold the suicide guilty, guilty of the gravest sin, the one irredeemable sin, and of the worst crime of violence, deserving punishment, even though the perpetrator of that crime has moved out of our jurisdiction forever.

Suicide, a sin against Life, a crime against...oneself? But who is the aggrieved, who is the victimized? If another chooses to take his or her life and has already done so, what can that now be to us?

How morally absurd it is to crave to inflict punishment upon one who has already inflicted the ultimate punishment upon himself! What worse could he deserve for what he has done than what he has done?

The Christians have laid their moral censure (*mortal sin*) upon suicide. They, whose model, whose first practitioners, were themselves suicidalists. Of course, things are different now. We can't compare ourselves to the Savior or to the saints. Why they acted as they did is a *mystery of the faith.*

We pass judgment upon the suicide into the empty air, or—all judgment meant to be cautionary and deterrent—we warn the still living against doing what the suicide has done.

Our condemnatory valuation of suicide is, I think, not so much high moral principle as it is mere resentment and grudge. Those of us who are still in the race, sweating, dirtied, bruised and sore in limb, breathing out gasps of weariness, pressing on mindlessly,—how we resent the one who, to escape the terribleness of Life, has taken the easy way out. We still have to put up with the struggle, but that one, the quitter, has shortcut the race, in mockery of the other runners, and, by so doing, has called the worth of the race itself into question.

We've got to keep going, no matter what, until we collapse in exhaustion. Damn the quitters!

The prospect of suicide renders human life merely provisional and conditional. Continued living, only so long as... Continued living, only if it keeps to certain standards. Continued living, only if life is livable. Otherwise, the race no longer worthwhile, out of the race!

Absolutists, life-absolutists, find such thinking repugnant. For them, suicide is a grave sin,—and a temptation. So, if they cannot put the suicide in jail, they will put him in Hell.

Even so, the damage has been done. The example of the suicide calls Life into question. By doing so, it embitters the lives of the survivors and bystanders. We dread a contagion of life-weariness.

The moral condemnation of suicide is only spite returned for spite. Death is silence, so Life can always get the last word in.

132

"Merciful Killing?"

There was a doctor in Michigan whose practice consisted in enabling patients to end their lives. He was by trade a pathologist, well acquainted with those morbid processes of the body that are irreversible. To spare the patient in a hopeless situation the agonies of protracted suffering, the doctor intervened and provided the know-how and wherewithal to cause death. He did not solicit patients, but came to their summons. He considered what he did an act of compassion.

Dr. Death provoked opposition religious, legal, and medical.

The religious said that life is a *gift from God* and that only God should have the power over life-and-death. The so-called mercy killing that the doctor practiced was a double sin,—suicide for the patient that solicited his own death, murder for the doctor who obliged.

That this particular doctor enabled the deaths of dozens of terminal patients, did so openly, and campaigned on behalf of the practice only magnified the moral outrage. The religious were not persuaded that the compassion the doctor expressed justified his acts.

If God does not defend his own prerogatives, the religious must do it for him. Regarding the suffering, Christians have always believed that suffering (especially someone else's) is salvific. "The Lord works in mysterious ways his wonders to perform," one of which mysterious ways must be gratuitous physical suffering. The limit of Christian compassion is at the point where it infringes upon God's power.

The religious allow medical people to intervene on behalf of Life (give God a boost);—that is what medicine is; but doctors must not intervene on behalf of death. The infliction of death is a sin, unless God does it.

The law is the powered arm of morality, and so the prosecutors too attacked the doctor, trying to secure his indictment on the charge of murder. The more they pursued him, the more the stubborn doctor dauntlessly proceeded to, and then proclaimed, his latest assisted death, at which provocation the law made its next attempt.

Yet, crime must have a victim. If a person solicits his own death as a relief from intolerable suffering, how can he be characterized as a victim? The families of those the doctor served considered him a benefactor and angel-of-mercy; they lodged no complaint against him.

Euthanasia is a crime against society, the prosecutor then said, as if a few deaths in Michigan would induce the entire society of the United States to go on a binge of mass suicides, the doctors all turning into assassins at the bedside.

"The Constitution does not recognize a right-to-die," a court pronounced,—a dereliction by our Founding Fathers.

God has the right to inflict death, the religious say. The State too has that right, at least in those states that practice capital punishment. But the individual has no such legal and Constitutional right over one's own life. Democratic liberties do not extend that far. If God and the Constitution require a person to suffer, that person must yield to superior sovereignty and do so.

The doctor's attorney fending off legal attacks, the prosecutors took a backup position on behalf of society. If euthanasia must go on, then it must be regulated, to insure that no patient is done in without due process. Some considered *Dr. Death* overly zealous, which might lead to heedlessness. Also, the publicity surrounding him might attract some who should be saved from his services by establishing some procedural safeguards.

There used to be an absurd assertion that suicide was against the law, as if there could be such a law, punishment for the infraction thereof would be impossible. Yet, the legal system is still trying to get at any accomplices to suicide. Sometime in the future, the last stand of the law against euthanasia will be the issuing of licenses for it. As in the cases of alcohol, marijuana, and gambling, social evils, if they cannot be legislated out of existence, they can at least be taxed to increase the revenues.

Surprisingly, there was as much medical opposition to *Dr. Death* as religious and legal opposition. (That euthanasia has always been practiced covertly by physicians few in the medical profession would deny.)

Besides the crude jest that euthanasia robs a doctor of future income, we must recognize that a relentless fanaticism for life can be as dangerous to the patient as one for death. Some doctors have a zealotrous belief in the limitless technological possibilities of their treatments and would push each to the ultimate of measures. Drugs and paraphernalia can extend life on and on; but, one must ask, at what point does life become degraded to mere existence?

For their part in the controversy, the psychologists put the terminally ill in the guise of victim. What the unfortunates were really suffering from, the psychologists said, was depression, which could be relieved by more drugs or by psychotherapy. All severely depressed people think of suicide, but that does not mean that they really want it. Those who solicit euthanasia are victims, not of the incurable illness but of quite curable depression.

As if feeling better about a hopeless situation is an effective therapy. "Sure, you have pancreatic cancer, but cheer up, won't you?" Like the religious, the psychologists tend toward the belief in suffering as salvific. Like the medical doctors, the psychologists want the interesting cases at the frontiers of their practice to go on and on.

A philosopher—take Seneca or Schopenhauer, for instance—would say that one's own particular life and one's own particular death too are a private and personal matter, the one thing that truly belongs to the individual alone.

In the situation of choosing death instead of protracted suffering, there are plenty of intrusions by other people,—the clergy and moralists, the lawyers and judges, the doctors and psychologists. Won't the libertarians tell them all to back off?

There are inconsistencies and hypocrisies among those who oppose euthanasia, of course. Many religions raise no objection to capital punishment. (Where is God's prerogative there?) The State sends off healthy innocent young men to die as soldiers. Judges condemn criminals to the electric chair or lethal injection. Doctors abort new life. The difference in the death-dealing is that, in these examples, one party inflicts death upon another, whereas the terminally ill wish to impose only upon themselves.

Most social issues become personalized. In this one, *Dr. Death* himself was a poor advocate for the cause. His appearance was cadaverous and sinister, his zealotry suspect, his determination and persistence fanatical. A few of his cases *might* have had medical solution other than euthanasia.

I wonder how the issue will progress now that *Dr. Death* himself has departed from the scene. (Was he able to find an obliging colleague for an assist in his own finish?)

We don't choose to come into the world. Despite our control over our own lives thereafter, we are denied any rights or say in our own demise. Strange that so-called free will should be prohibited us just when we need it most. Choose this-or-that, but you may not choose to die, they say. Or, if you do—(and a curse on you for it!)—, go ahead on your own and make a botch of it; medicine would lose its morale if it extended you any assistance.

But, really, doesn't the human being have a human right to give up and go? Hopelessness of mind and agony of body seem a perverse salvific. Under such dire circumstances, it is better to lose one's life than save it. A compassionate end, instead of a cruel continuation.

133

"The Ascendency of the Inert"

Death is desensitization and devitalization, but both processes may go on during living as well. Living needs to be stimulated by daily contact with the living; the animate is animating. Correspondingly, the inert inclines the living toward inertness.

I recently heard of a curious new toy called the *virtual pet.* It is a handheld electronic device that simulates the needs of a living pet. If the child pet-owner does not respond to the electronic pleading needs of the virtual pet, it sickens and may even *die*, which word, in this application, means the ceasing of electronic functioning. Not surprisingly, it was the Japanese who came up with the toy.

There is a lot less bother with an electronic pet than with an actual animate one, of course. The electronic version might even serve as a trial-run of a child's responsibility; certainly, neglect of a device is less cruel than neglect of a living creature. In actuality, however, children are caring for their electronic pets in lieu of real ones, and they think they are experiencing relatedness to a pet. Relatedness to...what? To a thing, an inert contrivance.

A living cat will rub against your bare ankles, a dog will lick your face, a bunny is a warm, smooth furry breathing bundle against your chest. Even a turtle will tickle your palm with its claws as it crawls over your hand. All such sensory aspects of relatedness to a pet are denied to children who own an electronic one.

Sensory contact of life-to-life is of the essence of vitality. The touch of an animate creature is enlivening.

The more contact we have with the living, the deeper and more intense is our own experience of living.

The entire history of the human race, throughout the development of the technosphere, is the story of the ascendency of the inert over the animate, and of a consequent desensitization and devitalization of the human. The electronic pet is just a recent instance of that process.

An infant who sucks a rubber nipple and clutches a cold bottle does not draw the life-nurturance of the infant sucking a real human nipple on a warm breast next to a beating heart. The child who fondles a rocket ship and fantasizes over lifeless outer space is deprived of the feeling of relatedness to life of the peasant child who cradles warm chicks in his hands or tenderly draws the fragrant soil around the emergent shoots of a green, living plant. The young man who is addicted to electronic pornography starves for the intimacy with life one feels in the vibrant naked loving body of a woman. The grown man who spends his days fondling tools and electronic devices suffers a daily desensitization to animate sensuality.

More and more in our modern lives, things seduce our senses away from natural sensoriness. Our senses become merely functional; and so does our living. Nature once made us live deep and intensely. Technology now makes our living superficial and distracted.

We have been indoctrinated into the Socratic belief that "The unexamined life is not worth living". But what about the unexperienced life, the unfelt life,—how can one call that really living?

The human problem is not that we don't think enough; no, we are addicted to thinking. The problem is that we have let ourselves lose our capacity for feeling. Life is in the senses and in the body; it is not in ideas in the mind or in the products manufactured from those ideas.— I tell you this, I, an idea-man, a writer of books, even of electronic books.

Natural animal sensoriness includes pain as well as pleasure, yes, but pain and pleasure in mix are of the inescapable innermost essence of being alive. Failing to realize and accept that, we anaesthetize our pain, but we anaesthetize our pleasure too. By means of technology, we keep life at a distance. We ourselves are detached from our own living.

In the nineteenth century, Emerson warned that "Things are in the saddle and ride mankind". Today we must recognize that things have trampled the human animal damn near lifeless.

As for death:—When we die now, we don't so much lose our living, as just cease to function, go out of operation, become obsolete, get heaped on the junk pile. Lives are as dispensable as are our machines. We tend to think of ourselves, of our bodies, as functioning machines. Death is just an unfixable mechanical failure.

How the naked savages—(and even the very self-conscious nudists)—appeal to our longing souls! Those people, primitive throwbacks though they are, really know what life is, really know how to live. We all want to be naked again, but we are incapable of it. Things have throttled the life out of us and hold us in their possession. We die as we live, a thing among our things.

It is the animals, not the primitives (who actually are quite sophisticated) who really know how to live. Animals live their lives in constant sensory touch of Life-Itself.

The human invention of the first tool was momentous. The touch of that tool was the first step of the process of technology and its consequent devitalization. "Tool of our tools," the Transcendentalists lamented; which we must modernize as "devices of our own devising", electronics being our contemporary controlling artifact.

Real living is naked and raw. We have become well-clothed and well-supplied, to our comfort but to our undoing. Enamored of the inert, we have lost our love-of-life. To us, Life is just an it, to be followed by the it-of-death. When we die, we are not so much stripped of life as dispossessed of our things. The wreckage of an American's death is the pile and clutter of possessions bereft of their owner.

In this year, 2020, the mass of all the manufactured—concrete, asphalt, steel, glass, plastics—in buildings, roads, vehicles, machines and products has come to exceed the mass of all the lifeforms on the Earth.

We have now reached an ominous stage in the ascendency of the inert: *Technomass* exceeds *biomass*.

So, it is not only the human that has become devitalized; it is the Earth itself.

Ultimately, the technosphere will obliterate the biosphere.

"Spoken Word, Written Word"

A spoken word is life communicating itself to other life through the medium of air. The mind that wishes to speak must do so through the animate lungs. Intention makes a breath meaningful. When I speak, I aspirate meaning.

In speaking to one another, we breathe our own breath of life into the other, as God did when he breathed into the nostrils of Adam, "Live!". Then Adam breathed, and one of his first breaths was a word of thanksgiving.

What human communication is more intimate, from the one who speaks to the one who listens, than the whisper, "I love you!"? Such breathed words enliven the breathing of the beloved.

To be mute, unable to speak, is to suffer a daily suffocation. We need to speak, as we need to breathe. To be deaf, unable to hear, is to suffer a daily smothering. We need to hear, as we need to breathe. The speaking is the out-breath, the hearing is the in-breath.

The spoken word is living and enlivening, intimate and personal.

The written word in a book is thoughts-in-a-box, an inert artifact. Yes, like the spoken word, it has meaning, but in a book meaning is embalmed. Or, say that a book is the petrifaction of thought and feeling. There can be no vitalization in reading petrified, embalmed thought and feeling.

Nor are the words in a book for anyone in particular. The meaning of the book is sufficient unto itself. The book is not even necessarily communication; it may never be read by anyone except the one who wrote it. It is still a book. Words spoken aloud to no one, in soliloquy, are a kind of madness, but it is not unusual for a book to be written for no one but the author himself.

The book is then left lying around. It may be filched and snooped into—(reading is a snooping into the mind and life of the author)—snooped into by anyone, no matter who. A book is common and vulgar, as are all mass-produced things. A book is nothing personal.

How *can* an author be intimate, when he writes for those he doesn't know? A letter may be intimate, yes, but never a book. Even if author and reader live next door to each other, they are as remote one from the other as was the carver of an ancient Egyptian hieroglyph from the twentieth-century archaeologist.

Why do we hold books so valuable, if they are as I have described them? Because they are a great repository of human knowledge, a voluminous inventory of much of human experience. A repository, like a mausoleum; an inventory, as in a warehouse. We can learn from the dead or distant,—that at least is the utility of books. Books contain their lessons, but no real lessons in living.

The written word is inert and impersonal. It may serve to stock our minds, but it does nothing to nurture our living or enhance our liveliness. The unlettered primitives are the most alive.

135

"Books of Others, Books of One's Own"

The origin of a new book is in an old book.

I don't think that a human must have seen art in order to become artistic. Nature, the visible world, is the stimulus to art. Sure, some art may imitate and emulate other art, but you don't need to have seen Van Gogh's works to smear a design over a surface, or to have stood before a Bernini sculpture to mold a chunk of clay. Perceiving senses in our bright and colorful world inevitably tend toward artistic expression.

Nor does music need music history. Music is as physiological as art. The throat hums spontaneously, voice can rise and fall in pitch, the ears respond, and the body sways in rhythm. Then, too, water rippling and birds calling stimulate music, as the sparkling silver of flowing water and the brilliant coloration of bird feathers stimulate art. We can sing without any songbook.

I do not deny that artists have looked at a lot of art and composers have listened to many compositions. The novice artist and the student composer analyze precedents and emulate models. Out of the precedents and models each period develops its artistic and musical styles; so the Baroque, the Classical, the Romantic, the Impressionist, Expressionist, and other such characterizations of periods in art and music.

All art is imitative, but the more imitative of precedent art the more feeble it is. The greatest artists are those who stay closest to the physiological roots in eye and fingertips and voice and ear.

Predecessors should be studied only for their technique, the how-to-go-about-it, the tricks-of-the-trade. Traipsing through all the museums of the continent will not inspire a single original canvas, nor would listening to a marathon performance of the nine symphonies of Beethoven cause the listener to leave the concert hall humming an original ditty.

The aesthetic is rooted in the physiological. Our education, then, should be directed to the senses, rather than to autopsies of the dead-and-gone. Many schools knock the art and music out of children by means of art and music classes. There is good education in apprenticeship—(education only in technique, as I said)—, but one artistic influence upon an impressionable young person is one influence too many.

Good new art is from acute vision, good new music from aural sensitivity, both phenomena mostly physiological. Literature, I am sorry to admit, has no such roots in the body. Literature is intellectual; as such, it derives from earlier intellectual literary exercises. Books come from books.

There is no physiological necessity for spoken language to become written language. Illiterate societies do not regret their privation of books. They train their memories and communicate quite satisfactorily to one another and to future generations through their mouths and ears, rather than through their intellects and eyes.

Uneducated artist there may be—(and don't we think the art of the Cave Men and modern *primitives* wonderful?). Uneducated music maker there could be,— (no composer of folk song or dance ever attended music school). Uneducated writer, however, there cannot be. One of the first tasks of our education is memorizing and copying the forms of the twenty-six letters of our alphabet. Thereafter, the tasks are to recognize words, their meaning and their correct spelling, then put some words together into a simple sentence, then sentences into paragraphs, paragraphs into pages, pages into chapters, chapters into books,—that gradual accumulation and adding-on and building-up of the elements of written language, until the student is literate (and literary) at last. Written language is all academic, never mind the word *art*.

You might argue that some writing, indeed the best writing, is sensory. What about poetry? Aren't poets sensorily sensitive? Isn't their writing as sensually perceptive as Impressionistic art or the birdsong of Respighi's *Gli Uccelli*?

Certainly, a perceptive one may report his perceptions in literary form; and so we have our poems and other vivid verbal description. But where did the poet get the word to describe (to simulate) that perception? Out of a book, of course. More often a poet looks for an experience that gives him an opportunity to use a learned evocative word than he has a learned word at hand to capture a fresh experience. (Poetry is less a matter of spontaneous rhapsody than it is a mulling-over in words.) Poems are out of the dictionary, not out of Nature, no matter the self-deceptive illusions of poets and critics alike. Perceptions there may have been, but a word is a counterfeit of a sensation. The whole idea of verisimilitude in literature is a fraud. (You might say that it is a fraud in art too.) "How much of real life that book contains!" What mastery of dictionary and thesaurus is more like it.

Art and music may be more or less derivative and imitative, but literature is wholly so. In literature, the technique is all, any lived personal experience merely provocative and suggestive. (The writer's own life is just material to be given a cerebral working-over.) Writers are copyists of earlier writers, as George Bernard Shaw from Shakespeare from North from Plutarch from earlier lost authors. And books are out of books out of books.

Emerson wrote that over-influence by genius is the bane of rising genius; he proved his point by over-influencing *me*. Emerson warned of infection, but he himself was infected,—by Kant, by Swedenborg, by Coleridge, by Goethe, by Plato. All writers are infected by having read other writers.

Can't a writer fend off influences, be original? No, because the dilemma is that you cannot become a writer without reading, and you cannot read without falling under a literary influence, whether of format or ideas or style. I used to think that my own subjection to my literary influences would be something I'd outgrow; but I never have. I have come to the self-effacing realization that writers merely mimic other writers and copy one another's books. (All writers are translators.) No wonder a new book is stale before it is published.

The museum pilgrimage and concert marathon I mentioned before will not make a better artist or composer, but reading more and more books does, in fact, make a better writer. There is a proportional relation between number of books read and quality of work written. Well-read writers are the best ones. (Not *all* well-read writers, of course; some become pedantic and muddled out of their surfeit of reading.) Reading a lot is the *sine qua non* of writing, for the simple fact that books come out of other books.

I had a professor once who complained that there is a type of scholar who reads 5 or 6 books, then feels competent to write a book of his own. But that scholar is not competent to turn author. Let him read 500 or 600 books. Then and only then is he qualified to write one of his own. (My own ratio may be about 300 to 1.)

In writing, all competence is in technique, all technique out of imitation. Direct perception of life and Nature is quite secondary and may be dispensed with by a little sleight of hand. It's not perception that literature deals with; it is meaning. Meaning, straight out of the dictionary, a book. Books are out of books.

The only difference between the insecure novice writer and the literary master is that the former imitates the works of other writers, the latter has come to imitating his own (which were earlier imitative). Literary originality is illusory; seeming novelty is only a cunning trick of adroit variation.

As a young man, I wrote the books of others. (*Eros...and Ebb* by Henry Miller and *The Test of Love* by Friedrich Nietzsche.) Now I am confident enough to imitate myself. (*Matters of Life and Death* from *Roman*

Ruminations.) Behold the hallucination of literary originality! And ain't I an idiosyncratic little plagiarist?

You might find it strange, but a writer's ambition may be not so much to find his name and book on the best-seller list as it is to find them in the bibliography at the back of new books. Why? Because the best-seller list is soon superseded by a later list with more recent titles, whereas that bibliographical entry is there in that book forever, insuring a writer's lasting influence upon future writers. Every book is out of previous bibliography and becomes an entry in subsequent bibliography, not only in scholarly works, where the bibliographic indebtedness is an explicit apparatus, but even in short stories and novels and poetry, where the bibliographical sources are not confessed.

I once found that I had written a short story—(an original inspiration, I thought it)—that could have come straight from the pen of Edgar Allan Poe. How could that have happened? Don't tell me that somewhere along the line I may have read some stories by Poe; ah, well, genius ever the enemy of genius by over-influence.

I'd better choose my reading carefully, if I want my writing to get better. Might as well infect myself with good germs.

136

"Writers Writing about Writing and about Writers Writing Writing"

That sort of thing has just got to stop.

Writers are readers, of course, but all that reading becomes too much of the living that they do. When they proceed to write about their living, then, they write about their reading. And so we get all those books about books, essays about essays, even poems about poems, in short, the round-and-round of my section 136 title.

Is literary criticism, writing about writing, literature? Self-portraits are art, but what kind of art would it be if artists drew only themselves and one another endlessly? An art of vocational narcissism. Fortunately, composers have no way of writing music about music. (Well, there was that *Young Person's Guide to the Orchestra*, but that was a piece of musical education, not incestuous music.)

Writers are interested in one another (an interest second only to their interest in themselves). They are searching for masters and models, techniques to imitate, and ideas to plagiarize. But they are not content with such mimicry and thievery. They have to speak up against their reading and write against other writers. There is a competitive struggle going on, a struggle for prizes, for prestige, for literary immortality.

There is also the dueling of self-assertive egos against one another. When a writer writes about another writer, he usually picks up the pen underhandedly, that is, with devious intent. Writing about the writings of a famous writer draws attention to oneself, insinuates the critic as peer, puts the master in his place, points out his limitations, and sets him up for supersession. Other writers, even the literary geniuses, are only the means for writers to promote themselves.

Some literary criticism is feigned homage, some is analysis and interpretation, some just carping. There is no end to opinions on how a book should have been written. In fact, any other writer who has read the book would be able to write that same book better than its author did. The critic might pretend that he means to help the common reader, the literary layman, to appreciation, but really he is out to get the author.

Some books are done to death by books about them. The Bible is the most prominent example. (And didn't I myself write a Bible-killing book?) Some authors too have their books overwhelmed by books about their books. There must be a book on Shakespeare for every single page by Shakespeare. The poor student has no time for reading Shakespeare, so burdened is he by the assigned reading of books about Shakespeare. Malevolent critics went so far as to strip Shakespeare of the authorship of his own works.

The book-about-a-book is a deadly weapon against literature.

Then, too, there is the cult of literary vocation. That cult was founded and has been proselytized by authors themselves. What with all their talk of *inspiration* (even divine inspiration, whether by pagan Muse or Jewish Jehovah), they make the mere writer an oracle and prophet. The book from the anointed head of the divinely chosen, then, is a relic, a sacred cultural relic. Every author is holy, every book scripture. And readers have come to believe it. They are converts to literariolatry. All literary criticism is biblical criticism, very worth reading.

(James Joyce proposed that, if a person wanted to live a worthwhile life, that person should dedicate the whole lifetime to deep study of the works of James Joyce.)

The ultimate goal of an author's literary criticism is to write about his own writing. All other authors put in their place and dispensed with, the writer can then devote himself to his fascination with himself in its guise of his process of writing. He will let the reader in on a secret,—how he writes what he writes, nothing less than the secret of divinely inspired genius itself. The oracle and prophet condescends to report the how of his revelation. And the reader finds it all most wonderful.

With unabashed self-assertiveness, the writer writes his vocational autobiography, his masterpiece. (I myself did that in *An Autobiographical Letter*.) There is no life in his life story, nor are there any other writers' books anymore. There is only the writer and his own books. A most exquisite contemplation of one's navel, in this case the navel as inkwell.

But if such a writer thinks that his last-will-and-testament will be the last word, he is mistaken. Younger writers line up for their potshots, in that same old way of feigned homage and putting-in-his-place. And so it goes, on and on, writers writing about writing, about others' writing, about their own writing, about writing itself, all writing writing writing.

I myself plead guilty to literary self-obsession. Am I not myself committing that very sin right here in this chapter of a book that is seemingly about something else? There is no escaping literary self-obsession. I confess but I do not reform. I commit the crime at the same time that I indict it. Thank God, at least, that I am not more well-read, that I myself have not written more books.

Writing about writing, as I have been, and writing about writers make me think of something else:—

137

"Types of Writers and Writing"

There is a type of writer who wants to communicate what is and the way things are. This is the recorder of the real world. His personal interest, his vocational mission, is to inform. To do so he is a fact monger and fact purveyor. Science, economics, politics, sociology, current culture,—he writes what the reader should know about the world we are living in. This type of writer works for a newspaper or magazine; expanding the pieces, he produces books on contemporary issues. Like all writing, his work should be interesting; more importantly, it should be relevant.

The real-world writer is especially valued in democratic societies, where citizens need to know about the world, in order to vote for effective problem-solving policies. There is also a usefulness of real-world information to making a living; the reader may acquire the knowledge needed to perform the work that society wants done. Any art in real-world writing is less important than the clarity of communication and practical applicability. Facts are functional.

Another type of writer is the one who wants to communicate what was and the way things were. This is not only the archaeologist and historian, but also the biographer and autobiographer, archaeologists of individual lives. A retrospective type, sometimes analytic, sometimes nostalgic. (Some of my own writing is of this type.) More fascinating than the present, the past may be escapism,—ancient Egypt, Greece, my Rome, the Middle Ages. The writer of this type is usually an escapist. Memory, whether collective or personal, may be escapist. Of course, the past is not only escapism; it too has its relevance, as maturity is understood by reference to the preceding childhood.

A third type of writer is the one who wants to communicate what is not now and never was, but what might be, or actually never could be, but is interesting to consider, anyway. This writer is a fictionalist, fantasist, futurist, or other visionary. The writing may be sheer entertainment, diverting storytelling, or it may be serious and intellectual, like religion and philosophy— (metaphysics is the fantasy of the intellect)—, or it may be aesthetic, like poetry—(poems are fantasies of perception and feeling). Whichever, the distinction from the first two types of writing is that this one has only tenuous contact with the real world; this writing is out of the imaginative mind, meant to stimulate the imagination of other minds. More escapism, but escapism of the most vaporous kind. Any relevance farfetched, such writing must justify itself by its pure art. Journalism may have a literary quality, history too, but fantasy must be literature.

Some rare virtuosos might produce writings of all three types—real-world, retrospection, fantasy—, but generally the writer's temperament determines an affinity to just one of the three. In writing, the writer meets his own needs, even as he tells himself that he means to meet the needs of his readers.

Correspondingly, readers will find themselves most drawn to the writing of just one of the three types, the reader's temperament seeking and finding writers of similar temperament and a writing that matches. Literary communication is to temperament, as much as it is to mind.

What benefit does a reader derive from each of the three types of writing? What satisfaction is there in each?

Regarding the first type:—If we read information and facts, there are always more facts and information to be read. What is significant, what is essential to know, really? The real-world writer thinks that what he writes is significant—(because it is, to him), but to the reader it may prove not to be so. The craving for facts cannot be satisfied, because the total of facts is innumerable. No matter how much I read, I can never find out everything, I will never come to know everything. I go on through life accumulating knowledge, but what is the culmination of it? I may know more useless facts than significant ones. As De Quincy regretted, "It is one of the misfortunes of life that one must read thousands of books only to discover that one need not have read them."

Still, we do need to know as much as possible about what is, and so we carry on our functional reading, the newspaper and magazines and manuals of operation.

Satisfactions are, necessarily, little ones, because there is no end to it. Our minds become cluttered. What does it all add up to? There is a creeping futility in our reading of information and facts. It is all a *Trivial Pursuit,* as the board game calls it.

There is more satisfaction, I think, in retrospective writing. That is because time and distance enable a more thorough consideration and so a deeper understanding. There is extractable significance in past collective or personal experience. The reader finishes a history book or biography with the feeling of not only knowing but understanding. There is a moral to the past.

The satisfaction in reading fantasy is recreational. Such reading is a diversion and time-killing, enjoyable while doing it but with no residue of significance thereafter. Reading fantasy is like eating a non-nutritive snack. Hunger may feel satisfied, but, there being no nourishment, one is quickly hungry for the next snack. There is an emptiness to fantasy, the emptiness of imagination. There is nothing there, really, except some brief stimulation and excitation. If one stopped snacking to evaluate, you would come to the conclusion that books of fantasy are the most unsatisfying of all,— especially the fantasies of religion and philosophy.

Beyond the inadequacies of the three types of writing there is the inadequacy of writing itself. What could I ever read will tell me what I most need to know? Where is that magical sentence that will penetrate my consciousness and transform my life? Nowhere, alas! How many books do I have to read—(and, like De Quincy, I have read thousands)—before I feel fulfillment from literature? All books are the excreta of others. How can I be nourished on excreta?

Despite my dissatisfaction, I haven't given up reading. Reading is the force-of-habit of the educated person, a habit made worse by the vocational necessity that a writer, in order to write some little, must read a lot. Don't think I'm any more satisfied with my writing than with my reading.

I sometimes feel a nostalgia for the illiteracy of the primitive. The primitive reads the Book of Nature, which, I believe, *is* truly satisfying. Nature is the real-world itself; no need for reporters, translators, or interpreters. Nature contains within herself the retrospective record too, for those who can read that. Nature is without fantasies, true, although she does have her whimsies.

We literary ones are illiterate in looking into the Book of Nature, an ignorance that our close readings of the books of the sage dead cannot compensate for. Our literary articulateness is not true wisdom, nor is our polysyllabic verbosity superior to natural simplicity.

We read of the real world and the past, with now and then a foray into fantasy. In none of those types of writing do we find the deep satisfaction we seek.

Reading is futile. Every writer fails the reader.

138

"Does the Writer Really Understand His Own Writing and Himself?"

You wouldn't think so, what with all those who step forward to explain it all for him,—the book reviewers, the literary critics, the readers playing literary critic, and the academics inculcating literary criticism into their students' heads. All that exegesis makes one wonder whether the writer himself is an incompetent who doesn't know how to communicate effectively, can't make himself understood without intermediaries, just doesn't know what he is doing.

A critic was once delving into the significance of the title of one of William Faulkner's novels, *Light in August*. He was doing so to Faulkner himself. The critic went on and on expatiating on the optical, calendrical, rhetorical, poetical, metaphorical, metaphysical, and meteorological meanings of *Light in August*. Since Faulkner was there, the critic thought it wouldn't hurt to get another opinion. "Why *did* you use the title, *Light in August*?" he asked. "Oh, I don't know," Faulkner shrugged. "It just sounded good to me."

Now, if someone has to tell you that you have been kissed, well then, you haven't. She can go on and on telling you where you were kissed, how many times, in what duration, by whom, with what intent, and so on—a full lip-by-lip analysis—, but you still haven't been kissed. Art is a kiss.

Music, visual art, and literature must all be received in an experience of direct apprehension. Direct, not second-hand or by hearsay; apprehension, not analytic explanation. Piece-by-piece fragmentary comprehension of art does not add up to appreciation. Sure, you might need some help—with the Italian of the opera libretto, with the fact that the naked woman with the snake hanging from her nipple is Cleopatra, with a dictionary definition of a word you don't know. Those little boosts aside, if you yourself do not experience the work of art by direct apprehension, you haven't gotten it and never will. After a complete explanation by someone else, you might delude yourself into thinking that you grasp it: "Uh-huh!". But you've only been told about the kiss.

You know, there are some people who just can't sit down to a meal without making a critical comment after each mouthful. Why can't they just enjoy the meal? When I myself read, I suspend my critical faculty. I have confidence that the author knows what he is doing. I go along with the author completely, eating course after course, opening my mouth for the food, not for commentary, until the very last crumb of dessert. I try for total receptivity; in that way, I believe, I derive the utmost benefit from the book. If I criticize and evaluate, it is only after thorough digestion.

A lot of what I have heard from critics is not elucidation, but only a confession of their incomprehension. The problem may be not so much incompetent writers as stupid readers, especially professional ones. Whenever I hear such a statement as, "What the author meant to say was...", I interpret that as meaning, "The way I misunderstood it was...". The author did not *mean to say*; he said it. It is a foolish presumption to correct and rephrase the thoughts of another person's mind.

Speaking of mind, another type of literary exegesis is the psychoanalytic, an exegesis of the author himself through the medium of his own words. If the literary critics read between the lines, the psychoanalysts read between the letters of each word. To them, words are symptoms. By analyzing a writer's words, you can get into his unconscious, discover and expose his repressed complexes. To the psychoanalyst, it goes without saying that the author doesn't really understand himself. He only knows his own writing superficially, at the conscious level, and is blind to his true self. A good psychoanalyst can explain the author to himself by reading what he has written.

Psychoanalytic psychologism! Many have come under the compelling influence of the psychoanalytic view that art is expression of neurosis. I believed it myself, until I took to writing and discovered differently. If art were expression of neurosis, insane asylums would be creative arts centers.

Herr Doktor Freud himself undertook the reductionism of art and literature in some papers he wrote on Leonardo da Vinci and Dostoyevsky. (He attacked no composer through his music, confessing that he was stymied in his attempt to reduce music to a complex.) Of Freud's followers, Albert Mordell was one who took on the writers. Not surprisingly, most of the cases Mordell chose were French and British Romantics, who certainly had their quirks.

You can no more psychoanalyze a writer from his writing than an architect from his building or a composer from his symphony.

Unlike the other arts, literature is words. Words have meanings, and some words of an author might have self-revelatory meaning. But to reduce a writer to his words is naïve. We writers are *illusionists*, as Anaïs Nin characterized the cunning in our craft. And I will tell you that a writer is not involved in his words, but detached. The seemingly subjective and sensitive is written with ruthless objectivity.

The psychoanalysts have also perpetrated, or, say rather, propagated the Romantic nonsense about art as therapeutic. The writer is writing away his troubles! Such further reductionism is obnoxious to those of us who practice craftsmanship and know that it is damn hard work that imposes more stress and strains than it ever relieves. More artists are beaten down and unhinged by their work than are ever convalesced and cured.

The psychoanalysts presume to be landlords of the unconscious; in fact, they claim to have built the building,—(or perhaps I should say, more accurately, excavated the cellar). They will blithely and glibly explain the author's unconscious to him,—shining no light in August, I assure you. We writers shake our heads at what we hear, because every artist is a true master of the unconscious, not the unconscious as the pit of repressed complexes, but the unconscious as the wellspring of creativity.

I will let you in on the work of my own unconscious in the composition of this book:—

I had accumulated some random essays over a period of many months. I was groping toward an organization of them and any related material I might write. One evening, I was standing at the kitchen sink with my wife, when the title, *Matters of Life and Death*, came into my head—didn't pop in, but emerged from my unconscious. My unconscious knows what I can write and should write. I accepted the direction of my unconscious and recognized what my next project would be.

Once I got down to work and began writing more, section topics and core ideas would emerge from my unconscious, one or more each day. I didn't sit down to write them out immediately. Instead, I let them incubate in my unconscious. No impatient tapping away at the eggshell! Meanwhile, I would write hatchlings from previous days. I always had a backlog of three to six incubating ideas. My unconscious would send up new ones, as I wrote out the old. I learned long ago that trying to write doesn't work; only writing does. Nor do I deliberate. I let ideas present themselves. When they do, I welcome them hospitably.

Gradually, the ideas coalesced into large themes. And so, this book has been proceeding, at the pace and in the directions given by my unconscious. Far from being a snakes' den of lurid repressed perversions and complexes, my unconscious is the creative wellspring. Yes, I have said that writing is intellectual, but I didn't mean by that only cerebral and rational-methodical. The intellectual is a latter organizational stage of the process. My unconscious is doing most of the creative work.

So, enough of this writers-don't-know-what-they're-doing, don't-even-know-themselves stuff. We know perfectly well, both consciously and unconsciously. We have our psychological problems, yes, sharing those with the human, not only with other writers. Regarding neurosis, art may be in-spite-of, but not because-of. As Nietzsche wrote, emotion never created anything; certainly pathological emotion never did. You just can't reduce art to psychologism.

Oh, and a by-the-way:—

Through this my writing about the psychology of the writer, you may have become annoyed by my narrow use of *the writer* as *he*. How could I be such a throwback to ignore the courtesy of our currently enlightened *gender-neutral language*?

You know, in English we have three genders for the human, grammatically speaking,—masculine, feminine, and indeterminate. The first is specific to male, the second to female. The third is in usage such as the British *one*—("One just doesn't do such things")—or our American *you*—("First you plug it in, then you turn it on, then you…"). The indeterminate gender sounds strange to us, the British *one* virtually dehumanizing, the *you* confusing—("No, I didn't mean *you personally*, I meant *you-anybody*.") In referring to the human, traditional usage favors masculine and feminine, not the indeterminate or the neuter either. To me, *gender-neutral* means gender-neuter, the hermaphroditism of *S/he* and the sex-change to *God the Mother* notwithstanding.

In so-called gender-neutral language, feminist ideology has been imposed upon traditional usage. I choose the latter. (Regarding the former, I may say that I have been successful in doing something the entire feminist movement has been unable to do. I've made one woman happy.)

I don't use the plural *writers* to sidestep supposed sexism, because I don't know the psychology of any and all writers. In this chapter, *writer* mostly means the fol- flowing:

Type: Literary worker. Gender: Male. Specimen: Myself.

I don't have an inkling of the psychology of the female writer.

I knew a brilliant poetess once, knew her intimately, in fact, yet her poetry was to me incomprehensible, she herself unfathomable. I have always had trouble with complex women, and she was one of them. She once remarked to me how she wished she were as intelligent as I; I told her she was a lot more intelligent than I. She only thought me more so, because I was ten years older than she and had thereby accumulated more knowledge and worldly experience. I only seemed smarter. In the end, she wised up and recognized me for the simpleton I am.

The female mind is a phenomenon quite different from the male mind. (I don't regret that as the cause of mutual estrangement. I rejoice in the stimulations of yin-yang complementarity.) As the female mind is different from the male, so is female writing. I can usually tell a woman's writing from a man's, just as I can tell a woman's voice from a man's on the telephone,—providing the writing is personalistic, not expository of information or facts. But that I may be able to tell that a woman wrote a particular piece doesn't make me presume that I can include her in my understanding of the psychology of the writer.

I consider women generally more perceptive about other people than men are. I find it puzzling, therefore, that men writers have portrayed believable women— take those of Shakespeare, Flaubert, and Ibsen, for example—, but women writers give us not men but manikins. The only manly characteristic of Jane Austen's men is their names.

I ask you to accept my use of *writer* in the restrictive sense I have said. I am sorry if I offend sensitivity on the issue of gender-neutral language, but we hidebound conservatives are hopeless cases, just too old and set in our ways to adopt these newfangled modern enlightened ideas and progressive linguistic forms.

Regarding women writers, I don't ignore or denigrate them; I just confess my woeful obtuse incomprehension and back off. The last thing I would ever want to do as a writer would be to write something controversial, get people upset, or, worse, start a war between the sexes.

139

"A Writer's Solitariness"

The problem in having a job for which you "go to the office" is that you have to put up with other people. The problem in having a job for which you stay home—as a writer, for example—is that you have to put up with yourself.

As the human is social, so should we be cooperative. Work is our main enterprise of social cooperation. "Let's work together." And so, there is the daily mass commute of scattered individuals to the company, where there is cooperative work to be done.

There is something satisfying in working with other people. We feel a sense of belonging, we enjoy camaraderie, we take pride in others' recognition of the worth of our efforts. We all want to be good for something. When others tell us that we are, we believe it.

The social aspect of the collective workplace is stimulating. Other people's personalities and the interactions with those personalities are endlessly fascinating. Contact with others draws us out of ourselves; we savor communication, humor, enlivening conversations, even if only gossip. We have an opportunity to express our opinions and influence, whether on the issues of the day or on the issues of the operation of the workplace itself.

Contacts in the collective workplace may lead to friendships or even to romance. There is a lot more going on in the workplace than mere work.

But some of what is going on may undermine, as well as bolster, the person. There is competition in the workplace. Because of that, there are devious dealings, power-struggle, sabotage of others' efforts, back-stabbing, undercutting and deliberate inflicted humiliations, a secret war of each against all, the victory sought being pay raises, promotions, status, power. Even where such schemings are guarded against or repressed, there are still incompatibilities and conflicts, that putting up with other people that I mentioned at the outset. Other people, in their self-assertion against our self-assertion, necessarily frustrate and exasperate us.

Just as there may be friendship, so there may be implacable hostility caused by workplace interactions. As there may be opportunity for romance, there might also be temptation to adultery fatal to marriage, the marriage that the job itself was supposed to support.

In the collective workplace, the contacts between the workers are considered incidental to the task at hand, but, in fact, those contacts may be more of the essence of the experience than is any work that gets done. Work with other people is an experience of other people, not a mere experience of work.

As for that work, it is assigned, rather than chosen, because the work meets the needs of the company, not those of the individual. There are many tasks to be done, some tedious, boring, or bothersome. The boss assigns the work and we have to do it, like it or not. Needless to say, there may be little satisfaction in doing work that one is compelled to do. Nonetheless, you're getting paid for the work you do, not for the chit-chat or flirtations. Some find the socializing a compensation for the tedious work, but woe to those who can't stand the job and can't stand the people either!

Now, a writer is a stay-at-home whose work experience is very different from those who go to office or factory.

Working alone as he does, what does the writer miss in his work experience? No stimulating personalities or conversations, no support or motivation or approval from fellow-workers, no jokes, and, of course, no opportunity for romance. Even though the writer's work is communication, as he works he has no one to talk to.

No one to talk to, but no one to put up with, either. The writer never dreads the next day's work because of what someone else might be trying to do to him. The writer's job is free of conflict, stress, and mean politics. Nobody can exasperate the solitary one.

The writer's work should be satisfying, because the writer himself has chosen it, every task of his own devising, a labor-of-love if ever there was one. The writer is free to do the work he wishes, as he wishes, when he wishes, how hard he wishes, or, if he doesn't want to work, he just doesn't. No boss lords it over him, no co-worker spies over his shoulder, there is no one at all to harry his workday. Of course he can't be fired.

The writer's work schedule is free of regimentation. No 7:22 train, no day-in, day-out 9-to-5, Monday through Friday for him. Henry Miller knew a writer who would write just one page a day,—that was his self-imposed discipline. If he wrote that page in ten minutes, well then, his daily work was done. Seemingly a light-load laziness, the page-a-day-every-day, that writer would turn out the equivalent of a 365-page book every year, productivity enough.

A writer's work may be short and sweet and occasional or it may be all-day and all-night nonstop, as he prefers it. Unless he is compulsive and self-driven, his work need not be taxing or tiring. Against that I might say that a writer is never really able to go into retirement and rest. His work is so married to his life that he usually goes on writing into his dotage. After all, he can't retire from his own life. His work goes on as long as his life does.

Most of it may seem idyllic, this writer's life I'm talking about. There is autonomy, freedom, self-expressive creativity, the potential for personal fulfillment, all with a wide margin of leisure. Yet, the bright picture has its dark flip-side:—-

What afflicts the writer is not workplace politics, but workplace psychology—his own. The stimulations of other personalities absent, the writer is an ever-present companion to himself, for good or ill. People serve to check the extremes of one another's idiosyncrasies. The solitary writer lacks those correcting checks; he is thrown upon his own resources. Alone, alone, always alone. Solitariness takes a toll on mind and morale.

A writer soon becomes bored with himself. He begins to suspect that his writing might be as boring as he himself is. His life becomes as narrowed as the four-walls confines of his study, as silent and devoid of stimuli as the hermit's cave. The writer has a past life and off-hours life of social experiences, true; he can draw on them as literary resources. But what if he exhausts all his material? What then? He becomes an empty husk staring at a blank page.

The writer's life is one of privation. The writer realizes what he is sacrificing and he endures it, for the sake of his art. Sometimes, however, he eats himself up at a faster pace than he nourishes himself and his art. Then he finds himself more stymied and frustrated than ever could a worker in a collective workplace. No co-worker was the agent of his frustration. The writer did it to himself.

Each day of solitude is contracting; sustained concentrated discipline itself is contracting. The soul, especially the social soul, shrivels up. A working exclusively out of one's own resources is a spending of self, a wasting-away. No wonder so few writers are worth knowing personally. Whatever was worthwhile in them has been poured into their books. The writer has used himself up in his works.

When he has come to that pass, the writer falls into a desperation to write a book impossibly better and richer than he himself is.

Morbidity is a writer's vocational disease. Thinking lapses into brooding, then self-doubt, feelings of inadequacy, drying up, moroseness, pessimism, misanthropy, all washed down with copious alcohol. No one can live with an old writer, because an old writer cannot live with himself.

If you ask a retired worker about his or her job, you may hear more about co-workers than about the rote tasks of the workday. The collective workplace feeds and nourishes the social self. Office retirees are sociable. If, on the other hand, you interview an old writer about his career, all he can do is talk about his books, the it-of-it, the inert products of his solitary labor. The books speak for themselves, really, leaving their author with nothing more to say, except redundancy. Often, the old writer looks back upon his books with as much revulsion as he feels for himself. He hates what the writing of his books has done to him.

The writer is the ascetic of our secular society. Like the mad flagellants of Christianity, the writer turns into a torturer of himself. Literary art means as much to him as salvation of the soul meant to the true believer. But solitariness proves the ruination of the person of the writer, as it was of the person of the hermit, a self ruined, and a life ruined, whether or not the striving for art or salvation turned out to be a success in the end.

Working with others has its dissonances, but in working alone stillness verges upon death. A writer spends, expends, his life emptying out the contents of his mind, until, it empty, he finds himself emptied, too. He becomes worse than tired out. He becomes moribund.

About a minor character in *Madame Bovary,* Flaubert wrote, "He shut himself up at the age of forty-five, disgusted with mankind, he said, and resolved to live in peace."

I myself did the same—(at the same age, coincidentally)—, abandoning an erstwhile social and social work career for solitary writing. The peace I am now living in has become quite grim. How much longer do I have to put up with myself?

140

"Literary Friendlessness"

A writer is little capable of friendship, at least in so far as his vocation has become his life.

The solitariness of the writer, a vocational necessity, gradually withdraws him from sociability. The writer loses both interest in others (except as they might provide material for his writing) and any social skills he may have possessed. Spending his days alone, that ingrained habit, takes away his initiative to socialize. He wishes to communicate only with himself.

The writer is a self-rapt one. How can anyone self-rapt, wrapped in himself, become or be a friend?

It would seem that writers would befriend other writers at least, supporting and encouraging one another through the rigors of lonely vocational struggle. Actually, there is little of such mutual aid. A young writer might respect an older one as a model and master, but in any such mentor-apprentice relationship there is patronizing by the older, the poison of envy and ambition in the younger. Between writers who are peers it is all competition. No one is so unappreciative of a writer's writing as is another writer. Self-rapt, the writer is not open and receptive, doesn't care about others' work, is too obsessed with his own, doesn't want to be distracted or bothered. Worse, a writer may worry that his writer friend might appropriate his material and do better with it than he himself has done and can do. Writers are sympathetic readers of only their own books.

There are writers' associations, certainly, in which an attempt is made at mutual support and encouragement, but in them there is less amity than ambition. Writers join writers' groups to advance their own careers, not to minister to insecure others. Contacts may be more crucial to literary advancement than quality of work is.

Between one writer and another there is inevitable bumping of heads, Thoreau and Emerson one case I know well. Friendship may be longed for, it may be attempted, but it will founder on the incompatibility and clash of minds asserting themselves.

What about a writer's attempted friendship with one who is not a writer? If the focus of the friendship becomes the writer's work, then that friendship becomes adulterated, by ego from the one, by hero worship or criticism from the other. A writer's book estranges him from everyone who has read it.

If a writer should write about his friendships and loves, that very objectification kills the friendship and love. Friendship and love are tacitly understood as they are experienced; explicitness and analysis of them are killing. When a writer violates confidentiality, friends and lovers are hurt by the treachery of exposure; writers turn them into enemies. A writer will exploit all his relatedness, until, at last, he has not much relatedness left.

To be a writer a writer doesn't need friends, but how he does need them to be a human being!

An exception to the general friendlessness of writers, a heartening case, was in the relationship between Petrarch and Boccaccio. Petrarch, who was the elder of the two, befriended and encouraged Boccaccio. Their relatedness, however, was not that of master to junior, but friend to friend. They even succeeded in appreciating and complementing each other's work, Boccaccio writing a *Lives of Famous Women* as distaff company for Petrarch's *Lives of Famous Men*, and both taking on in common the subject of the fortunes and fates of the famous. They had their literary differences, true, for Boccaccio admired Dante, whereas, to Petrarch, Dante was a ghastly spook of morbid medievalism. The bonds of friendship overcame any competition or differences of views.

The proof of that friendship came when Boccaccio, his youthful spunk forsaking him, was thrown into a fright of concern for his eternal salvation—(because of his supposedly immoral *Decameron*)—by a mad monk who pronounced a revelation of Boccaccio's sure damnation. Petrarch rallied to his friend, preventing Boccaccio's repudiation of his life and lifework and bolstering his morale.

Petrarch came to Boccaccio's financial aid too, even to the extent of a clause in his will bequeathing to Boccaccio money for clothing to keep him warm during the winter of his old age.

The friendship of Petrarch and Boccaccio is more admirable, humanly admirable, than all the works of the two of them put together. Their friendship may have been the *magnum opus* of each man.

Friends need to be in harmony, but—the case of Petrarch and Boccaccio the rare exception—writers send out too much dissonance and discord for the parallelism of shared lives that is friendship. The self-obsessed, self-assertive mind, ego and ambition, and the objectification of feeling all incapacitate the writer for friendship.

If you ever come across an essay on friendship, don't waste your time reading it. I am sure the author knows nothing about the subject.

141

"The Visitation"

One day after school, when I was sixteen years old, I was sitting at my Royal manual typewriter, staring at the page. There were three lines of type I had written two days before, but on that day I had not typed a single letter. Blocked and becoming tense, I gazed out the window down at Racine Avenue.

Recalling myself from distraction, I stared at the page again. My fingers clutched at the keys, but I did not stroke any of them.

The doorbell rang. At first, I did not hear it, so intense was my concentration. It rang more insistently.

I got up from the chair, went into the living room to press the button to release the downstairs door lock.

Just before I got to the button, the bell rang again, three short times. Three short rings was the code signal we used for members of the family.

I opened the apartment front door, so that, as I pushed the button, I could hold it down until I heard the opening of the downstairs door.

The downstairs door did open, and footsteps padded up the two flights of carpeted hallway stairs. I stood at the apartment door waiting.

A man arrived on the landing and approached. He was a tall man of athletic build, but he had a gray beard of age, and his head was mostly bald. He wore glasses to help the sight of his blue eyes.

At first, I thought that he might be an insurance salesman or someone else who had business with my mother. (In those days agents would make house-calls.)

"My mother is not here," I told the man.

"I'm not here to see your mother," he answered. "I'm here to see you, Norman. May I come in?"

I was taken aback that he knew my name, for then he had the advantage of me. Was he a policeman? But I had done nothing wrong. Or someone from my high school? But I was an exemplary student. I couldn't figure out what man I didn't know had come to see me at our family apartment.

He was an adult, a figure of authority. And he seemed non-threatening. I backed off and let him in.

He walked into our living room with an air of familiarity and immediately sat down on the couch by the door. He surveyed the room, taking in its details, but not in a way of looking at anything novel.

Ill at ease, I closed the door, then sat down in the stuffed chair by the window, facing my visitor.

"How are you feeling lately?" he asked me.

"OK," I answered.

I was about to ask him who he was and what he wanted, but he continued speaking:

"Not too down in the dumps, I hope. These Novembers in Chicago are such gloomy times. They make one morbid."

What he said was like hearing myself thinking. I had always hated November as the worst month, all overcast and damp and chilly, the light of day darkening toward winter. My visitor had spoken out loud a very thought I had had just before his arrival.

"Well, there's no use brooding over it," he continued. "Teenagers are given to brooding, introspection, too much self-involvement. You're not much different from anyone else your age. But you'll get over it, I promise that. Just hang in there, and try to be your own best friend."

I wondered at the man addressing me in such intimate manner, a stranger taking on the role of counselor. Again, I wanted to ask him the who and why of his visit, but he kept on:

Looking over my shoulder at my typewriter in the other room, the page in it illuminated by the table lamp, he pointed with his hand and asked, "Doing your homework?"

"No," I answered.

I resented the intrusion of this stranger into the house, his sudden intimacy with me, and now his prying into the privacy of my journal. I wished that I had shut the adjacent room's door behind me when I came to answer the bell, or at least turned off the table lamp.

"Something else, eh?" the visitor said, leading me through the conversation, as if he already knew all the answers.

"Mr., please..." I objected, but he continued on:

"Now, Norman, it's all right. Don't get upset. Why, you look like you'd like to crawl into a hole and hide. I know you, can't you tell? I'm the one person you couldn't hide from if you wanted to."

I stared hard at the visitor, baffled and frightened by what he was saying to me. Yet, there was something in his appearance and manner that reassured me, some uncanny affinity between us. I suddenly felt that he had a right to speak to me as he did. I relaxed and felt more comfortable with him.

"Writing, Norman…Do you think you're any good at it?"

"I don't know. I mean, I've always been good in English, and the teachers have given me the highest marks. Even had me read a composition of mine to the class."

"You're doing this extra writing because of your teachers' approval?"

"No. It's something I want to do."

"Is English the only subject you're good in?"

"No, but it's the one I like the most, that I feel attracted to."

"To even write something on your own, outside of class assignments," the visitor said, gesturing again toward my typewriter in the other room.

"Yes," I admitted. "But I'm just beginning. I really don't know what I'm doing or what to write about. Sometimes I just can't write a single word—no ideas. And so I give up."

"Not completely."

"No. For the day. The next day or as soon as I have time, I try again."

"Perseverance is the discipline of vocation."

It seemed strange that the visitor used that word, *vocation.* I had known that word only in terms of a religious vocation. Was writing too a vocation? I asked the visitor whether it was.

"Of course," he said. "It's like art. If writing is your vocation, it is not something you *do.* It is what you *are.* Right now you are groping toward what you are..."

I found that last sentence reassuring and comforting.

"...trying to express yourself in writing, your soul, your mind, yourself. You're even hoping that one day you'll be a writer, a great writer. You're starting out on your vocation..."

"Do you teach writing?", I asked the visitor.

"I have. But you'll teach yourself. You'll learn how to do it on your own. I did so, so I know you will. Sure, you've got to get educated in school, but, as far as vocation goes, you'll educate yourself. I myself have the vocation of writing, so I know by experience what I'm talking about. I am the consequence of what you are now undertaking."

"What do you mean?"

The visitor did not answer my question directly but instead carried on with his own purpose of his mission. "You know, Norman, there can be no question about writing-as-a-vocation, because it is what you are. But what about writing-as-a-career, a job? Do you think you could make a livelihood as a writer?"

In thinking of a career for myself, I had considered either teaching or writing or both, but I was now inclining toward writing.

"I don't know. I would hope so," I said.

The visitor leaned forward and spoke to me more personally.

"Let me tell you about myself," he confided. "I am fifty-five years old. I have spent most of my adult life either writing or trying to write or thinking about writing. Ever since I was a teenager, actually. I have written fifteen books, rewritten many of them, some several times over. I have spent years and years trying to get my books published, to make a living at it, but I have not been able to. In that, my career, I am a failure as a writer. I would have starved—not to be too dramatic about it—, if it weren't for my wife, who supports me out of love for what I am. And so, I have a vocation, have always had it. I'm stuck with my vocation. As for career, I'm a failure, as I said. No moneymaking to speak of. Would *you* be able, I mean, *are* you able, to endure such a fate and outcome to your writing?"

I felt a sharp pang of compassion for the visitor, at the same time a dread for myself and my own prospects. It was as if a prophet had come to pronounce a doom upon me.

The visitor leaned back onto the couch. The two of us sat looking at each other in silence for a few minutes.

"Why are you here?", I finally was able to ask him.

"To tell you what you're in for."

"But why should what happened to you happen to me too?"

"Because it has to, can't you see that? It's our fate."

The visitor got up and came over to me. I stood up, too. He took my hand and held it briefly in a comradely embrace.

"Accept your destiny," the visitor said. "Don't hate it, because, if you do, you'll only be hating yourself. *Vocation* means you're on your own. You must sustain yourself, whatever the world thinks, and if the world ignores you. Don't give up. Persevere, and you'll find fulfillment. Fulfillment is more important than success. Be faithful to yourself."

The visitor took another look around our living room, turned to the door, opened it himself, then swiftly descended the stairs.

I wanted to go after him, call him back, but I heard the downstairs door draw shut. I ran to the window and looked down. The angle to the sidewalk was so steep that I could not see the visitor leaving the building.

I went back and shut the apartment door. Then I lingered at the window a long time, trying to understand and assimilate what had just happened. The visitor had been a friend to me, but I didn't know who he was. Or did I?

I drifted back to my typewriter, sat down, and faced it. I had second thoughts, yes; the visitor had forced second thoughts upon me. But he had used the word *vocation*.

Closing my eyes, I caressed the keyboard in front of me.

I then dropped my hands to my side and fell back against the chair.

I would write nothing that day. But maybe on the next...

142

"Not Enough"

I have worked long and hard on my writing, but long and hard has not been enough. I have let my living intrude. And I have succumbed to inertia and to demoralization.

The artist is an obsessive; that should include litererary artists. Dedication must be total. Every waking moment, every experience of life, should go into the writing of it all. The artist lives to work, the creative process the real living. So difficult and slow-developing is mastery of literary art that one must devote the whole of oneself and one's life to it.

I did try to feed my life into my art, even when there was not that much living going on. When, however, my living became so very interesting—my travels, my romances—, I abandoned transcription and just lived in my living. Activities, experiences, and events carried me along in their excitement, all to the neglect of reflection, rumination, and writing. I thought that I lived to write, but for long periods of time I just lived to live. Those were years lost to the mastery of literary vocation.

True, there were some other years of day-after-day, straight-through assiduous writing. I can pursue the monomania, get down to work and stick with it. I have been capable of perseverance,—ten books in one seven-year period.

But there were times when I just ran out of gas. Then I lost entire years to inertia,—1976, for example, or, earlier, 1967, when I dried up and was stultified, couldn't write a single sentence to carry on a project I had started. I have languished in some deadly doldrums.

What usually incapacitated me from my writing was turmoil in my personal life,—dislocations, severe financial straits, failures to get a job, the ruin of an affair. Then, worse than inertia, I suffered a deep demoralization.

I am not one of those hardy ones, like Nietzsche or Henry Miller, who can write through their miseries. No, I need a secure calm around me, in order to be enabled to write. During my bad times, I would become stripped of initiative, struggling against a paralyzing self-doubt that verged upon self-loathing. (Now we're really getting down to "The Morbidity of Authors"!) If I thought of myself as a nothing, what of anything good could a nothing write? When my personal life was a mess, how could I write anything but another mess? Instead of writing, then, I wasted away in reading and drinking, a consuming consumptive.

Of course, if you live a long life, even wasting most of it, there remain plenty of hours and days in which to get some work done. (Only the first half of *Ars longa, vita brevis* is true.) And so I have gotten some work done. But it hasn't been enough.

The dedicated, monomaniacal literary artist must be an ascetic. Unfortunately, I have a hedonist streak in me and have lapsed into self-indulgence, when self-discipline was what I really needed. I have permitted myself pleasure and happiness,—two nemeses to a writer.

—(You know, a true writer takes no pleasure in drinking. Alcohol is the depressant that detaches him from the world and its allure, the toxic fuel of the process of literary brooding. A true writer is incapable of any sensual enjoyment. As for me, I have done most of my drinking for the pleasure of it. Nor has sex been, to me, mere research.)—

Worse yet, I have sometimes had an I-can-take-it-or-leave-it attitude toward writing. After all, if I was really no good at it, it was a waste of time, time I could better spend at some other enterprise,—even a paying job that I might rouse myself enough to find some interest in.

Actually, I never had any real interest in job or career. Since I was sixteen, I knew that I had an exclusionary vocation. I considered myself a writer and have ever since, even through those protracted nonproductive periods of inertia and demoralization.

The writer expects his life to be turned into a product, intangible consciousness solidified into a tactile bricklike bulk of bound pages. "There's my book, the proof that my life has meant something." That's the artist's illusion, that living must be proved by output. Nature herself must laugh at the notion that living should be anything other than an in-itself.

If you turn out to be a failure as a writer, you might then consider yourself a failure as a human being, one whose whole life has been a failure. Such self-accusation and despair are what come from the monomania of art. Really, there is no correlation between literary eptitude and eptitude in the art of living. So what if my books are bad, if my living has been good. (That my dedication has not been enough is indicated by the fact that I would find absurd the vice-versa of the previous sentence, "So what if my living has been bad; at least my books are good.")

My writing has at least kept me interested as I've gone along through life. Writing is the best antidote to boredom. Still, it hardly shows literary dedication to be writing just to dispel yawns and a nodding-off. You're supposed to keep yourself interested, only in order to write something that is interesting to others. But that others show no interest in your writing doesn't mean that you and your life are not interesting.

At times I have wondered whether my writing has been not a vocation but a mere hobby, recreational time-killing. I quickly deny that to myself, for, if I were not dedicated, would I have persevered through all these years of failure and futility?

I should give myself some credit. My writing may not have been all-or-nothing, but there has been a lot of it.

Just not enough.

"Lost Works"

Even so,—

Whatever did I do with all those other books I've written?

Sure, I've got a stack of my completed works all secured in a vault, hidden away where no one can find them. I count the boxes of manuscripts. There are only a dozen books there. I've written many more than that, I know. What happened to the others?

It's hard to imagine, but I think that I have actually written books that I've lost, or even forgotten completely. How is the latter possible? You might lose a manuscript, yes—it might get burned up in a fire or stolen along with your car, for example—, but how could you forget having written a book, after you must have spent so many months or years writing it?

I guess I'm just too productive, like Haydn and his 104 symphonies. The more you crank out, the less you remember of any one particular work. I suppose that, if you write so much, as I have, you just might completely forget a completed book. Life is long, genius bountiful. And, as for losing works, what with the manuscripts accumulating and my former life so vagrant, I might have been a little careless.

Maybe I haven't really forgotten very many of my own books, but I have certainly lost some of my manuscripts along the way. I know that, because I can remember their titles. I usually decide upon the title when the book is well along or finished, so, if I can remember a title, there must have been a book that went with it. But the books are gone; left behind, lost, given away,—something.

If I think back autobiographically and chronologically, I may be able to recall most of my lost works.

Let's see. I started out in adolescence. *Notes of a Nonconformist*, my first book. Well, it was just a journal and commonplace book, anyway. Juvenilia, they would call it. I might have destroyed it; probably did. Maybe I should have kept it. A writer's idiosyncratic themes emerge very early in his work, sometimes at the very beginning; hmm, *nonconformity*. Never mind the juvenility of *Notes of a Nonconformist*; there might have been some themes in it that I could still exploit with my mature mind.

When I was twenty, I really got down to literary work. I wrote *Sensations*, which was sensational. I had a handwritten original and a typed copy, both now disappeared. *Sensations* was a peculiar book, eccentric in substance and style. Strange that I should write such a wayward work when I was barely starting out. I wish I still had that book. It was a literary curiosity.

What else from those years of my young manhood? Well, there was *Summer Notebook*. I remember starting it and I remember that summer, but I forget what happened to the *Notebook*. Maybe it was noteworthy, but now it is in oblivion. Then came *Words*, a great title, quite succinct! I must have found that book too wordy to keep; anyway, it is gone, too. Talk about titles, how about this one: *Remnants of a Dead God*. Very portentous. I hadn't even read Nietzsche yet, when I wrote that book. What was in it I have no idea. It might have been another wayward foray. Then, when I went to Italy for the first time, I worked on *European Journal*. Where is that one today? It must have dropped out of my pocket onto some Italian roadside while I was hitch-hiking.

Then there's that damn *Soliloquy*. I'm sure I wrote not one, but several books with that title. (I'm not against reusing titles. I've used the title *Love* several times. A writer has to write about what he knows.)

I've got a *Tropical Ecstasy* in my inventory, but that was a recent book. I must have written a different *Tropical Ecstasy* while I was living in Brazil. I can't imagine that I spent two years there without writing anything, especially since I had been on such a productive hot-streak.

My years in Rome on my second stay are well accounted for, in terms of books I've written—(*Roman Ruminations,* a trilogy!)—and still have, except for that *Eros...and Ebb*, my most painful loss. But after that there is a gap. . . .

Come to think of it,—I mean, thinking of soliloquies and Rome—, I wrote something called *Roman Soliloquy, Book 2. Book 2*? What about *Book 1*? Both lost!

Didn't I write a play once? I remember writing it, but I can't recall the title. As I said, I usually write the title during or after completion, so I must not have finished the play. If I had the manuscript, I might finish the play now. But it too is gone.

I know that I haven't perpetrated much poetry. Some verse here and there, yes, but not a book's worth. I did throw away some love poems written to me and for me by her. I threw them away when the love died. I've got enough of my own output to try to keep and keep in order, without being custodian for some poetess. I got my revenge on her by making a gift of my massive *Trilogy*. Oh yes, *Trilogy*, another lost one, another lost three!

In my thirties and forties, I took all those wilderness trips. I know that I wrote a book called *Into the Quetico*, but not a scrap of it do I have. Did I drop the manuscript on some portage trail, or did it slip over the side of the canoe? On one excursion, I had a fishing partner named Bill, who was writing away at his own book. Scribbling and paddling, a pair of literary *voyageurs* we were! I never did get to read Bill's book. I'll never get to read my own either. The wilderness just swallowed it up.

Speaking of travel books, I wrote one about the five months' camping trip through the West that Jan and I took in our camper. At least I think I did. (Why can't I remember? It was only thirty years ago.) If I did write a book about that trip, I haven't got it.

In this, my middle age, wasn't there a *History of Western Values*, or something like that? Well, just because I once thought about writing a particular book, doesn't mean I actually got down to writing it. A title does not a book make. Sometimes I get mixed up on what I have actually written and what I only intended to write but didn't.

I'm living a more settled life now, so I won't lose so many manuscripts on the road, as I must have done during my vagabond years. There'll be fewer lost works of mine from here on out, I'm determined. I'll take better care of my books.

What about my future works?...

Whatever do I do with all those books I haven't written yet?

144

"Leave It Alone, or, The Cure for Self-Vampiry"

Once you get infected with literariness, you become self-devouring, vampirizing your life itself. Not only is every thought, every feeling, every experience *grist for the mill*; they are all blood for the pen.

A college girl in a poetry class has a little fleeting feeling. She gets the inspiration to put it down in a poem. After some frowning and chewing of the pencil, she succeeds, at least in her own mind. "Look, my feeling in a poem! A good poem, too."

Having written one poem, she is now a poet(ess). She wants to write more poems. But where will they come from? Her feelings, of course. Well, she hasn't had any more fine feelings lately. Without the feelings, both inspiration and subject-matter are lacking. Now she wants to feel something, in order to write another poem. If only she might find a young man to fall in love with, then she'd be able to write a whole sheaf of poems. Another Elizabeth Barrett Browning, a model she is studying in her class.

Literariness has got her now. She stalks herself, waiting to pounce on any little emotion that might arise, any happenstance of the day that might have hidden aesthetic significance. All the better if she suffers a distress or a grief, which she can turn into a more powerful poem. "A poet cherishes his chagrins/And sets his sighs to music," diagnosed Thoreau, a versifier the girl should have read, because she herself is afflicted with the pathological literariness of Thoreau's admission.

Nietzsche wrote that poets are the most unfeeling of human beings, because poets exploit their own lives ruthlessly, life itself only the means to premeditated art. Nietzsche needn't have restricted his indictment to poets. Most writers do the same.

I myself have never written a poem, but I suffer from the literary affliction. Every day I leap out of bed wondering what experience of that day (or remembered experiences of earlier days) I can siphon off to feed the literary. I plunder my own mind. I make all time worktime, turning living into a mere means. Ravenous and rabid with literariness, I suck my own blood-of-life.

It seemed like a high and noble ideal, at first, that turning of ephemeral living into enduring literary art.

Wouldn't my life, wouldn't life itself, acquire meaning, if I could succeed in semanticizing it? Yes, I'd capture life and make beautiful sense of it all.

What I wound up doing was rendering life through a meat grinder, shrink-wrapping the result, and offering it to the hungry. You start out with a high ideal and vocational devotion, but the prophet only turns into a butcher.

After you've written something and judge it of value, the mania of ambition adds further derangement to your mind and to your living. Your living is wrenched out of your life and deposited into your writing. When you live to write, you are just about done for.

The artist inevitably makes a ruination of his living. Not only if he should fail—(failure in his art is what he conceives of as ruination)—, but also if he should succeed, for the more that has gone into his art, the more has been sucked out of his living. When living has become merely instrumental, lifeblood is completely drained from the one who had been living. The writer becomes a living-dead, a vampire. His book is his coffin.

In our contemporary culture, we are pressured to tell all about ourselves and our lives. The writer does tell all. Nothing is withheld as sacred and private; the writer's life is all raw meat to be ground up for vulgar public consumption. It's a putrid meat, bloody with self-vampiry.

Our would-be poet might still cure herself by giving up her attempted poetry. As for myself and other lifelong victims of chronic literariness, there is little hope. Prognosis for myself is more and more autobiography unto the total sucking-out and complete draining of my lifeline.

Like the wasted alcoholic and the aging drug addict, all I can do is warn against what I have done, the affliction I suffer from:

"Youngsters, don't you do as I have done, don't you wind up like me! Never mind *art*; or, if you are enamored of the idea, put your art in your living. Don't exploit your living for any other purpose. Don't suck out your blood of life. Love your living. And leave it alone!"

145

"A Writer's Shame"

When I arrived at the hospital to see my mother, there was something that I wanted to tell her. There was also something that I wanted to withhold.

The news that I had for her was that I had just gotten a new job,—director of a residential youth camp for inner-city children.

To that point, my work history had been irregular. After college, first there was the Peace Corps for two years, then a brief stint as a social worker in Wisconsin (where I had also been a day-laborer and an insurance agent), next two years teaching English in Rome, then three years at Encyclopaedia Britannica, from which I quit, so that Jan and I could roam the West in our camper, then my part-time job at Berlitz, teaching English again, plus some summers working at the camp as the naturalist and program director. What did it all add up to? I was almost forty years old, yet had no profession, let alone a career.

In fact, I had a vocation, the only endeavor of labor that had concerned me since I was sixteen, namely, writing. But that too added up to nothing. In 1981, I had taken Jan to Rome with me to photograph for our book. Yet, now, three years later, there was no published *Rome* book or any prospects of one, either. *Rome, The Values of Cosmopolis* was another quixotic literary venture of mine.

In the early Eighties, I was actually working three jobs more or less at the same time,—doing my writing, teaching for Berlitz, working at the camp. From the first labor there was no income, from the second moderate income, from the third a small and only seasonal income. I was a hard worker, but had little to show for it. My mother never said anything, but she must have wondered what my university education had been for. I didn't seem to be making my way in the world very well. Fortunate for me that I had a working wife.

Compared to my brother, there was not so much to disapprove of in me, but, still, I should have come to more than what I was.

I arrived at the hospital with the news that I had been appointed camp director. That might have seemed a frivolous job to my mother, so, when I told her the news, I explained the importance of the position, comparing it to that of a principal of a school.

In fact, the job was only full-time seasonal and the remuneration some few thousand dollars, pay at social service agencies generally low. I didn't tell my mother those particulars. I wanted her to think that I might have found a career at last. I wanted her to think well of me.

The new position actually changed my work life very little, for I would have to continue some teaching at Berlitz, and I would carry on with my vocation. All I was really doing was heaping the workload higher without substantially increasing our income. When Jan and I had returned from Rome in 1981, our marital money pool was reduced to $300. Temporary part-time jobs returned us very slowly to shaky solvency.

It wasn't job or career that preoccupied me as I visited my mother in the hospital; it was my vocation. The Rome book had come to nothing. My mother did not inquire about it, so I didn't have to revisit that failure.

But then there was that notorious book that I had just finished and was attempting to market. I actually thought that I could get it published soon.

That book was what I withheld from my mother. I knew that she would disapprove of its irreligiosity. Her negative judgment upon my working career—even though mostly unspoken—was bad enough, but her disapproval of my book would have been a moral judgment against me. A writer of integrity does not write for approval or cater to the biases of readers, of course. The reader can take it or leave it. It's not so easy to say the same thing when the reader is one's own mother.

In judging my work history, my mother had a right to be disappointed. Of my writing, she would have disapproved. That was why I withheld any talk about the book.

I felt guilty for what I had done, my writing a sin or crime, my silence about it a secret sin or crime. The more we disappoint others, the more we find ourselves to blame. At that time, I felt only a small portion of the sense of failure and futility I have endured since. Even so, thoughts about my work history and my writing were disquieting and demoralizing. I wanted to come to something, I really did.

So, I told my mother about my job but kept the secret of my new book. Jobs had always been for me temporary expedients, until I had written enough, published enough, to be able to pursue my vocation exclusively. Those temporary expedients have dragged on through decades.

My notorious book, I thought, would be a secret I could keep,—until the book was published. What then? I visualized my mother reading it, not understanding but being appalled. Then my shame would be out. Did I want to succeed in my vocational ambition, only to scandalize my mother and bring shame upon myself?

As it turned out, my mother would die before my book was published some nine years after that day I visited her in the hospital. I have written many books since then, but I still have one of those same old part-time jobs, one that has become a nearly lifelong temporary expedient.

We disappoint others by what we do and by what we fail to do. Others' disappointment in us undermines our morale, infects us with self-disappointment. We try to persevere in the pursuit of our authentic self, we try to maintain our integrity against others, but we only wind up judging ourselves as the world has been judging us.

146

"Killing Off"

Sometimes a writer should kill off one of his books, before it kills him off.

A writer works away with the intention of finishing his book and getting it published. The more he works away, the more his time and self are invested, the more momentum his project takes on, the more necessary it seems to finish and publish. Who would ever write a book, only to destroy it? Yet, there are situations in which that must be done.

I am not talking about the self-doubt, severe self-criticism, and perfectionism that caused the dying Vergil to make his appeal to his executors to destroy the *Aeneid*. Vergil thought that his epic wasn't good e-nough—(the ghost of Homer haunting him at his deathbed?)—, but he must have known that it was still pretty good. Unfinished, yes, imperfect, certainly, the *Aeneid* nonetheless should not have had euthanasia committed upon it. It posed no danger to its author, whether during life or afterwards.

No, I am not urging destruction of an author's work out of punctilious perfectionism. Instead, I am talking about works that are pernicious in themselves, harmful to society and potentially lethal to the author and his good name.

Consider how parenthood may go horribly wrong. Husband and wife long for a child to lavish their love upon. When that child is born, father and mother rejoice in what they have produced, are proud of themselves and each other, and ready to pour out their love. Their child is of them, their flesh and blood and family name.

But what if that child goes from brat to delinquent and on to criminal and pervert? Then the parents curse what they have wrought. The monster-child poisons the marriage, makes the parents blame themselves and each other for having brought such a child into the world. And the father thinks that, if he had the power, he would kill his own child, do away with the botch. But society has taken that right away from him. So the father must suffer the notoriety of parental association with the criminal, the shamed surname.

A literary project is like a pregnancy; once started, and especially once it is beyond a certain point, it must be carried through. (Yes, an author may abort a book, as a woman may abort a fetus, but only in the first trimester. Thereafter, personal investment becomes a consideration.)

As in parenthood gone horrible, an author may write a book that turns out to be a botch,—not an artistic botch, but a moral botch. He may have written the book out of bitterness or grudge or spite or meanness or iconoclastic vandalism or plain hatred or other such perversities of the soul. Not every book is written to enlighten and edify, believe me.

Just like individuals, books may be delinquent or criminal or perverted. What is a book, but an individual who has found a way to propagate himself? If that self is a monster-self, the book will wreak havoc upon society.

Books of cruelty, violence, pornography, and horror are the worst monsters. They should make their authors recoil in revulsion, but they do not, because their authors are as corrupt as what they have done; bad words are like bad blood. Such books should be destroyed before others are corrupted by them. (Their authors, however, may be too far gone for any moral self-regeneration.)

Destruction to such books and their contagion and corruption! Books may be as criminal a contraband as heroin and assault weapons. Killer books, written by killers. Books that should themselves have been killed.

I have described the dire extremes of books that deserve to die. But there are others, not so harmful to society but still harmful to their authors. Books written when the author was down, depressed, muddled, in emotional turmoil, not at his best. Such books may not be plague upon the world, but they are a case of disfiguring disease in the author.

Our contemporary society urges writers to bare all, but why should the author invite readers into his toilet, where he proceeds to vomit or defecate in front of them? No, spare us such crude realities. We are none the better for sharing them. Do not brutalize our sensitivity.

As with the parents of a child that has gone wrong, it is painful for the author to admit that his book has gone wrong, wrong because he was in a bad state-of-mind when he wrote it. The book itself may even be impeccable artistically and aesthetically, but, if its spirit is rotten, that overrides any literary virtues.

Painful and difficult too it is for an author to recognize and admit that his offspring is bad, wrong, and deserving of destruction. No, the book was written, and it must be published. There is a blind inevitability to the whole process.

To create, then to destroy,—that goes against the whole nature of the artist, as infanticide is against the nature of parenthood. We treasure everything we create, hoard it all, find our own value in what we have done, insist upon its value, even when it is the most obvious botch. For an author to destroy a completed book of his is to nullify the entire period-of-life of its creation, as to murder a newborn nullifies the nine months of the pregnancy.

It would be a wise and recovering author who recognizes that that particular book of his was a bad experience of illness. To save society from contagion and himself from re-infection, he must kill off the book that he has written. Maybe the next book will be a healthy one. If not, it too must die.

Sometimes the greatest benefaction to society an author may perform is for the creator to turn destroyer.

147

"Success/Failure"

The beginning of vocational wisdom is the realization that success may be as bad as failure.

In a job or career, others' recognition of the quality of one's work is crucial, because that recognition, that valuing of the employee, leads to raises and promotions. The work of an unrecognized worker goes for naught. One who does good work rightly resents others' failure to recognize his or her productive efforts.

On a job for hire, we work for others' approval. Sometimes that approval can be secured by means other than quality of work. You can ingratiate yourself with the bosses, become skillful in office politics, win the owner's daughter. A successful worker may actually find little satisfaction in the work itself; the satisfaction may be all in self-advancement. Success gratifies ambition. Failure on the job, on the other hand, may be taken as a negative judgment upon an entire life, the broken ego accepting the verdict from others.

Vocation, the practice of an art, is different. When you practice an art, the work is all. The work-in-itself.

Hemingway said that recognition is the ruin of a writer, for if it comes too early it spoils him, if it comes too late it embitters him. But can't early recognition be a stimulus, recognition-at-last a consolation?

The problem with success achieved or denied is not timeliness; it is worthiness. There is also a potential for the corruption of the writer and his work.

There have been writers whose success was immediate, sudden, and overwhelming. Famous in a day! Their very first book sells in the millions, royalty checks fatten the bank account, the author's name and the title of his book become nearly omnipresent in the current culture.

But what of the intrinsic worth of the book itself? Popular enthusiasm is no sober judge of that. The author was surprised by his own quick success; he doubts himself and his book. Never mind. The public now wants him and more books of his. And so, he forgets his commitment to art and becomes a commercial writer, perhaps to further popular success. Ambition then runs roughshod over disciplined objectivity. Now he will write to please...others, not himself. Success proved the unmaking of the artist, as it was the making of a literary entrepreneur.

But does a writer really know the worth of his work, unless others tell him so?, you might ask. Well, that is what art is,—sureness of judgment. The artist must be an expert on intrinsic worth; if he is not, he is no artist.

He can apply an objective standard to his own work. Appeal to the opinion of others for validation is insecurity and insidious ambition both. Vulgar acclamation is nothing but a babelous din.

Any writer who succeeds too soon, too much, and against his own expectations should suspect himself. Even if success is deserved, he must beware of what it may do to him. As art is an ascetic discipline, so success is a voluptuous self-indulgence. Success corrupts, and spectacular success corrupts absolutely.

The artist needs the same detached objectivity toward the public's response to his work as he directs to that work itself. The writer must satisfy himself and find that satisfaction in the working and in the work-itself. The arbiter is oneself. True literary success is in the doing, not in the done; and it is personal, not public.

Failure presents flipside hazards; the dirty coin is two-sided. Where success encourages, failure demoralizes; where the former gratifies ambition, the latter frustrates it; where success makes the writer believe that he is more than he is, failure makes him think that he is less,—both distortions of accurate self-estimation.

Opposites though they are, success and failure share the yielding of competent judgment to others, the sacrifice of integrity to ambition, and the finding of satisfaction in others' response, rather than in one's own sure judgment. Failure is hard on the mind. Success is hard on the soul.

The worst sense of failure is not that after an early attempt—(such a false first step might be constructive to self-criticism and future development)—, but the conviction of a lifetime of failure in an old writer.

Much of success or failure may be actually due, not to the book itself, but to the cultural climate, whether congenial or unreceptive. Some milieus want frivolities and fads. I do not go so far as to assert that all great books are untimely ones or that all great writers can be understood and appreciated only by posterity. Even so, timeliness may determine success or failure. Timeliness again! What does it have to do with intrinsic worth?

Besides recognition, what does the successful writer have? The book he wrote, the book as achieved art. Besides neglect, what does the failed writer have? Why, the book he wrote, the book as achieved art. It might be the same book offered up in different cultural climates.

The book is the proof of the writer, the only proof.

You might object that writing is communication, so, if the author fails to find an audience, he fails in communication, he fails in his writing and his art. If writing is soliloquous, isn't the writer a madman?

Is the composer who plays his new piece for himself alone mad? Is the artist who stands back and admires his new painting—one seen by no one else—mad? So, too, the writer may read the words of his book, words read by no other human, and be sure of himself and his work. Yes, music wants ears, art wants eyes, literature wants a receptive mind, but, all those lacking, worth is intrinsic or elsewise nowhere.

"Having been mellowed by failure, I now find myself embittered by success." So spoke a writer whose recognition came at long last. He was wise at first and persevered in his art, only to succumb to ambition in the end.

One way or another, success or failure is the bane of every writer. Looking to the other for validation is treachery against oneself.

Blessed are the writers who remain ignorant of the ideas, *success, failure*! Blessed are those free of the vice of ambition!

"Work alone is your proper business, never the fruits...Stand fast in Yoga, surrendering attachment, in success and failure be the same, and then get busy with your works." (*Gita*, ii, 47f.)

148

"Psychological Survival as a Writer"

The key to psychological survival as a writer is to care nothing about reactions to what you have written. To the creative literary artist, a finished book is yesterday's turd.

Ah, but the expectancy, the anticipation of what you will write tomorrow!

This period of *Matters of Life and Death* is becoming more productive of pages than even my sojourn in Rome, hitherto my most productive time of life.

Moral of the story: Don't die too soon. You might write better yet.

149

"Literary Immortality"

The ancient Roman was preoccupied with his *fama*, that is, his reputation, both while he lived and as judged by posterity.

The word *fama* is from a root word that means talk. One's *fama* was how one was talked about, repute whether in admiration or in*famy*.

Some of *fama* was collective, some individual. The former was a family legacy handed down by illustrious ancestors. (If illustrious ancestors were lacking, some affinity could be made up, a phony family history concocted, the slim proof of which might be a similarity of family name to that of some great family of the past.) The *familia* had its *fama*. One duty to the ancestors was to recall that *fama* to contemporaries and enhance it, in order to pass on greater *fama* to children and distant progeny. Family reputation was transmissible. The Romans had the peculiar notion that character is an heirloom.

Every Roman general and politician developed an ego that found its gratification in individual personal *fama*. Great deeds swelled a man's stature among his peers and ensured him a recognition and place in the long line of the greats of Roman history. One's statue in the Roman Forum itself! Deeds earned the immortality of being spoken about forever.

What about those incapable of doing great deeds?

"Exegi monumentum aere perennius," proclaimed Horace of his own *fama*. But what had Horace done? He had been a soldier, yes, but an infantryman bringing up the rear. Once, he even fled from the field in a panic of cowardice. And yet, such a deedless impotent one claimed that he merited "a monument more enduring than bronze". Was that Horace's satire on the Roman's obsession with one's own *fama*?

Not at all. As the great conquerors and statesmen attained their self-memorialization by their deeds, Horace did so by his words.

What, great words as good as great deeds? Who said so? Horace did. Tongue-in-cheek? Maybe so, but confident self-assertions sometimes secure persuasion of others. If one's peers do not speak of one, if they show no recognition of one's *fama*, you might as well do it yourself.

Julius Caesar had been a skillful self-promoter, his device of referring to himself in the third person being one artifice to keep his name on everyone's lips. (In those days, books were read out in public. *Caesar* is a recurrent word in *The Gallic War*.) Caesar objectified himself, detached himself from himself, in order that he might praise and promote himself.

The conqueror of Gaul seemingly earned his *fama* by conquest; yet, deeds may be forgotten when all the witnesses to them have died. Thus the necessity of words as eternal witnesses to the deeds. In order to secure his *fama* in posterity, Julius Caesar the general became Julius Caesar the author.

But back to Horace: No war hero, he, no statesman, no world-beater. Just a poet, an idle inactive sort, ostensibly a useless type in a dynamic society like the Roman Empire, where there was so much that had to be *done*. A statue of Caesar, yes, but a monument to that lazy little ode writer? It seems un-Roman.

Caesar wrote words about his deeds so that those deeds would be remembered. Horace wrote words about his words—(literary autoeroticism)—and on that flimsy foundation built his "monument more enduring than bronze, which will outlast the pyramids," etc.

In order for Horace's claim to be plausible, a revaluation was necessary. The Romans had always been doers. Horace had to convince them that they were talkers, and, further, that the good word was of equal value to the great deed. (Horace was asserting Greek values over Roman ones.)

Literary men have been making the same attempt ever since, promoting the primacy of culture (and therefore of literature) over politics. The less the scope and freedom a modern person has to act, to accomplish great deeds, the more we have come to believe that mere written speech is enough to earn immortality. Everybody wants to be a somebody; even a nobody does. We believe Horace's joke.

The fame that used to follow the deed in Rome now follows the word in modern Europe or America. Words speak louder than actions. I don't have to do anything; I just have to come up with a memorable book of words or two. Then, the Pulitzer Prize or a National Book Award, modern versions of the ancient laurel wreath, unto the Nobel Prize for Literature, the equivalent of the statue in the Roman Forum. And maybe one's image on a postage stamp, to be sent all over the world.

As for posthumous literary immortality, it consists in a book perpetually in print or a big passage from a writer's lifework in a textbook anthology force-fed to generations of students.

Contemporary politicians still follow Caesar's course of composing self-glorifying, self-memorializing memoirs and autobiography, but, really, the writer acquires just as much *fama* by skipping the deeds and just writing the words. The words, not the deeds, may be the means to immortality. (Has anyone ever heard of a politician being described as an *immortal*?)

Because of our modern democratic individualism, the immortality belongs to the individual alone; it does not accrue to his family, as it did in ancient Rome. Contemporary *fama* is narrowly egotistic.

An author's name on the title page, in mere eighth-inch font, proves a more enduring proclamation of fame than a name incised in two-foot letters on the stone face of some rock pile. Horace was right about himself. He can boast that, like the pyramids of Egypt, he is still with us.

Ancient Roman *fama* is a value that is modern American too. (How much of self-estimate derives from the estimate by others.) Our American version of *fama* is *celebrity*, a recognition trivial in itself yet esteemed by all. In ancient Rome, Horace notwithstanding, you generally had to prove yourself one way or another. Our American celebrities earn their *fama* merely by being identified as celebrities; they are do-littles, without much real significant impact.

Authors, despite their lofty conception of their sacerdotal role in literary culture, frequently hanker after the *fama* of vulgar celebrityship, a television interview perhaps. Might as well bask in being known while one is still alive, posthumous immortality so uncertain. "What if they don't talk about me after I'm gone?", the author agonizes, as if, in that case, his life would have been as wasted as his words. The author worries that his posthumous reputation, instead of *nil nisi bonum*, will be just plain *nil*.

Horace would chuckle over his peerage with Caesar, he having taken the easier course to immortality. There need be no inflicted wounds from a pen, none of the risk incurred by those who attempt great deeds in dangerous times. Julius Caesar was done in by his deeds, a casualty of assassination because of what he had done and intended to do. I can't think of any writer who was assassinated because of his bad words. (Heretics perished as a result of their obstinate opinions, not their literary ineptitude.) A paper cut is nothing threatening. So, the literary way,—not only an easier route to immortality, but a safer life meanwhile.

The author hopes to earn his immortality in a word. That word is his own name, to be spoken by the human tongue forever.

We don't speak Latin, but we know the meaning of the word *fama*. We want it. An author especially wants it. In all his books, he writes his name again and again and again, as Julius Caesar once did. The author prays that posterity has a good memory.

150

"Admittance"

I approached the high stairway leading to the door.

Before ascending, I checked myself to see that I was presentable, because I knew that admittance would be granted only to persons of quality. I believed that I was a person of quality.

Satisfying myself on my presentability, I ascended.

Arriving onto the broad porch at the top of the stairs, I looked at the door. How solid and imposing it was, much more so than it had appeared from the bottom of the stairway.

I drew myself up, erect and confident.

There was a bell to the left of the door. I pressed the bell, just one time. I then took a step back, in order for the person who answered the door to see me clearly as a person of quality, not as a supplicant.

I waited patiently, but no one answered the door.

After a minute or so—what I thought a sufficient time so that I didn't seem too insistent to those inside—I rang the bell again, this time twice.

Once again I stepped back a single pace and waited to present myself.

No one answered.

Might the bell be out of order?

I was reluctant to knock, because knocking is threatening, like an attempt to break in. The door seemed so solid, anyway, that I doubted whether my knocking could be heard within.

I decided to ring the bell again, three times now, each time a firm long ring, so that my ringing was sure to be heard.

While ringing, I myself could not hear the bell through the solid door, so I couldn't determine whether the bell was working or not.

There was no stir inside the door, nor turning of the doorknob, nor any other indication that someone was about to open the door to admit me.

A strange situation! I knew that there were people inside; I even knew the names of some of them. They were always there. How could it be that not a single one heard my ringing of the bell?

I stood waiting until it became clear to me that no one would answer the door.

Well, such a grand mansion must have other entry doors, I thought to myself. I'll go around to the side to see whether I might get in through one of the other doors.

No matter by which door, whether the grand main door or some side door, the important thing was to get in.

I did find another door. No bell for that door evident, I would have to knock. I would not pound away on the door, but, instead, tap, loud enough to be heard, but not so loud as to be threatening or irritating to those within.

Tap, tap, tap.

I took the one step back and stood waiting.

No answer, so, after a few minutes, tap, tap, tap, tap, tap.

I was now becoming impatient.

I must make an effort to control myself, I thought, because the manner of my entry would determine the kind of reception I would get once I was inside.

Because I hadn't announced my coming, no one inside would be expecting me. Even so, having arrived, I deserved entry, welcome, and acceptance.

Might this be the wrong place? No, I knew the building I wanted to enter. Might it be the wrong time? No, they should grant me admittance anytime I showed up. This was certainly my time.

That side door still shut tight, I continued around the house.

I found another door, narrow and short, one I would have to squeeze through, ducking my head. This door had no bell; it didn't even have a doorknob. This must be a past-use, permanently sealed door, no longer open to entry by anyone. Well, that shut door was no particular rejection of me personally.

Making my way to the back of the house, I then came upon a large picture window.

I looked in. There were many people inside, conversing and enjoying one another's company. I recognized some of them. Yes, that was the assembly I deserved to be a part of; I was their peer.

Of course, I would not knock on the window; that would be rude and offensive.

Instead, I just stood there, hoping that someone inside, in a glance toward the window, would see me, recognize me, and direct me around to a door, where I would be let in at last. Once in, I would not complain about their earlier negligence or demand an apology. I would be forgiving.

I felt awkward standing there, as if I were a voyeur, rather than a potential member, but I didn't know what else I could do.

I tried a few subtle waves at people I thought might have seen me, but no one responded. Now that they had all achieved admittance, they seemed to have no interest in who might be outside seeking entry.

I felt a bit silly waving and I wondered whether I might have a pitiful look on my face in my plea for admittance. Yes, very awkward and embarrassing for me.

No one inside taking any notice of me, I placed my two hands on the glass and drew up so close that I almost pressed my whole body against the window, so desperate had I become to be admitted, to join those among whom I belonged.

What might those inside think of me, if they saw me doing that?, I wondered. My earned stature and renown would be subverted by such a first impression.

I backed off and resumed just standing and hoping to catch someone's eye.

Little by little, I began to seethe in frustration. Why wouldn't they let me in? I fully deserved to be inside with them, yet they refused to admit me as one of them.

On impulse, I felt a delinquent urge to pick up a rock and throw it through the window. That would get me attention and reaction! But of course I would do no such thing.

If they ignored me, if they didn't want me inside with them, if they believed I didn't belong,—well, I had no choice but to accept their verdict.

They weren't worthy of me, I lied to myself, in re-buttal to their judgment that I was not worthy of them. I belong in a better group in an even grander mansion, I also told myself, but I knew that that was not true either.

I had other such thoughts attempting to justify myself and my worth, but they were just emotional reactions to the futility of my attempt at entry.

At last, I understood that I would not get in. It didn't matter that I deserved to be in among them; if they didn't want me, I just wouldn't get in, that's all.

I turned around and walked away.

151

"Wishes"

One night in my study, lamp turned off, as I sat languishing in the midst of my manuscripts—some of them decades old, some of a few years past, one uncompleted—, I fell into a drowsy stupor.

My half-closed eyes detected what seemed like a glowing light in the corner. I was startled back into alert wakefulness.

The light throbbed and expanded. Then, in a puff of small explosion, a bulb-headed genie appeared.

"Good evening," he said blandly.

I lurched up into erect attention.

"Yes," the genie said. "You recognize me for what I am. And, yes, I am here to grant your wish. Even a genius can use help from a genie.

"I say *wish*, not *wishes*. You know, that three wishes stuff is too much of a good thing. As if people really wish for this-that-and-the-other-besides. *Three* wishes! Why, if most people considered it carefully, they could reduce the three to the one supreme wish."

Astounded, I was speechless before the apparition.

"Take you, for instance," the genie continued. "There must be some one thing you want more than anything else. I am the wish-granter, and I will grant you your supreme wish."

"But I..."

"Haven't thought about it, my man?" the genie said, anticipating my response. There was a little mockery in his voice. "Why, sure you have. It's just a matter of winnowing out the secondary wishes—those are not all that important to you, are they?—and then you'll know what your supreme wish is."

"Why are you here, really?", I succeeded in asking the genie, my voice a gasping whisper.

"To grant your supreme wish, as I told you," the genie answered.

We sat in silence for a few moments, the genie and I, he in the aura of his little fiery glow, I in the darkness. I felt a sensation of fire in my face, as if I had become all lit and apparent to the genie.

"Well, let me narrow it down for you, since you seem so reluctant," the genie offered. "Reluctant to have your supreme wish granted? Don't you mortals really want what you want?"

I couldn't answer.

"I'll give you two choices," the genie continued. "I know you, but I'm not sure which of your two greatest wishes is really your supreme wish. I'll tell you what your two great wishes are, then you must choose the one you want. And that wish, that wish only, I will grant."

"All right, yes," I said to the genie, my fright by now being dispelled by the prospect of having my most heartfelt wish granted.

"Writer, writer!", the genie exclaimed, that little mockery in his voice again. (I suppose that the one who grants wishes might be a bit contemptuous of those needing ones whose wishes he grants.)

"Here is your first choice," the genie proposed. "You pick one of these manuscripts of yours here lying about.

Any one you choose. And I will see that it is published to a success you can't imagine. Everyone will buy and read it, the critics will appreciate and praise, not find any fault, you will become a culture-hero during your lifetime, a literary immortal thereafter. And you'll make and enjoy a fortune to boot. There, how about that choice?"

A prospect to dispel a lifetime of frustration! Yes, that was my supreme wish, as the genie knew.

I was about to beseech the genie to grant that, my supreme wish, when he stopped me:

"Wait, wait. Not so fast. I have another possible supreme wish of yours. Consider this possibility: You know, you've been in some creative doldrums for a long time, haven't you?..."

Yes, the genie did know me.

"...If this might be your supreme wish, I will grant it: A flash of the greatest inspiration of your life will come to you tomorrow morning. And you will write the best book of all of yours, one of the best books ever written, in fact. You will be filled with the joy of extended creativity, let's say two years of steady creative composition, each day one of excitement and satisfaction, until you complete the book, at which time you will feel fulfillment. In short, I will grant your wish for the ultimate creative experience. Beginning tomorrow."

"And that book? Will it be published?"

"No, no," the genie answered, waving his bony little forefinger. "That would overlap into the first choice I gave you. That book, as soon as it is completed, will vanish utterly.

"One wish only, one or the other, not both."

I fell back into the chair and stared at the genie.

He let me consider a bit, then said, "Well, there are your two choices. Which do you want?"

My uncertainty and wavering suddenly ended.

"The second," I told the genie. "Please!"

"So, you'd rather be creative in what you will be doing than rich and famous for what you have done?", the genie said.

"Yes, that's right," I answered.

And I felt a deep conviction in the rightness of my choice.

The genie began to laugh, at first agreeably and sociably. He laughed and laughed, but the tone of his laughter gradually changed from humor to mockery to cruel scorn. And as his laughter changed, so too his image changed, from genie...to demon!

He stopped laughing and glared at me.

"Your supreme wish! *Your* wish!", the demon barked at me in ridicule. "I *can* grant wishes, yes I can, but I will grant neither one of the wishes you considered. Because I want you to go on wishing! I want you to consume yourself in wishing! I will give you...nothing!"

He glared at me with an intense ferocity.

Although I was terrified, such rage overcame me that I leapt from the chair and lunged toward the demon in my study corner, my hands clutching for his throat.

In a puff of smoke and with a little lingering stink, the demon disappeared.

I fell back into the chair, exhausted. Through my half-closed eyes, in my stupor, I perceived the stacks of my completed manuscripts around me and a blank page still in the typewriter.

The next day, I burned down my study with all the manuscripts inside, hoping to burn up the genie-and-demon with them. The upwelling heat of the conflagration carried the flaming pages into the sky.

When all had died down, you might have found a charred page carried by the wind, but on that black page there wouldn't be one legible word.

And so I cured myself of wishing. From that day to this, I have had not a single wish. Nor have I had any further encounter with genie or demon.

152

"A Writer's Aging"

There is a hardening of the arteries of imagination, just as there is a hardening of the arteries of the blood of life.

In a writer's youth, ideas surge up with the physiological energy of the young. The world, just being discovered, provokes interpretations of a thousand points. The young writer is barely able to keep up with the ideas that occur to him. He feels an artistic potency as accompaniment to his sexual one.

What he writes may be poorly done, but there is plenty of it. Superabundance and superfluity of ideas bring satisfaction, irrespective of questions of quality. Scribbling away, scribbling away, chasing the ideas-inflow, the young writer is carried along, each day of his life one of expectancy and excitement. The greatest excitement is the sense of himself as a creative artist.

Then, with a few more years and some maturity, the writer discovers his idiosyncratic themes, focuses on them, and, necessarily, pushes aside extraneous spontaneous ideas. He develops a discipline. Selecting what he thinks his best ideas, he labors over them, shapes and reshapes them. He comes to place less value on inspiration, more on craftsmanship. That very process of reworking the same or similar material excludes wide-ranging and wayward ideas from entry into his mind. The mature writer's mind, like his life, is narrower but richer.

The mature writer devotes years to his few themes. Whether a success or a failure, he feels that he was destined to write what he does write, in the way and manner he writes. Now and then, remembering the over-flowing cornucopia of inspirations and ideas of his youth, he might wonder about other possibilities, but he eventually becomes resigned to his narrowness and limitations. A writer cannot write about anything and everything; he's got to find his forte and stick to that. And so, in his maturity he produces those few books that express what the writer thinks he is and can do, his peculiar books, culled from the abundance of the ideas of his youth.

After those books, what then? Having spent the years of his mature discipline concentrating on his themes and excluding the extraneous, the writer has lost receptivity to fresh inspiration. Unlike the young man, whose each day is open arms and open mind, the mature writer has enclosed himself in a cubicle of his own making. He finds it hard to imagine anything new.

Perhaps he tries, anyway, thinking that versatility is as admirable as mastery. But virtuosos do not become so in middle age. The mature writer's book on a new uncharacteristic theme pleases neither him nor his readers, who already know what he can do and expect him to keep doing it.

Then comes the day when the writer must admit to himself that he has artistic atherosclerosis. Sure, he could persist, whether in his proven competence, the same old stuff, or in more desperate rambles into the different. He has long ago forsaken inspiration, has attained and expressed (pressed out) his worked-over themes, and really has nothing more to write, except to write more just for the sake of writing more. He has spent himself. The flow of the arteries is sluggish.

Well may the old writer look back in nostalgia at the excitement of the potentiality he felt in his youth, or at his first conviction of the mastery of his themes and treatment, or, if successful, at the readers' acknowledgement of his worth and an appreciation of his work. Retrospection, the fate of every writer, even those who do not write from their reminiscences.

Gradually, the writer lapses into his vocational senescence. Inspiration gone, themes exhausted, books written and rewritten. Achievements perhaps, but no prospects. He has written himself out, and he knows it. He indulges his nostalgia, tries to banish second thoughts, and take some pride in what he has done, but, like all the old, he must live in his memory, in his memory only, because his imagination is gone.

And then the writer lapses into the inactivity and passivity of old age.

He becomes only a reader.

153

"Terminal Desperation" (a soliloquy)

"I've got to finish this damn book, before I'm finished myself.

"Now, where was I? Pick up where I left off. Where was that?

"My memory is getting as feeble as my body. My head hurts. Can't remember where I left off. Yesterday's page must be here on the desk somewhere…Did I write a page or some pages yesterday? I think I did.

"Why did I waste so much of my life doing everything else but what I should have been doing all along? If only

I had worked harder at my writing! If only I had worked harder, I would have already finished my masterpiece. I could hold it all bound together right here in my hands.

"My masterpiece! Here it is, just a jumbled pile of papers. I can't even remember where it was that I left off yesterday. Why did I wait so long to get down to it?

"Feeble, I feel so damn feeble, worse every morning than the day before. But my mind still has its powers, doesn't it? If the body can just hold out a few more months, I should be able to finish my book. If my body holds out...If my mind holds out!

"No, let me face facts. I'm old and sick. Too tired, worn out. What kind of a book can I still write, except one that is old and sick and tired, just like me? If only I had gotten down to it when I was in my prime. Why didn't I? Well, I did, only to give up on it. A quitter. Too daunting a task, my unrealized masterpiece!...

"Damn it, I won't give up now! I'll prove it to myself that I've still got it in me. And I'll show them all, too. My life hasn't been wasted. I've just been laggard in harvesting the crop of it. 'Laggard in harvesting the crop of it,'—I like that phrase. Think I'll put it in my book somewhere.

"I used to be able to tumble out of bed onto the chair in front of my typewriter and just whale away at the keys, word after word, sentence after sentence, page after page, book after book. Maybe that's my problem now. I've burned the candle down to the nub. Or is it *nib*? And, as for those books of mine,—well, they're all right for what they are. But I'd give up the whole lot of 'em in exchange for this masterpiece that I know I've still got in me, the one I've got to write before I die.

"Where did I leave off? Ha! Not only can't I remember that, I don't even know what it was that I've been writing about. You're senile, old boy, Mr.Alzheimer himself.

"No, my masterpiece is about...what? Oh, something profound, that's for sure. The wisdom of a wise old man. Everything I've learned in my long life, eighty years, put down on a few hundred pages, a counsel for the ages. Pages for the ages! And the key life-lesson I've learned was...Well, that's the substance of the book, the life-lesson I've learned.

"If only I had gotten down to it sooner. Oh, I said that already, didn't I? What's the point of regret? I'm working away at it now, aren't I? There is still time to finish it. I feel pretty good today, for a change.

"My daughter thinks I'm senile, that's for sure. She supplies me with paper and typewriter ribbons and encourages me. But she doesn't believe I've still got it in me, I know that. I'll prove it to her. If only she would leave me alone and not keep looking over my shoulder. I can't stand anyone to see my work until it's completely finished and polished; she knows that. She wants to peek just to see if I'm writing gibberish. That's what she suspects, because she thinks I'm senile.

"God damn the day that I decided to be a writer! It set me on the course of all my lifelong frustration. Frustration, continued into what should be my *golden years*. It's not gold I've got, but lead. Lead and shit.

"She loves me, I know that, although I think her love is mostly pity now. She figures that if I work away on my book I won't sit and brood about my ills. She doesn't know that my work is a worse wear-and-tear on me than any aches and pains of my body.

"Still, I've probably got her in suspense. They're all in suspense, really. Suspense to see whether I can still write anything worthwhile, much less turn out my life's masterpiece. That's a bit thrilling, isn't it, the suspense of all those who know me? Even if I don't finish the book, I'll enjoy stringing them along in the suspense of it. And if I die before it's done, well, let them imagine what it could have been if I had lived to finish it.

"It's a compulsion, I know it is. Write a book, then right away write away at another one, then another one, and another, another, another. Mustn't let any idle time creep in. If you do, you're washed up.

"Inspiration's the whore that you can never let get out of your bed, even if she tells you that she'll be gone just a few minutes to make wee-wee.

"Oh, God, I'm sick of it all! Sick of my life, sick of my writing, and sick of myself. But I'm going to finish this book if it kills me...Where did I leave off yesterday?..."

154

The "Wayside" has become a byway. Now back on track in *Matters of Death:*—

"Death-Watch"

Arnold Bennett, a British all-around literary man, wanted to have something of real life in his novels. He was a relentless observer, watching, watching, watching, so that his art would truly imitate Nature. Fancy and imagination should be grounded in reality, if fiction is to be at all believable.

Romantic novels commonly have a death in them, but what did Arnold Bennett know about death? He wanted an agonizing death for one of his characters. How could he describe it in a way that would be realistic and convincing?

As literary luck would have it, Bennett's own father was, at the most opportune time, *in extremis*. And so, as Bennett tells us, "All the time my father was dying, I was at the bedside making copious notes."

What diligent research and devotion to craft! Ogling Arnold, finding out the reality of death, so that he could mimic it in his little tale. And didn't his father render a fine final service to his son's career advancement.

"What's it like, pop?"

"Just like this, sonny boy. Watch me carefully, and I'll carry it through to the end for you. That's a good, hardworking boy!"

So I imagine the scene; but perhaps Bennett's father was not such a willing collaborator at that. He may have had other things on the mind attached to his distressed body. Anyway, I hope Bennett included his father's name on the acknowledgements page, if he did not inscribe the dedication of the book to him.

I've never read the novel that contains the results of Bennett's real-life, I mean real-death, research. For those of us who don't read Romantic novels, movies and television shows provide deaths aplenty. The deaths may be abrupt or protracted, histrionic or a simple falling-asleep. We don't take any of it seriously, because we know we'll see the same actor or actress alive again in some other movie or TV program, perhaps to die again. Our show business would make us believe in reincarnation.

Some portrayed deaths feature a display of grief by the bystanders. What about your dad's death, Arnold? But then, you couldn't be taking all those notes on your father's expiration and other notes on your own grief at the same time. Grief would have been distracting, not to mention all those tears dripping and smearing the notes. The literary artist has to concentrate on one thing at a time.

Still, Arnold, your research was mere observation, after all. You were on the outside looking in, as it were. In literature there is too much second-hand reportage. Because you saw something, Arnold, doesn't mean that you understood it. Just ask those who witnessed the Crucifixion.

No, if Arnold Bennett wanted to give us a real, realistic death, he should have given us his own. Well, I know it's probably hard to die and at the same time write about undergoing the experience, but maybe Arnold could have hired a secretary to transcribe whatever realization about death Arnold could have communicated in his last gasps.

Writers, report your own deaths. Then we devotees of realism in literature can really learn something. Then we'll be convinced.

It is only at his own death that the fiction writer may, at long last, tell the reality from the fantasies.

155

"Staring into the Face of It"

At twenty-six years old, Ralph Waldo Emerson married Ellen Tucker, still in her teens. The young couple's experience of marital passion, love, and joy lasted only sixteen months, for Ellen died of tuberculosis, a common fatal affliction of the time. The widower sank into bereavement.

Emerson recorded that Ellen had told him that she could do him "more good by going than by staying". How could that be true? How could it be of more benefit to a husband for a young wife to die, rather than to continue in love?

Ellen probably meant that her lingering incapacitation would become too much of a burden on her husband. Did she lack faith in her husband's commitment to her? Love must endure common burdens willingly. Or did Ellen feel herself inadequate as a wife, due to her helpless state? A man would be better off with a healthy, helping wife than an ever-incapacitated one. Yet, Emerson himself and other members of his family were afflicted with tuberculosis, some succumbing to it. Or did Ellen think that she was failing to make him happy?

Whatever the thinking behind her statement, that you-would-be-better-off-without-me must have sounded like a cruel rejection to her husband.

Emerson had loved his wife. The ordeal of grief at her loss severely tested his faith.

A year later, he reported doing something strange: "I visited Ellen's tomb and opened the coffin."

We shudder at such an act. First of all, did he really do it? Did he force open the coffin to stare upon the disintegration of the face of the beloved? We want to think that his meaning was only figurative, that he was posing a what-if. Love finds it hard to accept loss, seeks reunion with the beloved, wants to be with, and gaze upon, the beloved. But to open the coffin and look...into the face of love?...or into the face of death?

If Emerson really did open the coffin and look upon Ellen, what could his reaction have been? From an aesthetic standpoint, revulsion. Emotionally, horror and dismay. Even from the religious or spiritual perspective, demoralization.

There were no known witnesses to the opening of the casket, nor did Emerson himself say any more about it.

We ask some further questions: Did Emerson shed new tears and suffer renewed grief at the sight of the disintegration? Did he later regret what he had done, if, indeed, he really did do it? Did he venture to reach out and touch the corpse of his dead wife?

Whatever the particulars, it is apparent that Emerson had not disengaged himself from Ellen after a year of separation by death. Could the opening of the coffin help him achieve acceptance at last, resignation, understanding of reality, or some spiritual lesson? What good could come from such a ghoulish act?

Ralph Waldo Emerson was a light of idealism, optimism, and affirmation of human worth and potential, a steadfast believer in the ultimate good of it all, one who further believed that the divine was in the human and that the human could approach the divine. In all, as wholesome and aspiring man of faith as our country ever produced.

How could he have been like that, continued to be that, after staring into the face of death's corruption of human love? He was a seer, but he should have shunned such a sight. There can be no reunion of souls by an act of exhuming the body.

Three-and-a-half years after opening the coffin of his first wife, Emerson married his second wife. When they had a daughter, they named her Ellen Tucker (after the Ellen of the sixteen months of marriage, we would hope, not after Ellen the moldering corpse).

Of the children of that second marriage, the first and most beloved was the boy Waldo. But he died at five years old, causing Emerson a parental grief.

Fifteen years later, while relocating the coffins of his mother and his son Waldo to a new plot in Concord's Sleepy Hollow Cemetery, Emerson remarked on the good state of preservation of his son's coffin and reported that, "I ventured to look into the coffin."

On that occasion, like the first, Emerson did not explain anything about his reason for doing so or record his reactions to what he saw.

Hadn't he had a full dose of raw reality with Ellen, without feeling a need to do it again with Waldo? How many times can we stare into the face of death without having our living contaminated by the experience?

Two peculiar macabre incidents in the life of a noble man. I doubt they contributed anything to his love-of-life or spiritual health. Perhaps morbid Puritanism was a spiritual tuberculosis with him. The Christian ever verges upon a fixation on "ashes to ashes and dust to dust".

Death is not really known or dealt with by staring it down. Looking upon the corpse is only seeing the aftermath. Nor can lost love ever be regained, even by the most loving and longing of glances.

156

"The Writer as Spouse"

Emerson's first wife had told him that she could do him "more good by going than by staying". Lidian, his second wife, who gave him four children and lasted through a long marital lifetime, said to Emerson, "Dear husband, I wish I had never been born. I do not see how God can compensate me for the sorrow of existence."

We would expect a nun or pious virgin to look to *God* for compensation and consolation, but Lidian was a married woman; why didn't she look to her husband, her life helpmate, to help her deal with her sorrows? Yes, she had lost a dear child—one of the most acute of human sorrows—, but she still had three other children, a husband, and their home and life together. Why did Lidian have to resort to the distant deity, bypassing the husband close at hand?

Emerson seemed twice-blasted in his attempts to please his wives, the one wishing to be dead-and-gone, the other wishing she had never been born. Hardly testimonials to his qualities as a husband.

We might expect a writer to be the perfect lover and spouse. Take a poet or writer of romances, for example. Of all the types, who better than such a person, one who has explored the depths of human feeling, has cultivated sympathy and empathy, knows the exquisiteness of emotionality, has, in fact, become the master of love and so the best of all possible lovers?

Do you think that poets are never hated, that romance writers never get a divorce?

Those writers who take feelings for their competence are actually masters of only their own feelings. In order to simulate emotionality in their poems or in their created characters, they infuse their own feelings with imagination and hyperbole, a whipping-up of themselves. They recognize, of course, that they do not themselves feel the entire range of human emotionality, so they become acute observers of the emotions of others. They do so only to gather further materials to enrich the emotional content of their writings. Their vocation is a feigning of feeling, a fictive emotionality. One who wishes to love them, who expresses emotion toward them, becomes mere source material. A writer will analyze and fictionalize your love, but he won't love you back. That's not a formula for giving emotional satisfaction.

Writers are actually detached from feeling, because detachment is a necessary discipline of art. They keep all feeling, including love, at a remove. They want mastery over love, not immersion in it. And so, writers are no damn good as lovers, or, consequently, as spouses either.

Emerson esteemed his wife Lidian, but he was mostly impervious to her emotional, and even physical, needs. In their marriage Lidian suffered a chronic invalidism, not only during her pregnancies, as may have been the fashion of the time, but in-between times. She was subject to "dyspepsia and debility", headaches, anemia, and various other ailments whether real or hypochondriacal. She was housebound and bedridden. Emerson, off on his lecture tours, was necessarily absent for much of it, but I don't think that he was really present for Lidian, emotionally present, even when he was at home. She had to resort to God for emotional support.

"Give all to love" was the first line of one of Emerson's poems. Emerson should have taken his own poetic advice, given more to love of Lidian.

Emerson was not only a poet, whose expertise was supposedly in fine feeling, but a philosopher too, the "Sage of Concord", a reputed paragon of wisdom. Shouldn't he, then, have understood Lidian better, shown more practical human wisdom in his relationship to her?

That is another illusion regarding the competence of the writer as a spouse. Just as the Romantic is self-indulgent regarding his own emotionality, to the exclusion of a giving emotional relatedness, so the intellectual is wrapped in his own ideas, to the obtuse exclusion of the minds of others. He understands...himself. But he is no more competent at understanding others than would be anyone in any other vocation who has had some experience of people. And the writer is too self-rapt to make the effort.

Emerson felt esteem of Lidian. Yes, esteem and respect are components of love, but they are not love-itself. Emerson, the poet who wrote "Give all to love" and the philosopher who wrote an essay entitled "Love", lived in a lifelong ignorance of some essentials of love-itself.

He used to have extended conversations on love, sex, and marriage, not with his wife, but with Margaret Fuller, an intellectual mate of his. There was that detachment that so incapacitates a writer for loving relatedness. All Emerson did was arouse Margaret Fuller's virginal love-longing, a further futility.

Writers are the worst lovers and spouses. Their emotionality is artistic, their human understanding only a self-understanding, their detachment deadly. The most grim fate for a young woman is to get married to a poet and philosopher. Living with such a superior individual, she'll get to know what lonely really is. Let her take the case of Lidian Emerson as cautionary, as deterrent.

Nor will a writer's wife find recompense for her privation in the reading of her husband's books, seeking to discover in them what she herself is missing out on. Imaginary romance is no substitute for real love. What a woman really needs is a simple straight-forward spontaneous love from a simple straight-forward spontaneous lover, a type opposite to that of the writer.

A writer himself is satisfied if his spouse is his fan. A writer's spouse is never satisfied, cannot be satisfied, because, as she discovers, a writer is the most unsatisfying of lovers. A writer is in love, yes, but with himself, his mind, and his books. The spouse is just a bystander to that love affair.

157

"Soap Bubble Death"

In a discursive musing in *The English & Italian Notebooks,* Nathaniel Hawthorne conjured up a fantasy of ideal death: If only we could vanish like a soap bubble. Pop! Gone!

As it is, we leave our loved ones with the distasteful and demoralizing chore of disposing of the remains of our corrupt carcass. Their last, most vivid memory of us is our corpse.

What humane consideration and compassion Hawthorne showed in his imagery of the soap bubble death. Yes, if only we could spare the survivors the trouble, the very troubling consequences, of our death. Hawthorne wanted to wish away death-as-it-is, not for his own sake, but for the sake of the survivors.

Yet, if our entrance into life is messy, so must be our exit. God had no aesthetic sense in his creation of the processes of birth and death; nor did He show any consideration for pain or sensitive feeling. We are thrust rudely in and wrenched rudely out, both raw realities offensive to refined human sensitivity. As they are, birth and death are affronts to our dignity. Rethinking them, we could come up with more wholesome alternatives, like Hawthorne's soap bubble.

Humane thoughts are neither rescue nor redemption. I think of Hawthorne himself, of his own deterioration of mind and body. He aged rapidly and became unhinged, toward the end composing compulsive gibberish. Those who loved him had to suffer in the witnessing of the wreckage of his mind, as well as that of his body. Hawthorne's mind became a corpse before his body did.

Ah, Hawthorne, humane in your imagination, wishing that death was a mere bursting soap bubble.

The death of our mind too should happen like your fantasized death of the body. Mind-death, pop! Body-death, pop! Just two soap bubbles. Pop, pop! Gone.

158

"A Writer's Wake"

Hawthorne's neighbors and friends must have read either his books or his mind, for William Ellery Channing reported about Hawthorne that, "One of the things he most dreaded was to be looked at after he was dead."

As if there could be such a thing as post-mortem embarrassment. Yet, our self-image may be daunted by the imagining of what we must inevitably become,—my living body, sooner or later, to be a repulsive corpse. Let those around me now delight in looking at my body while it is animate, but must the very last (and most lasting) impression we leave upon others be a demoralizing one?

Hawthorne himself was a handsome man. (When a young woman encountered him on a path, she exclaimed in awe, "Are you a man or an angel?") But Hawthorne was shy, averting his beautiful eyes when they were stared into by a young woman who was enchanted by him. He didn't want to be looked at, even while he was alive. As he lay in the coffin, his eyes shut and sunken, how could he avert from the gaze of others? A living, handsome, shy man, when dead a horrid wreck, but still shy, or imagining himself that way.

Hawthorne didn't like to be looked at, whether at his best or at his worst. And yet, he was a writer who wanted his words to be looked at. What is a writer but an exhibitionist, of mind if not of body? The truly shy never speak up and so would never write. Hawthorne may have been reclusive with his body. Not so with his mind.

"One of the things he most dreaded was to be looked at after he was dead." Now, every writer writes with the intention of communicating as living mind to other living minds. The book outlasts its author, however. The book is a kind of coffin into which the writer has committed the corpse of his mind, the words, paragraphs, and chapters like cells, organs, and limbs comprising the body itself.

When a man writes a book and offers it out for widespread distribution, what is he doing but soliciting attention to the corpse of his mind? What he should really dread is not that bystanders at his wake will find his physical remains repulsive—(how few, comparatively, there will be who will actually attend the wake)—, but that they will find his mental remains repulsive.

As with number of bystanders affected, so with the extent of the time of the demoralization. After all, a corpse is put out of sight in a day or two, but a book lies in state eternally. A library is a mausoleum of minds on exhibit; every writer clamors for admission to that mausoleum.

Ellery Channing wrote further that Hawthorne was "swallowed up in the wretchedness of life", which accounted for the fact that "as a writer, he loved the morbid...his plots and thoughts are often dreary, as he himself was in some lights."

Whether life is found wretched or not depends upon one's temperament and attitude, but there is no such subjectivity in regard to the undeniable wretchedness of death. All thoughts of death are necessarily morbid, Christian hopes notwithstanding. Imagine what the corpses arising at *the resurrection of the dead* see. One another! Hawthorne will shy away from that particular seeing and being-seen.

I myself have a little dread at being looked at after I'm dead—not my body (for I have ordered it to be turned into sterile ashes)—, but my mind. And so I have gone over all the literary work of my life and scrutinized it with regard to likely postmortem impressions. I have torn a few books of mine to shreds, in order that they not demoralize my survivors, not to mention embarrass my posthumous self. My self-censoring has been a self-administered embalming, freshening up the literary corpse as much as possible to look presentable. If the dead must speak, let them speak some nice words. *De mortuis nil nisi bonum* in my case should be translated as "<u>From</u> the dead nothing but a good word".

If I had a truly refined aesthetic sensitivity, I would destroy everything I have written, my books like my body mere soap bubbles. I cannot bring myself to do so, because, like every writer, I want to be "looked at". Being read is the proof of my living. Destroying all my books would be like obliterating my life, so close have been the products of my mind and the process of my living. Such life-in-the-work is a complex that all writers share.

Hawthorne wrote to make a living—(at times he had to scrape along)—; his writing was what made his living-itself. Did he have any anxiety or embarrassment regarding posterity's viewing of his books, *morbid* and *dreary* as Channing described them? That would have been a more appropriate apprehension than his dread of a distasteful defunct corporal shell.

As it was to turn out, Hawthorne made a good show at his wake. Emerson, one of the attendees, confirmed that "The corpse was unwillingly shown...only a few moments to this company of his friends," but, against Hawthorne's dread, the appearance was "noble and serene in its aspect...a calm and powerful head".

"No, no, don't look at me!", the writer pleads. That is a little hypocrisy. Being looked at is what the writer wants most. A writer's deeply longed-for immortality is one of perpetual self-exhibition.

159

"Fated Exits"

One symptom of Hawthorne's mental deterioration was his compulsive, repetitive scribbling of the number 64. When Hawthorne died—in 1864—some found premonition in his Pythagorean fascination with numbers. Hawthorne knew when his number would be up.

Mark Twain was born in 1835, the year of Halley's Comet. In a vain conceit that his life had galactic importance, that he himself was a comet come unto literature, Twain expressed the conviction that he would die with the return of the Comet, jumping back on it, as it were, and blasting off into the infinite and eternal. As fate would have it, Mark Twain died in 1910, the very year of the return of Halley's Comet. His life did have cosmic significance, after all.

As for myself, I came in with the dropping of the atomic bomb. Accordingly, I expect that my death and exit will be accompanied by nothing less than Universal Doomsday. My life must have a significance nothing less than apocalyptic.

160

"Posthumous Works"

Most writers' careers trail off, like a sentence they just can't manage to finish, their creativity and powers become attenuated by senility. Not so Ernest Hemingway, who punctuated his career on July 2, 1961, with the exclamation point of a shotgun blast.

Heroes must come to a tragic end. Hemingway, a self-styled hero, wrote the climax of his autobiographical epic as an abrupt (but inevitable) finish. His obsession with potency, juvenile thrill-seeking, fascination with life-on-the-brink-of-death, creative compulsion, wringing-out of all experience, physical and psychological wear-and-tear, and the depressions induced by alcohol and chronic pain combined to do him in, or, rather, made himself do himself in. If the electro-shocks at Mayo proved no cure, the shotgun blast at Ketchum did.

There is no real necessity for a writer with failed powers to kill himself over the fact of his decline. The achievement of a body of successful work entitles him to emeritus status; he may rest upon his laurels, as comfortable a bed as an old man can find. I think Hemingway's self-inflicted end was due more to psychological, than to vocational necessity. The hard drinking was worse for his love-of-life than the hard writing was.

A violent death is often the making of the legend of the hero, but Hemingway's, being self-inflicted—(and, at the time, explained away as an accident, a clumsy blunder)—, was tainted with negative self-judgment. Blowing the gray matter of your brains onto the walls and ceiling of your living room may be an artistic statement, but it's a messy image, one that befouls the reputation of one who would be a martyr-hero of literature.

No matter the reason or provocation or extenuating circumstances, Hemingway did it, after all, to himself. Suicide is a libel against self-worth. But, as I said, I think Hemingway killed himself because he felt done for as a man, not as a writer.

In fact, Hemingway was by no means done for as a writer. In the years following his death, there was a continuing output of posthumous works, *A Moveable Feast* and *Islands in the Stream* and short stories too. If Hemingway had not yet achieved literary immortality, he had, anyway, found some means to literary life-after-death. Dead as he was, he just kept cranking out more and more stuff. Composition after decomposition.

The critics were not very kind to Hemingway's posthumous works. They evidenced his decline, the critics said; the man just couldn't write as he did in his living prime.

To me, such criticism seems most unfair. Of course a dead man has reduced powers; what did the critics expect? I myself was in awe that a dead writer could write anything at all, and not just a single farewell either, but book after book and story after story year after year into the decade following his death. The critics should be appreciative of the effort, indulgent, making allowance for any decline in quality. A dead Hemingway could still write better than most of his still-living contemporaries.

I can't say that I dug deep into Hemingway's posthumous production. Not a particular admirer of the living writer, I avoided the hypocrisy of becoming a fan of the dead one. Even so, (and beyond the further hypocrisy of *de mortuis nil nisi bonum*), Hemingway's posthumous perseverance in vocation earned my unreserved admiration. To be able to go on writing even after one was dead! Had anyone ever been able to do it before? I know that I myself will be done when I am done for; my last breath will be my last word.

Some hold that suicide is cowardly. Yet, for Hemingway, it was an act of raw courage. Finished as a writer? No, he'd show them. If he had dried up as a living writer, why, then, he would kill himself and go at it again as a dead man. There never has been such courage, or such dedication to vocation, either.

I wouldn't have the nerve to kill myself to start out on a posthumous literary career. First of all, I write from my experiences, and it seems to me that, after death, experiences are few and far between, if any. So I don't think that what I'd be able to write after death would have much life in it or be worth reading. It would be nothing about nothing. Then, too, how could I reach my agent to participate in negotiating the publisher's contracts? Nor could I spend my earnings. No, my dying wouldn't do much to enhance my career. I have no inclination to follow Hemingway's course and precedent.

Today, sixty years after Hemingway's death, I don't hear of any new works of his. Maybe he has written himself out at last. And he may have become demoralized over that annual memorial they hold for him in Key West, the so-called tribute being nothing but sloppy drunkenness and caricatures of Hemingway's physical appearance. The ridicule of his own fans may have silenced Hemingway at last.

Really, it is better for a writer not to go on writing after he dies. His stuff, necessarily feebler than what he wrote while alive, must inevitably detract from his lifetime reputation. Better to be dead-and-gone, getting in the last word *before* one dies.

My advice to writers, taking the Hemingway case as cautionary, is: Try to get it all done before you're done in. If you fail with a posthumous work, as you must, you'll never live it down. Just die and be done with it. Your works should outlive you.

161

"Death of a Poet"

> Hart Crane jumped in the middle of the ocean;
> Hart Crane jumped in the middle of the sea:—
> The end of the life of Hart Crane,
> The end of the writing of his poetry.
>
> Why did you jump to your death in the ocean?
> Why did you jump to your death in the sea?
> Could any of your verse be any worse
> Than the splash of your suicidal sea chanty?
>
> There's no critic in the middle of the ocean;
> There's no critic in the middle of the sea.
> What was it broke your heart, Crane?
> Your life or your work or your homosexuality?
>
> You could've made a poem in the middle of the
>   ocean;
> You could've made a poem in the middle of the sea.
> But you dropped your pen and you dropped yourself
> Down into the deeps, down into your death, down
>   into obscurity.

Hart Crane jumped in the middle of the ocean;
Hart Crane jumped in the middle of the sea:—
The end of the life of Hart Crane,
The end of the writing of his poetry.

162

"Bruni's Book"

When the great Florentine humanist Leonardo Bruni died in 1444, he was given a fine funeral by his city and interred in the church of Santa Croce, where, later, a monumental tomb was built around his body, upon the bosom of which had been placed Bruni's masterwork, *The History of Florence.*

Did the Florentines put Bruni's book in his casket with him in a gesture of "Take your book and get out of here!"? By no means. The gesture was a respectful memorialization of a great man by the community that Bruni himself memorialized in literature. Florence couldn't put Bruni's intangible learning and eloquent speeches in the tomb, but they could bury the book with its author.

The book-with-the-body,—what more appropriate sendoff could an author receive? Yes, let's bury an author's books with him, the corpus of creation with the corpse of the creator. If a man is what he has done, an author is his books, both in this world and out of it too.

There may be some problems encountered in book burying, of course. If a writer has spent his life on one slim volume of verse, poems and poet would fit nicely in the same casket. Bruni's book, although hefty and learned, did not crowd him too much in the casket, I presume. But for those prolific authors, who, during their lifetimes, turn out scores of books, either the size of the casket must be increased or condensed versions of their works, epitomes perhaps, will have to do for the burial. We can't have the books usurping too much space, to the discommoding, displacement, or—God forbid!—the ousting of the body itself. (Imagine Isaac Asimov going out with all his output.)

The Florentines placed Bruni's book on his breast. His history of his hometown must have been from-the-heart. Depending on the type of book an author specialized in, different placements might be made: Bertrand Russell's works on his forehead, John Ruskin's over his eyes, politicians' volumes of speeches over their mouths, James Beard's cookbooks on his belly, Henry Miller's smut over his genitals, TV scriptwriters' hackwork under their asses, Arthur Frommer's travel guides under his feet, and so on. For writers too versatile for such easy symbolism, their books might be arranged around the edge of their body, forming a fine literary circumference and halo.

Some editorial selectiveness might have to go into it. Not all books are an author's best work, worthy of carrying into eternity and showing off to God and his angels. Embarrassments should be left behind on Earth to be forgotten ephemera. A casket is not a junk box into which anything and everything may be tossed.

I have mentioned my own fantasy of being buried with a pen and blank paper, but in that I just confessed my work compulsion. The dead do no work, so I should give up the idea, as well as my intention to spend my afterlife time, as my lifetime, on endless revisions of my imperfect, defective, and fault-filled writing. I must take my own writer's counsel about dying and letting go.

As for arrangement, my books should be tossed in with me in a haphazard heap, just as I produced them. Might as well throw them all in, too, for I myself have been my only judge of quality, and I can't tell the good from the bad, or even whether any of it has been good enough to take with me.

Still, I've got to continue sticking by my work, even unto eternal fidelity. Besides, I'd like a little something familiar to read on my long journey to the other world. (If only I can resist that compulsive temptation to tinker with it some more.)

Regarding Bruni's book, the Florentines might have had some notion that it would serve as Bruni's credentials in arguing his worth before God, just as the book established his credentials on Earth. (The Florentines assumed God's literary appreciation.) Applying that notion to myself, I'm afraid that my eternal salvation is in extreme jeopardy.

Book-burning has a sinister association with censorship, but I think that it would be an appropriate ceremonial accompaniment to an author's cremation, if that is the manner of disposition he prefers. Burn-the-books and bury-the-books are clear analogies. I like the cremation idea better, because the smoke of fire ascends to heaven quickly and directly, without subterranean detour. No long waiting-around for the resurrection of the body-&-books. Other authors might disagree, exclaiming, "All my lifework up in smoke? No way!"

No artist's canvas is ever buried with him; unique, it is too valuable to be lost to the living. But books are replicable and so less valuable. Very much like their authors.

The Florentines honored Bruni by putting his book with him forever, but, if an author has been a failure all his life, it would be cruelty, spiteful and malicious, to bury the botches with their perpetrator. (That is another morbid idea that tends to make me find the prospect of death and eternity depressing.)

We hear a lot of schoolmarms' prattle about "books that live", but every author knows better. The author buries his own book himself, just as soon as he has finished with it. His book is nothing alive to him. An author's life is like his books, really. When it is finished, it is finished off, dead and done for.

Bury me with my books, yes, but don't pretend that either I or my books are still living. Books are born dead. How suitable, then, that they should join their author when he too comes to the same state.

163

"Why Authors Deserve to Live Forever"

"Everybody has got to die, but I have always believed an exception would be made in my case."

So wrote William Saroyan, vainly as it turned out, because he died shortly after making that statement, half truism and half appeal.

Some would interpret that remark as a feeble witticism from a desperate man, a selfish little narcissistic wish of a coward.

Not at all. It was not for himself that Saroyan said that. Writers are benefactors of humanity. It was on behalf of writers that Saroyan must have expressed the wish for exemption from death. I agree with him completely. If only the second half of his statement were as true as the first.

Yes, writers should be granted a special exemption and dispensation from the inevitable.

A reader arrives to argue the point:

"What? Exemption from death? Why should there be any such thing? Even if there were, why should writers be the ones to enjoy it?"

All right, dear reader, let's consider other candidates. You might suggest, for example, holy men, those who lived lives of such sanctity that death inflicted upon them seems an injustice. But death is the crowning achievement for holy men, I say. How else can they proceed to sainthood, not to mention to an enduring cult of the veneration of their memory by the living? The saintly deserve to die. It's the best thing that could happen to them.

"Wait a minute, Mr. Author. I'll choose some other candidates, if you don't mind...What about the great men of the world, the seemingly indispensable? They should be exempted from death, in order that they may continue in their work."

There is too much frenzied doing going on in the world. The doers wear themselves out, wear us out, wear the world itself out. We don't need them around forever. There is no shortage of ambition. Other doers will rise up. The movers-and-shakers should die, give the world a rest.

"Men aren't so important to life as, say, women are, I'll grant you that. Ah, women, yes, they are the truly indispensable ones! They bring life into the world, they nurture life. We need women. Women should live forever."

No, women are needed only during their child-bearing and child-rearing years. When they get old, neither Life nor their children need them. Life gets done with women, so it is only fitting that they depart the scene. Women ought to die, like everybody else.

"What about people who do so much good, like doctors and nurses?"

Are you kidding? They spend their whole lives fighting death. They are the sworn enemies of death. When death gets them at last, they are only getting their just deserts.

"Priests and nuns and ministers and rabbis,—all our spiritual guides and counselors."

Experts on death, those people! They should die, just so they can find out for themselves whether they knew what they were talking about all that time.

"All right, then, I propose teachers."

When the lesson has been learned, who still needs the teacher? Besides, teachers become pedants and fuddy-duddies, stultifying instead of stimulating intelligence. No class of people more deserves to be removed from the world than old teachers.

"I suppose you incline toward the self-importance of the so-called artist. Shouldn't artists—real artists who beautify the world, I mean—shouldn't artists—and composers too—be permitted to live forever, so that they can continue to enrich our lives?"

Artists are mere decorators. Composers are noise-makers. Nature has painted prettier scenes and made more melodious music than those pretenders ever achieve. Death to artists and musicians!

"You want writers and only writers to live forever, I know what you're leading up to. Very convenient for yourself, I'm sure. Just why should writers, of all people, be the ones privileged to live forever? Why can't we do without them?"

Because writers are the ones who provide the only really indispensable service to Life and to the living.

"And what might that be?"

We give meaning to Life. With meaning, lives become worth living. If there were no writers around to give meaning to lives, why, I think that the population would kill itself off in a day, nothing to live for, and they'd all be dead, and this whole question we're considering couldn't be brought up, because there'd be no one to bring it up. Writers deserve to live forever. Life-Itself can't do without us.

"But there are plenty of writers, always will be."

Do you think that the full meaning of Life is so simple that it can be captured by a single writer? No, it's a great cooperative vocational enterprise, what we writers do. It's the ultimate altruism. And we need all of us and more. We've got to stick to our task, work together, find the meaning of Life together, for the benefit of the human race and of Life-Itself.

"But if a writer has written his book, found the meaning of Life as far as he was capable, why shouldn't he die, just like the woman who's had and raised her baby?"

The miracle of meaning isn't attained so easily as is the miracle of Life. One book, one generation of books, does not exhaust the answers. Writers need immortality on Earth, so that they can get their job done. Killing writers off like everybody else—as if we were like everybody else—is a waste. No wonder people find Life so demoralizing. Their saviors keep getting killed off one after another. First Homer, then Shakespeare, then Saroyan. What, am *I* to be next? How can Life mean anything without *me*?

164

"Reviews"

(Letter from a publisher:)

Dear Mr. Weeks:

Thank you for your book proposal, *Matters of Death.* You deal with a subject that is of interest to everyone sooner or later. I read your proposal with great interest. You have some interesting ideas and seem to write well.

Unfortunately, the most important consideration for a book of the kind you propose is credentials. We would be looking for someone with academic or medical degrees, preferably a person who has written articles on the subject, conducted seminars, has a platform, become well known. You seem to be new to the subject you treat. Therefore, we cannot pursue your proposal further. I do not think your book on death is viable.

Thank you for thinking of *** Publishers, and we wish you success in your future endeavors.

Sincerely,

***, Acquisitions Editor

P.S. I have enclosed a copy of our current catalog. Notice that we now have an 800 number for direct orders. Of course, our titles are also available through on-line bookstores and at book dealers near you.

———

(Excerpts from some reviews that might have been written about this book):

There is a crying need for a self-help book on death, but *Matters of Death* does not meet that need. It is difficult, in a short review, to tell all that is the matter with *Matters of Death.* Death matters so much, but a light or frivolous or inept treatment of the topic is another matter altogether.

There are only three chapters in the book, so let's consider each of them:

The first chapter, "Death Interpreted", provides a historical background of beliefs about death and the afterlife and funeral rites and customs. Some of the information presented here, especially about the Cave Man era, is suspect, because undocumented. You can't understand either life or death without having read an extensive bibliography.

Even worse than the pop archaeology is the irreligious or antireligious bias the author shows in his treatment. If a person has no religious faith to sustain him at the time of death, what else does a person have?

The author's irreligiosity vitiates the book from the outset. The only hope this reviewer has is that when the author's time comes he will rediscover his lost faith. If this book were to be read by many, the author would have on his conscience a great harm caused.

The second chapter, "The Morbidity of Authors", hardly seems to belong in a book of this kind at all. The psychology of an author, as presented here, is, indeed, a very morbid one. Mr. Weeks presents his fellow authors as self-centered and unlikable, neurotics and misanthropes whose demise readers might welcome. Part of this chapter might have made an article in a publication for a narrow specialized audience—for example, an article in *Writers Digest* advising how a writer should go about dying. There is even bad verse in this chapter!

"Incidents of Death", the end chapter, attempts the poignant, but is mostly pathetic. It is nothing but a maudlin mishmash, every death related topic the author could think of just tossed into the book. Yes, there are some interesting ideas here, but interesting ideas do not make a book. In this last chapter, the author has gone literary, and the result was disastrous. He writes about expiration without inspiration.

Instead of the 100 seemingly random sections of *Matters of Death*, what we really need is a short, simple, practical manual on death, something along the lines of *A Twelve-Step Quick-and-Easy Program for Facing and Dealing with Your Death*. There is no such usefulness in this misguided effort. For those interested in a competent medical treatment of the subject, we recommend *How to Die*, by . . .

* * * * *

. . . The flower of the Flower Children has wilted at last. They are getting old, these members of the Sixties generation. Gone are the days of *sex, drugs, and rock-'n'-roll*. What obsesses them now is death,—their own, of course. And so we have *Matters of Death*, the latest narcissistic self-obsession of that moribund generation. They present death as they presented sex, that is, as if they themselves discovered it...The only compensation we can find is that their proclamations on death will be the last words we'll hear out of them. Then they and their tiresome act will recede into the oblivion they deserve...

* * * * *

...not a book for browsing on a beach towel. And don't give this book to grandma as a birthday present, either...

* * * * *

...like a travel guide written by one who has never been to the place he purports to describe...

165

"A Writer's Realization"

While writing, a writer knows what he's about and what his book is about, but he does not yet grasp the book's potentially deep significance for him. It is only many years later, in reassessment of what he has written, that the deep meaning may emerge.

The writer is competent in his material, certainly, but only as the transcriber of his arising thoughts. He lacks the perspective to see those thoughts in the broad scope of his entire life. He is master of the particular what, but ignorant of the overall why.

Literary critics attempt an exegesis of his book, as if the author were not the master of his material. (A browser knows better what he has just read quickly than did the one who worked long years to write it.) In actuality, the critic does not discover the deep meaning; the critic only remedies inadequacies in the communication; (at least the critic does so in his own mind). No one but the author can provide the true and ultimate exegesis—the meaning that transcends the contents of the book itself—, and he only much later, when he has acquired the lifelong perspective that extracts the meaning from the context.

Writing a book is an act of conscious life processing itself. Life too being a process, it is a very different life at different stages of the author's lifespan. The author changes, in the processes of his mind as in those of his body. The processes of life, mind, and writing enrich one another. Eventually, in the fullness of maturity, the author may come to understand the deep meaning of what he has written.

When I read something that I myself wrote, say, when I was still an adolescent, I am, first of all, embarrassed on behalf of myself, embarrassed over my rawness, naïveté, and mumbling and stumbling in the literary craft. I have a similar feeling as when I look upon a photograph of me in my awkward adolescent years. But what is the point of self-criticism of juvenilia? As I looked young, so I wrote young. Inexperience deserves no censure.

Just when I have asserted that an old writer will understand what he wrote as a young writer, I now recall a contradictory experience. In 1992, I came across a sentence I had written in 1972. How could I have written that sentence? It seemed like an idea I never had, there was in it a word I don't have in my active vocabulary, and the style was as succinct as I have always aspired to be but never succeeded. Strange, brilliant sentence! A sentence of mine, surrounded by other sentences of mine—(those others I did recognize, they seemed familiar)—, my own sentence alien to me. I couldn't imagine myself writing that sentence.

I could not have been quoting, because I am honest in my attributions. So, I know I wrote that sentence.

Discovering it was as uncanny as if I were to find, at the bottom of my desk drawer, a photograph of myself in intimate familiarity with a beautiful woman I have no recollection of. It must have been a very different self-of-me who wrote that sentence, a sentence that was a little extraneous random process intruding into the greater process I was living and writing at the time.

If a writer lives and writes long enough, he will eventually discover such sentences of his own strange to himself. He may even find one of his earliest books incomprehensible. (In his youth, he must have been much more complex than he has since become.)

Now, if a writer were truly the creative artist, he would drop and forget each book as soon as it is finished and proceed to other, totally different books. The protean artist, the rarest type!

No, generally the writer remembers, and so redoes, his previous work. He reiterates his personal themes, he cultivates his idiosyncratic style. A reader can recognize a later book as the same author's by the memory of having read a former book. My hair is gone now, and I have a gray beard, but I still recognize that teenager in the photo as myself,—something in the eyes, perhaps, or the expression. Once-me, still-me.

The author does a rewrite or redo not only within the same book but from book to book, all variations on the theme of who he himself is. (He suffers the illusion of constant being, oblivious as he might be to the becoming; he thinks that his processes constitute an identity.)

After having written, reread, ruminated on, and redone a dozen books of his, the author may come, at last, to some self-understanding, that is, if his work has been a cumulative unfolding of himself, rather than a haphazard collection of opportunistic projects.

I myself have drawn together the scattered threads of my life into a series of interrelated books, until I have made my life and my work coherent to myself. Having achieved that—and having exhausted most of my auto-biographical material in the process—, am I washed up as a writer? Yes, unless I reinvent myself as a different person and launch upon a new process of self-creation.

When asked to explain anything in any of my books, I have answered, "I am neither a critic of, nor a commentator upon, myself." In candor and confession, I am both, of course. My remark meant only that I did not want to pile up more words on the same old exhausted material. Better if they would ask me what I'm working on now, what I plan to write in the future. I prefer spurs to the laurel.

A writer should not consider one book of his better than the others, except in the sense that one day is better than another or arrived spring preferable to worn-out winter. Each book was his process at the time, the book-as-it-had-to-be. One book was snow, another fog, a third a warm, balmy breeze, a fourth hot summer languor, and so on. If an author does have a favorite of his own books, it is just as one might express a preference for one season over another, one type of weather over another. Yet, our life is to be lived in all seasons, in all kinds of weather.

There is no better; there is only different. If a writer were to say, "That was my best book," he would concede that when he wrote it he was at his life's best and has deteriorated since,—an admission no one likes to make. And besides, how does the writer know that his so-called best is past? He would never write another book if he believed that. He will write more books, the writing process continuing as long as the living process, even unto geriatric literariness.

I have written badly at various times in my life. I threw a lot away. (More, you might have wished.) I have been disabused of my naïve idea that I would get better and better as I went along, reaching a culmination of genius in late middle age. In truth, I am as envious of, as I am embarrassed about, some of my juvenilia. We lose as much as we acquire as we go about processing our lives through words.

My literary mentor, Erasmus, said to me, "We shall not cease to make our writings more polished and more complete until we cease to breathe. No book has had so much work put into it that it cannot be made more perfect."

Accordingly, during these recent years of my freedom from a daily collective workplace job, I have rewritten and redone some books I wrote decades ago. At first, I was motivated by perfectionism (as well as by a self-protective desire to censor out my former ineptitude). I would write the same books better. And did I do so? I made them smoother perhaps and did improve them, but only in so far as I was able to return to the frame-of-mind, the particular process I was in, when I wrote them. That required as much creative imagination as retentive memory. I made all those old books of mine more presentable; whether I improved them in substance is doubtful. I can edit my past books, but not my past lives.

Even so, the very undertaking of that extended campaign of revision forced the stages of my old lives back on me again. In rewriting, I relived. More importantly, I was impelled to find overall coherence in those old books of mine, the scattered threads. I found more satisfaction, because more significance, in the redoing than in the original composition, (although the creative excitement of discovery was lacking, of course). Ah, persevering craftsmanship!

All my books taken together and assembled like jigsaw puzzle pieces do not complete the picture of who I am—I mean, who I have been—, because I have not been the totally committed artist; my life has not been at every moment and point contiguous with my literary work. Still, there has been enough congruence between my living process and my writing process to form a coherent picture,—of the writer, not of the man.

"Know thyself!", said the oracle at Delphi, one of the many Mediterranean sites I have made pilgrimage to. I do know myself, even though I no longer believe that there is a solid self to be known. I know many of my selves, anyway. I have had some success in self-explication, whatever my reticence or silence about some aspects of my life. I didn't tell all—only a fool does that—, but I did tell some important things.

No life is ever completed until death, nor is a literary vocation, either. I write on and on, as I live on and on. I have been a series of sometimes disjointed psychological processes, but I have lived in the continuity of the physical body. The many and the one,—the paradox of our lives; also the paradox of my literary art.

I've got all my old books, just as I've got all my old photographs. Today is another day. I put a new type-writer ribbon in the machine, as a new roll of film in the camera. More processes of the autobiographical process waiting to be reported. I am the documentarian of my own life.

And at last, at long last, I realize what it is that I have been up to these past fifty years.

"Dreams of the Dead, Thoughts of the Dead"

"It upsets me to dream of dead people," she said to me.

Then she reported that the images of her dead parents had appeared the night before in her dream. And when she awoke, she was upset. Not that the events of the dream in themselves had been nightmare. No, what was upsetting was the mere appearance of her deceased parents in the dream. Why had they intruded into her sleep? Did they want to rearouse grief? Or did they want to force upon her an apprehension of her own approaching death? When an old woman dreams about her long-dead parents, she might really be dreaming about her fear of her own death.

It is through dreams that the dead may return to our lives. While awake, we can refuse to think of the dead, but, when we are asleep, the dead return to our presence. We can remove them only by waking up.

Yet, the appearance of dead loved ones in a dream need not be distressing. Sometimes, the appearance takes on a consolatory aura of fond reminiscence. Then the dead are not intruders but guests. Such a dream may be a loving family reunion.

The dead live on in memory and make their epiphany in a dream. During our waking hours, we are too busy and preoccupied with immediate mundane reality to spare much thought for the dead. And so, it is we ourselves who relegate the dead to dreams.

If we thought more of our deceased loved ones, we would dream less of them, although if, in the anguish of bereavement, we think too much and obsessively of the dead, then they might dominate our dreams too. The dead must have their due, whether in thoughts or dreams.

Those who have been significant to us are a permanent presence in our lives. Seemingly, we may have forgotten them, but they are there still, sooner or later demanding their due of attention.

Our dreaming mind does not distinguish those who are dead from those who are not dead but are gone forever from our lives, the as-if dead. If one has been significant to us, that disappeared one will reappear in our dreams, no matter whether neglected or seemingly forgotten by day. Sometimes our dreams try to do right by one we did wrong to, or else make the one who did us wrong now do compensatory right. Or one who refused to love us will now do so in a dream.

Dreams reconcile us to death and to loss, make permanent the emotional ties we may have thought broken by death or desertion. We never really separate from those we love. A dream is a tryst, not with the dead, but with a remembered living one we loved.

Through all the hundreds of generations of humankind, the living have dreamt of the dead, a continuum of the memory of relatedness. Such dreams need not be upsetting, if only we understand them aright. The appearance of the dead in a dream should not be an omen of death; it is, rather, a tenacious memory of life.

Our conscious mind necessarily thinks of the deceased beloved as dead, but the dream, free of the constraints of the full truth, ignores the event of death and gives us our beloved as living again. The dream provides a therapeutic ministration to our mind. The living of the dead once again in our dreams enriches our living by linking us to the continuum of life.

When we wake up, the conscious critical mind re-asserts itself by stating fact and truth. When we remember having dreamt of the loved one, our first critical thought is "But she is dead". The conscious mind, restricted by reality, would kill off the dead.

If we never dreamt, we would be freed of the dead once and for all, or at least it would be within the power of the conscious mind to exorcise all active memory of the dead. But that would not be good for us. Something of the living in us dies when a beloved dies; because of that, the revival of a beloved in a dream revitalizes us. If only we would accept our dreams and not criticize and analyze them.

In the Christian mythology, the dead go on to Heaven, where, I would hope, they dream of the living beloved ones they have left behind. Nor should those in Heaven find such dreams distressing, even if they look back upon their living on Earth as an ordeal they endured, like the ordeal that their own death was to those who survived them. And so, the dead dream of the living who dream of the dead in a great, unbroken continuum of loving memory.

The highest honor we can show to the dead is to dream of them, for our dream acknowledges their life-long significance to us. The memory of the death of a beloved is upsetting only to the conscious critical mind; the fond reminiscence in a dream is both balm to the living and homage to the dead.

"Ah, yes, I did love my parents very much," the old woman sighed. "They were very fine people."

167

"The One Impossible Dream"

Last night, I dreamt that I was driving on a winding mountain road. Rounding a curve on slick pavement, the car plunged over the edge. An overhanging branch that I might have grabbed through the open car window was out of reach. I was but a moment from certain death...but then I woke up.

Have I ever dreamt of my own death? Could I ever dream such a dream?

When we dream, there seem to be no limits to our imagination. What to our awake consciousness would be the most fantastic of fantasies and the greatest outrages to rationality are the common stuff of dreams. Even when they take their subject matter from the familiar, dreams run through a riot of the surreal. Anything may happen in a dream. Anything. And yet...

I may dream of dangers to myself, but none of those dangers ever really does me in.

Perhaps, in another dream, I am flying, soaring through the blue high above the Earth. But then I begin to lose altitude, descend, fall, accelerating faster and faster to the hard Earth below. I flail my arms in desperation, only to plummet down toward impact. Just as I am about to be killed, my descent slows down into a soft glide. Extending my feet, I touch the Earth without harm, as if saved by invisible parachute. I do not die.

In such dreams of danger, one way or another I am rescued.

Or take the nightmare of the child. A fearsome beast arises and draws near to devour the child. Just as the jaws would clamp upon the child, however, the dreamer awakes, crying and shaking but still very much alive. (I myself have recurrent dreams of a devouring lion out to get me, and I am no child.)

In a nightmare dream, one is saved, not within the dream itself, as in the second falling-to-Earth case, but by escape from dreaming. Awaking is always an available door of escape from impending death in a dream.

Have any ever died from the fright of a dream? Given rescue within the dream or rescue by awaking, I doubt it.

But what of those dreams in which the dreamer might see himself in a casket, the mourners all passing in front of him? Am I not dead in such a dream? No, for if I were, how could I see the mourners pass in front of me? That kind of dream is not a dream of my own death, but, rather, my playacting my death. My seeming death is a live-show of which I am the star. Yes, how they'd miss me if I were gone! But I'm not really gone. I'm still very much alive, enjoying their paying respects to me.

Death is extinction, as I should know in my dreaming as I do in my awake consciousness. But just as the author of an autobiography cannot include in his text a narrative of his own death, so in the autobiography I compose by night after night of dreaming I do not dream of my own death.

For, if the dreamer becomes extinct, how can the dreaming go on? The dreamer wants to dream and keep dreaming. There must be no end to the dreamer, lest the dreams too end. The dream-self is immortal, kept so either by turns of the plot within the dream or by waking-up escape from danger, and never mind the parodies of my death and other such mockeries of death itself.

Actually, our conscious mind proves scarcely more able to admit our mortality than does our unconscious. As we can escape from death by dream trickery, can't we also do so by artifices of thought? The daydreaming conscious mind may deny one's eventual extinction by notions of personal continuity through one's children, through the memories of survivors, or through one's deeds and accomplishments. (We authors live forever through our books.) Even the irreligious believe in such immortality.

As for the religious, they believe that just as waking up may deliver us from death in a dream, so there will be a waking-up from actual bodily death into a new life,—*the resurrection of the dead.* "No, I won't really die. Death is just sleep. I'll wake up again," they try to convince themselves. Buttressed by the authoritarianism of divine revelation though it is, such a notion is, psychologically speaking, little different from the waking-up escape out of a death-threatening dream.

The ego wants personal immortality, both within our lifetime and afterwards, on Earth as it will be in Heaven. We do not long for, or dream of, our death and extinction. We long for, and dream of, our living on, one way or another. Living on is the most precious concept of our mind, whether conscious or unconscious.

Living on and on the deepest human wish, what willfulness the suicide must have to repudiate that wish! What the suicide craves is extinction and its oblivion, the extinction that the healthy mind both awake and asleep dreads and denies. The suicide is the hero of anti-Nature, spiteful though he is.

Wouldn't it be a wonder if, at the moment of bodily death, as one drifted off, just before the mind failed along with the body, there was one last dream, and that dream *was* of one's own death? That would be a dream coming true. Has any moribund one dreamt such a dream?

There have been reports from those pronounced dead but later revived by medical craft. Those dreamers reported their near-death experience as a peek into afterlife, of continuing living on, and of joining beloved others who have died but continue living on. So, perhaps one cannot dream of one's own death even as that death is the arriving reality that refutes all dreams and fantasies.

"I dreamed I died," said the selfless one. But those words could never be said, because there are no selfless ones.

Anyway, we can dream only about what we know, and fantasize upon that. What we know is our own life. Our own death cannot even be a fantasy; it is an unknown. And therefore we cannot dream about our own death.

168

"The Counseling"

"Are you afraid?", the counselor asked.

"Just a little," the young woman admitted.

The night before, the young woman had had a nightmare. She dreamt that her body had become a monstrous tumor and that blood was flowing out of every orifice, even her eyes, blinding her. In her dream, she was lying on her bed, but the bed turned into a bathtub, and she lay naked in the tub, helpless as the blood from her punctured body filled the tub. As the blood rose to her chin and began to flow back into her mouth, she began to choke and cough and try to spit out the blood. And then she awoke, and she was coughing up phlegm. She sat on the side of her bed and coughed and cried.

"Well," the counselor said, "It's only normal to be afraid."

The counselor was a mature woman heading into middle age. She was a nurse, and so had experience in medical crises. She looked across at the young woman with compassion, but the young woman thought that there was a professionalism about her concern.

"The procedure won't take that long..."

"*Procedure!*", the young woman echoed the counselor's word in her own mind.

A procedure is just something to be done, like an office procedure or an administrative procedure. Strange that medical people don't use normal accurate words like *surgery* or *operation*. To them it was just a *procedure*. Not so to the patient.

The young woman mulled over the word *procedure*. Yes, it meant something to be done, but it required a proceeding, a *procedure*, a going-through-with-it.

"There may be some bleeding afterwards..."

"Bleeding," the young woman thought. The word forced her to remember the nightmare again, her life hemorrhaging away, her very breathing choked with her blood.

"Your temperature and blood pressure are normal," the counselor continued, looking at the chart. "Do you feel all right?"

No, she felt terrible, the young woman thought to herself. Physically she may have been all right, but not really all right, because there was need for this surgery she faced. But something was sick in her heart or mind; she felt a deep distress; the nightmare was just a sign of it. This life-and-death stuff,—isn't it terrifying? We take life for granted, until there is a prospect of its ending. The medical people are confident in their science, they virtually guaranteeing their *procedures*, and yet...

"I'm OK."

"If you're not feeling all right, we can always delay, you know. A day or two of delay wouldn't hurt."

"Delay, why delay?", the young woman responded in her own mind. She was there, and she wanted to have it done now. Having it done would be the cure for anxiety and the end of her nightmares.

"Let's do it and get it over with," the young woman said.

The counselor recoiled a bit at the hardness of the tone of the young woman's voice. The counselor then questioned herself. In suggesting delay, when she should have been counseling acceptance of the immediate, was she making the young woman's anxiety worse? She had counseled many, but you never knew what they really thought about it, what they really felt, how they would really react to the crisis. She wanted the patient to go through with it, but sometimes she herself had anxieties and doubts. No matter how hard she tried to objectify it, life-and-death stuff was frightening to the counselor too.

"All right," the counselor said.

She had an impulse to put her hand on the young woman's shoulder or take her hand in her own, but she refrained.

"You're doing the right thing," she told the young woman. "You'll see later. Everything will turn out all right."

The young woman rose.

"Right through here," the counselor said, as she directed the young woman through the door.

The young woman went in.

And the abortion was performed.

169

"Unwanted Children"

The ancient Greeks and Romans resorted to exposure of unwanted children, that is, they would abandon the forlorn infant in some remote place to die from thirst and hunger and cold.

There may have been various reasons for the practice. A newborn may have come into the world defective, malformed, or so sickly that its future was despaired of. Or the rearing of yet another child would have imposed a crushing economic hardship. Or the child may have had its legitimacy suspect or been produced by incest or had some other shame attached to it.

And so, the child was taken from its mother, put out of home and community, and left to die.

We have no way of knowing how common the practice was. Any ancient remains of exposure have long since weathered away.

Exposure of infants is a cruelty, yes, but less than if a father or mother committed a direct violence,—smothered, strangled, or beat to death the unwanted baby.

A husbandman who notices one of the animal litter to be weak and unlikely to survive will remove that one, freeing the mother to devote her attentions to the healthy and lightening the competitiveness of the siblings in carrying on their life struggles. The farmer or pastoralist culls his flock or herd; he used to do so in his own family. Exposure of an infant must have seemed to him not so much a murder as necessary household management; exposure as a method was a nonviolent way of letting Nature take her course.

We indict the ancient practice of infant exposure as a specimen of pagan cruelty. Yet, the problem of unwanted children and the repellant recourses taken by those burdened with them are not a peculiarity of any particular culture or time.

In Christian Rome, fishermen netting the Tiber for fish would sometimes find the corpse of a drowned newborn in their net. They made an appeal to Pope

Innocent III. The vivid imagery of what he had been told caused the pope nightmares. He devised a solution, or, at least, an alternative for unwilling mothers. In an external wall of the church of Santo Spirito in Sassia, along the Tiber, a boxlike opening was made, with a door, and, behind that, a revolving platform the size of an infant. Those who were so desperate as to abandon their newborn—(and, in a Christian society, many girls were made so by the stigma and shame of illegitimacy)—could come in darkness and anonymity, place the infant in the box-in-the-wall and entrust it to the care of the unseen nuns within. There was a bell that the young woman could ring to call the nuns before she hurried off. By that device, an orphan was created out of what would otherwise have been a corpse.

As for the ancients, pagan parental feelings must have been as tender as Christian ones—(in intimate family matters human nature predominates over culture)—, so it must have been a wrenching decision to expose a child, except where the hopelessness of its physical condition might justify it.

The ache of parental longing is suggested by the myth of the foundling, which expresses the wish that the abandoned child will live and thrive despite its exposure. The founder of Rome, Romulus himself, was just such an abandoned child who survived. There were even tales of an abandoned child left with some ring or identifiable keepsake of the mother, which, kept through life, eventuated in a reunion with the mother many years later, with full acceptance of the child and forgiveness of the parent. We don't really want to abandon our children; if we do so, we regret it and wish otherwise.

It has been suggested that the ancients used to abandon their children at a designated spot, so that a childless couple might come there and rescue the abandoned one. Those who could not parent would pass off their child to those who could. But I think the quick rescue of exposed infants unlikely. It was, rather, a vain wish and self-deceptive fanciful scenario. Exposed children, like exposed kittens, surely must die.

Exposure of infants seems like a thing of the historical past, but from time to time we read or hear of a newborn found wrapped and sometimes dead in a trash container, or of a nurse on her way to the night shift who stumbles over a baby-in-a-basket on the threshold of the hospital. Exposure of infants, whether to their death or to rescue, still goes on. Again, cultures are different, but human predicament is the same.

The best solution to the problem of unwanted children is contraception. The ancients tried various folk medicines or concoctions for preventing pregnancy. Modern pharmacists puzzle over the little information we have about ancient efforts at contraception and wonder if any of them worked, and, if so, how. It is doubtful that honey was an effective spermicide. Today we have several effective contraceptive methods, so it would seem that the elimination of the problem of unwanted children is within our power, if young people take consideration of life.

But the sexual drive is heedless, so a late recourse, the last resort, is abortion. The ancients tried that too, using certain abortifacient plants, which may have worked to kill the fetus by poisoning the pregnant woman. In our own world, we have a methodology of abortion that is efficient, effective, and reasonably safe for the woman. How many abortions may have been attempted in ancient times we have no idea, of course; but we have enumerations of our own abortions. According to United States government statistics at this time of my writing, seventy million abortions have been performed in our country over the past forty years.

For the rescue of unwanted children of our time, we have the legal process of adoption, a formal transfer of parental responsibility from those unwilling or unable to those who are both willing and able. Some of us hold abortion in the same abhorrence we hold exposure, so we urge pregnant women not to abort but instead to put their child up for adoption. There should not be corpse, or orphan either, but adoptee. The helpless abandoned must be reclaimed for life.

Children are generally wanted, accepted, and nurtured. But there has been, is, and will always be human situations where the birth of a child is dreaded, wished away, and sometimes dealt with by methods that must be considered appalling, sinful, or criminal.

Subjected to exposure or killed in the womb, smothered at birth or abandoned, lucky if rescued by a childless peasant couple or by the legal process of adoption, the unwanted child has a tenuous grasp on life. Some will live, but many, certainly, will die, not as unfeeling Nature would determine, but as the minds of human beings decide and choose.

170

"A Scene in a Hospital"

She awakes all groggy, and in the first moment of consciousness she impulsively reaches to her belly. The bulge is gone; she has been delivered.

She did not undergo the full ordeal of labor; she slept through it, a sleep induced by the chemical anesthetic. She doesn't feel well, but she knows that she will feel better later. She is sore below.

She wants to shake off the grogginess now, wants her senses to return, wants to see and cuddle the baby.

The hospital room is quiet. She is alone there. It is an overcast day, which makes the room dim. No one has turned on a light for her. They wanted her to sleep off the anesthetic and wake up on her own.

For a moment she almost nods off. She rouses herself, tries to clear her head, and directs her attention to her soreness, because pain intensifies wakefulness. She feels the ache of her emptiness, as if her insides have been scoured out.

A wave of depression comes over her, but she has been told that that should be expected. Pregnancy is taxing, the labor of child delivery stressful, even when under an anesthetic. Weariness and ache will pass; they need not lead to postpartum depression. If depression there was, there was medication for it.

She reaches for the call-bell and pulls it to her by the cord. She puts her thumb over the bell, but then hesitates. She is in suspense, yes, but her physical state causes an inertia.

She wants the grogginess past before she sees the baby. She doesn't care about the ache of her body, but she wants her mind and senses clear. She doesn't want to feel depressed at the moment she first touches her baby, that moment that should be magic in a woman's life. She wants the first touch to be perfect.

After a few deep breaths, she raises herself up to a sitting position. The natural light in the room seems a bit brighter now, the cloud cover dispersing, some sunlight penetrating the closed blinds. She contracts her thumb and presses firmly on the button of the call-bell.

She is impatient for the nurse to respond.

In a minute or two, but at an interval that seems longer, a nurse comes padding towards the room. The nurse hesitates outside the doorway. The young woman can see the tips of the nurse's white shoes and a white patch of her uniform.

There was a second padding of feet; another person apparently joins the nurse outside the doorway.

The young woman waits in anxious expectancy.

The nurse walks in with the obstetrician, the two of them advancing gravely. The nurse draws near to one side of the bed, the doctor to the other. Their approach so close has a suffocating effect upon the young woman.

There are a few seconds of silence, during which a dread arises in the mind of the young woman. Something is wrong; she can tell by the manner of the nurse and the doctor.

At last the doctor speaks:

"Mrs. Alderson, I'm sorry to tell you…Your baby was stillborn…The delivery seemed to be going all right, the baby had a heartbeat before when we checked, but during the delivery the heartbeat stopped. We did what we could. We attempted to revive the baby, but we could not…I'm so sorry."

The young woman hears the words as if in a dream. The nurse and the doctor are unreal, and she herself is detached from herself. She just stares ahead, her eyes glazing over.

At that moment her husband rushes into the room, passes the nurse and draws near.

"*I* should have been the one to tell you," he says. "But I just couldn't."

The husband takes his wife's face in his hands and kisses her. He then begins to sob slightly. The young woman remains impassive.

"Is there anything I can do for you?", the nurse asks.

The young woman does not respond.

The husband sits down in the chair close by the bed.

"You should recover well," the doctor tells the young woman after a few moments of standing around. "We know you will have a difficult time ahead. We will have someone help you through it...What is important for you now is to rest and recover your strength and get well. Be patient with yourself. Time will heal you...It will take time. I'm so sorry."

After some awkwardness, the doctor takes the young woman's hand and feels her pulse. Then he withdraws, the nurse behind him, leaving the husband with his wife. By now the husband has regained his composure.

The wife cannot commiserate with her husband. She feels numb and weak and wretched.

She begins to think about the nine months of her pregnancy, about telling her husband the news, taking care of herself, following the diet, concerned with nutrition for two, enduring the morning malaise, monitoring the increasing bulge of new life, the discomfort but the expectancy, the hope, the...And it has all come to nothing.

She tries to dismiss such thoughts from her mind. Still, she suffers a sense of failure, and, in her heart, an emptiness. Empty even of love for her husband. She has been emptied out.

Something of her own living has died with the death of the baby.

Could she see the baby?, she wonders...See it, why see it? What would it look like, a pitiful dead thing? If physically perfect but dead, she wouldn't be able to look at it. If deformed and dead, she might be grateful that it was dead, but then she would accuse herself of a botch. No, dead babies are not brought to their mothers to cuddle; they are better disposed of unseen. As if the baby never existed. She would have to begin to forget immediately, forget for the sake of her own life and health and sanity.

"I'm very tired," she says to her husband. "I think I need to sleep now."

She lets herself slide down back into the bed.

The husband stands up. "You'll be all right," he says. "At least *you'll* be all right. I love you."

"Need to sleep now," she says weakly.

Her husband goes over to the window to shut the blinds tighter, for the sun has now come out strong and has been shining through the blinds upon his wife on the bed. The horizontal slats of sunlight make the skin of her face look sallow and sickly.

"Yes, sleep," he says.

He kisses her on the forehead and strokes her cheek lightly. "I'll stay by you, just outside."

He tiptoes out and closes the door behind him.

The young woman lies on her side, places her hand over her face, and falls back into the groggy stupor.

171

"An Accident"

I don't remember how I heard about it, whether it was through a personal contact with someone who knew the family, or whether it was in the newspaper, or whether one of those little domestic tragedies, the *human interest* the television news shows so exploit, following up their tale of grief with chit-chat about the outrageous tie the weatherman is wearing.

However I heard about it—and it was a long time ago—, I cannot forget it. It is almost as if I were a witness, someone who saw what was happening from across the street, someone who might have intervened to prevent the accident.

What happened was this: A man hurried out of his house and to his car. He was late for an appointment, would have to make quick time. As he got into the car, he did not see, he did not detect, his three-year-old daughter on her tricycle just behind the car. The child may have stopped there when she heard her father open the car door. The man put the key into the ignition, started the car, put it in gear, and backed down the driveway. As the car backed into the street, the man heard a scraping and grinding from beneath the car. He braked, put the car in Park, got out and looked. He saw the tangled wreckage of the little tricycle and the mangled body of his daughter. He had run over his own child.

What happened next I can see in my mind's eye:

The frantic father let out a cry of anguish, threw himself on hands and knees to try to pull his little girl out from underneath the car, failed in that, ran back and forth in a panic, cried out again. Then he reached into the car, snatched the key from the ignition, ran to the trunk, pulled out the jack, and, with trembling hands, tried to set up the jack, fumbling. At last he had the foot of the jack planted firmly. He inserted the handle and pumped up the side of the car. Then he reached under and pulled whatever part of the child's body he could reach. The body, dragged out from under the car, was limp, her little limbs crushed, the delicate white skin bloody, scraped raw and blackened by dirt and grease.

Horror in his eyes and blood on his hands, the man ran back into the house and past his wife, who started in alarm.

He grabbed the telephone and quickly dialed 911, giving them an incoherent message that the operator had to straighten out by asking clarifying questions. Instead of hanging up the phone, the man let it drop to the end of its cord.

His panic was communicated to his wife.

"What's the matter? What's wrong?", she demanded, apprehension in her voice. She hadn't grasped his words to the 911 operator.

He repeated to her what had happened—what he had done—and ran outside, his wife following.

When she saw the wreckage of her little girl's body, the mother dropped to her knees before the child, attempted to pick her up in her arms, but the child's body was limp. Father and mother then both knelt by the child, touching her, talking to her, now and then looking anxiously down the street for the ambulance to arrive.

Some neighbors or passersby may have been drawn to the scene, only to recoil from it.

The ambulance arrived, the parents were asked to stand back, and the paramedics got to work. The child was gently placed upon a board, strapped to it, and put into the ambulance.

So as not to interfere with the paramedics inside the ambulance, the parents would have to follow in their own car. The husband's car was still raised on the jack. The wife ran inside the house, took up the key to her own car and climbed in. The husband followed meekly. As the wife's car left the driveway, the husband stared at his car and the tricycle.

Arriving at the hospital, the parents' car close behind, the ambulance pulled into the emergency entrance, from which a nurse and an intern emerged to take over from the paramedics. The child's body was hurriedly wheeled down the corridor.

As the parents sat waiting, suffering their stress and tension, the first thoughts and judgments about what had happened began to arise.

"I didn't see her," the husband said in weak explanation.

No more explanation was necessary, because the wife knew what had happened as soon as she saw the twisted tricycle and her child's body.

In just a few minutes, but at what seemed in the parents' suspense a very long time, a young doctor emerged from behind the swinging white door and informed the parents what they already knew, that is, that their child was dead.

"I killed her," the husband said. There was crushing grief in his confession. "I didn't see her. I should have checked behind the car. Why didn't I?..."

There were no more words, as husband and wife collapsed into each other's arms. They were husband and wife, but no longer parents, for the girl was their only child, the treasured darling of their little family.

During the days that followed, the fact of the accident was sometimes denied, sometimes subjected to "if only", sometimes attributed to God, and, worst of all, sometimes blamed on the husband, even though no words of blame were spoken. A father had killed his own child. Carelessly not deliberately, yes, but he had killed her.

Without any words, there was accusation; without any words, there was confession of guilt. And grief, and deep, deep remorse.

The shock to the parents was incapacitating, even as there was so much that had to be done,—informing the relatives—(telling the grandparents would be especially difficult)—, making the arrangements for the funeral, choosing burial dress and casket.

The child, partially covered by concealing bouquets of flowers, was placed in the casket in such a way that the injuries were away from the sight of the mourners. Some cosmetic artifice of the funeral home employees worked to hide the raw horror of what had happened to the child. At the wake and at the funeral service there was uncontrolled and uncontrollable weeping. At the burial service, the mother nearly collapsed and had to be supported.

The couple's parenthood was abruptly finished, but their marriage went on. Whatever love they had for each other was put to its severest test. The wife had to forgive what really should have needed no forgiveness; the husband too had to forgive, both God and himself. The marital happiness went out of their lives, when the life went out of their child.

With the passage of time, the intensity of their grief abated, but mourning would linger as long as they lived.

Some months after the child's death, an acquaintance of the couple was thoughtless and insensitive to bring up the possibility of the couple's having another child. But they never would. They had made a ruin of parenthood. The death of their child estranged husband and wife from each other. Fate had been cruel to them, and they became cruel toward each other.

Whether there was eventual acceptance and healing and reconciliation, or whether the event of the death of their child was a permanent rupture in their marriage, I do not know. Together or alone, that man and woman suffered a lifetime with the vivid memory of one particular day. On that day, one life had been lost, but two other lives were destroyed in their continuance.

Survivors too die in accidents.

"Suicidal"

At one time in my life, among the various jobs and careers I have had, I was a social worker with adolescents.

There was a sixteen-year-old girl in our juvenile shelter home who had repeatedly tried to take her own life. She would find some sharp object, a true knife if possible, and slash away at her wrists and inner arms. We tried to keep all sharp objects away from her, but, short of tying her up in a straightjacket, that was not possible; even a metal-edged ruler would serve her compulsion.

A worker would find the girl with bloody arms, she staring down at them and shrieking in a panic that this time she might have succeeded in what she was trying to do. The worker would rush in, stanch the blood, and bundle her off to a hospital, where the medical staff would subdue and suture. After treatment and counseling, the girl would be returned to our care in the shelter home, where she might pick at the scabs of her self-inflicted wounds. And immediately she began plotting her next attempt.

What inner demon of self-loathing was afflicting that unfortunate child and tempting her to destroy herself? There must have been some harm done to her and her self-regard when she was very young, some terrible cruelty committed upon her, some insult to her so hurtful as to make her want to hurt herself in the worst way humanly possible.

How horrible the irresistible compulsion to kill oneself! Self-hatred is the most festering of all hatreds, violence against oneself the most disturbing of all violence. The suicidal compulsion,—the most appalling phenomenon of human motivation.

Some few may become suicidal out of a rational process, suicide the conclusion from weighing life and death against each other on the scales and judging life the lesser. World-weariness inclines toward a longing for the surcease of death.

And there have been those suicidal fanatics of ideological conviction,—the Christian martyrs, the Japanese samurai committing *seppuku,* the kamikaze pilots, and our contemporary murder-suicide terrorists. In those cases, the mind has been throttled long before it makes a decision to throttle the life of the body.

It seems bizarre to kill oneself over a mere idea, even if that idea may be considered a prime value. After all, the idea might be wrong. Righteous self-inflicted death is the worst error a mind can make.

So, the world-weary and the suicidal fanatics of ideology. Much more common than such derangement of the mind, I believe, is the sickness of soul and self, like that of the sixteen-year-old wrist-slasher. The stresses of life may have become so severe, the battering so thorough, the prospects for the future so seeming hopeless, that suicide appears as the only feasible release, desperate though it is.

Sometimes, the psychiatrists tell us, attempts at suicide are meant as pleas for help;—that is how they would diagnose the wrist-slashing of our hysterical girl. Yet, she had been given the best of available professional help—(but not love, because social workers may counsel, but they do not love)—and still she made further attempts.

An emotionally afflicted one falls into a downward spiral:

First, inadequate coping, then insidious feelings of failure and helplessness, a consequent erosion of self-regard that soon turns to self-loathing, a determined rejection of both the despicable person and the hopeless life, which leads to thoughts of the means of ending self and life, then the trying of those means, which, if the compulsion persists and is not broken, eventuates in successful suicide, effective termination of wretchedness.

I soon left my job working with adolescents and so never found out the fate of the girl who made so many slash attacks upon her lifeblood. Adolescence is a stressful time of life, a chronic crisis of self-regard. Attempted suicide is the most extreme form of common adolescent self-abuse. There have been many tragedies of violent ends to the lives of those who had so much life still before them.

All throughout life, actually, we all suffer blows against our liveliness and love of life, such as a sequence of bad luck, humiliating failures, betrayals, financial ruin, suffered cruelty or violence or war, deaths of loved ones and the demoralization they cause, accidents, grave illness, personal disasters of all kinds. Any of those blows might result in the rousing and activation of the suicide compulsion. Some recover and go on living; some fall into the downward spiral and succumb. Life and death straddle the pivot of one's personal morale; a slight tipping may cause a compulsion to die to overmaster the natural will to live.

They used to judge suicide a sin, or, absurdly, a crime. Such judgment in moral or legal terms is irrelevant, because suicidal compulsion is all psychological, pathopsychological. There is no point in condemning the dead, nor can they be punished. But suicidalists might be saved; or they might save themselves.

Suicide is a failure, a failure of the instinct to life. The suicidal compulsion is the only demonic possession that is real. Whether suicidal ones can be rescued and exorcised cannot be known except in the outcome; yet, we must rally to one another and to our natural wholesome instinct, bolster one another's ability to cope, nurture our tenacious love of life in one another. Our daily kind treatment of one another may be the most effective prophylactic against suicide.

A tragic death is the final act of a tragic life. Let us intervene to rewrite the script, not sit back in passive audience to the witnessing of the wreck of a human soul.

173

"The Widowhood of an Unmarried"

There was a young woman whose preparations for her wedding were stopped by the sudden death of her fiancé.

After an ardent courtship, the couple had set the date and proceeded with their plans. A church was chosen, a banquet hall booked for the reception, bridesmaids and groomsmen recruited and outfitted, the relatives and friends informed and invited, some scouting done for a new home for the couple, in short, all the necessaries in anticipation of a long married life together.

It was as the young woman returned home one evening, her finished wedding dress in the box in her arms, that she received the news. Her beloved had died, victim of what would be determined at autopsy as an undiagnosed heart defect.

The engagement was over. There would be no wedding. Death had intruded.

The young woman collapsed into the grief of lost love. The hope she felt for her future now turned to despair.

Instead of standing at her beloved's side before witnesses and pledging a lifetime partnership, she stood weeping, surrounded by the same people who would have attended her wedding, and stared at the coffin that contained the body of the man she loved. What would have been a line of people congratulating the couple was now a doleful trooping of mourners mumbling their condolences.

As the body of her beloved was lowered into the grave, it seemed to the young woman that her own life was being buried with it.

The sudden death of the young man was a shock to all who had known him. His friends sympathized with his fiancée, now bereft, deprived by death of future happiness. Some of them held tighter to their lovers or thanked their own good fortune in having living, breathing spouses and prospects of long, fulfilling marriages.

She would get over it, friends thought. It was a terrible thing that had happened to her, but she would get over it. She was young. She would know love again, and, with new love, perhaps a marriage after all.

As much as the families and friends commiserated with the young woman, offered their sympathies and encouragement, and then thought that they knew how she would heal, none of them understood her at all. She would recover from the tragedy, but not in the way that they thought.

First, there did follow weeks of tears and sleeplessness, sharp pangs of remembrance of love, dashed hopes. Then months of missing him, that chronic ache of bereavement.

When she had recovered some, time having done what healing it could, the young woman came to an understanding of what her beloved's death would really mean to her life:—

She would go on without him; she had to. But she would go on without any other man. From very early in their acquaintance, she realized that he was the one for her, the only one for her, the man destined for her female fulfillment. Now that he was gone, there would be, there could be, no other. She came to that conviction, not in a perverse urge to torture herself or in morbid fatalism, but as a simple realization of a truth for her.

The mourning for what had happened gradually lifted, the fantasies of how the couple's life together might have been faded away. The young woman eased into a resignation almost religious in quality. She could accept now, would accept, not only the death, but the consequence of that death, the consequence for her own life and future.

She would live purely and virginal, the rest of her life a renunciation of sex and sexual love. She vowed so out of fidelity, for she felt that her betrothed was already her husband, if not by ritual, then by the consummation of mutual commitment to each other.

She belonged to him only, as he belonged to her, forever. His death had not really separated them; nor should her life, the rest of her life, do so. She would go alone among others, because he would always be with her, if not by her side then in her heart. She was already married to him eternally; death was neither annulment nor divorce. Death was only an imposed separation of their bodies, one that did not sever the union of their souls.

And so, she lived out her seemingly solitary life. What to others may have been interpreted as an unhealed wound or bitterness or contraction from life was no such thing. Her love lived, and she lived in her love. In that love, she felt no grudge or privation or paltriness of living. She had found the one for her, had been loved, and still loved; in those thoughts she found her happiness.

Others wondered why she never married. She did not do so, she would have told them, because she was already married, she who had never been married. She was not a widow, really, but a wife. She may never have recited the words, "'til death do us part", but what she believed was, "Death shall never do us part".

Others may have pitied her, but she felt no pity for herself. For she knew what human fulfillment was. She felt fulfilled in the faithful steadfastness of her love.

174

"No Longer There"

She opened her eyes and was surprised to see the back of her husband's head still on his pillow. At first, she thought she didn't know what day it was. If it was a Saturday or Sunday morning, he always slept late, so his head should be there on the pillow. But if it was a weekday, he should be gone to work. He left for work so early that she never saw him on the morning of a weekday.

What day was it? Why, Friday, certainly. What time was it? The sun was already well up.

She propped herself on her elbow and looked over her husband's body to the clock on the dresser. 9:15. Even she did not usually sleep so late. Yet there she was, still in bed, and there was her husband. He had overslept.

She gently touched his shoulder and whispered his name. He did not respond.

She sat up, shook him harder, and called his name. His body was still.

Feeling a sudden panic, she leapt out of bed and ran to his side of it. Pulling back the covers, she looked at his face, the left side of it that was visible. She called his name again, but he did not hear.

She threw herself on her knees at the bedside and took her husband's head between her hands, looking hard at the closed eyes. His head was a weight, like an inert object.

She cried out in alarm and flung back the covers onto the floor.

Pressing her body against his side of the bed, she kept calling his name, caressed his face and brow with trembling fingers. She lifted his hand, but it fell limp back onto the bed. She laid her head upon his chest; she could detect no sound within. She pressed her cheek against his mouth and waited for an exhalation that never came. Then she took his head in her hands again and kissed him full on the lips, trying to blow the breath of life back into him. It was only her own breath that came out of his mouth.

With the palms of both hands she caressed his body and called out his name, each time more feebly. She could not see him clearly now, because of the tears of her realization.

Suddenly, she recoiled from the bed and from her husband's body, backing away to the farthest wall. She stood there weeping and gasping and crying out, "Oh!". Her whole body shook in uncontrollable convulsions. She felt faint and backed into the wall for its solidity. The beating of her own heart frightened her.

After a few minutes, she took some deep breaths and wiped the tears from her face with the sleeve of the nightgown. She thought of calling 911, but she knew the futility of it. Why suffer the intrusion of strangers into her bedroom, when she knew it was past hope?

She approached the bed and slowly got back into it on her side. Lying down, she put her arm around the shoulders of her husband's body and drew it to herself. Cradling his head, she whispered his name repeatedly and held him close to her. Then, whether she fainted or fell asleep, she was not sure later, but she lapsed into an unconsciousness with her husband in her arms.

When she awoke, it was past noon. Her first perception was of the body of her husband still in her arms, her first awareness the recall of her earlier waking up. Gently, she disengaged herself from her husband. And, with her wakefulness, the tears welled up again.

For the next few hours, she wandered the silent house, taking in all its domestic details, now and then going into the bedroom to look upon the body of her husband. In her dismay, she thought she might find the bed empty—what had happened just a dream, a nightmare—, but her husband's body was still there, tangible and real.

Her panic had left her, but she felt a deep stab of the cruel shock.

At last, she made the necessary phone call. The ambulance came to remove the body.

When the paramedics rushed into the house, they were at first eager to attack her husband with resuscitation efforts. It took only a cursory examination for them to determine what she already knew. When she first touched her husband, there was a residual warmth to that part of the body that was under the covers, but his face was cold. From the first contact with his face, she knew.

She was permitted to accompany her husband within the ambulance.

Afterwards, the informing of the families and friends and her husband's co-workers. There was a large turnout for the wake and funeral, many people approaching the widow and offering their condolences. A pressing crowd of people. Then, when she returned home, she was alone in the empty house.

In the first few weeks, the widow didn't sleep in that bed. Then, she crept back into it but couldn't fall asleep, as she lay staring at the dim outline of the empty pillow. It was only after many months that she could find comfort and rest in the bed.

Even now, each morning when she awakes, she remembers the usual Saturday or Sunday sight of her husband's head on the pillow. Now the pillow was always empty. He was no longer there. Would never be there again.

175

"An Empty House and the Ache of Absence"

Familiar surroundings have become hollow and empty.

The very furniture seems bereft, the bed no longer to be warmed by the body of the beloved, the stuffed chair never again to bear his impress, the dining room table-top bared of his elbows and the contact of his forearms and palms. The dressers and closets are shut repositories of clothes never to be worn again.

Household tools and implements have lost their usefulness in the absence of the one who used them. Every item in the house now seems a keepsake, memorabilia to be looked at for the rousing of memories, but not to be touched. The house has become a museum of memories.

Mere things, familiar things, but all of them associated with the lost beloved. Each one calls forth an image of his contact with them. These things are relics of lost love. Even though the survivor has no use for them, she does not consider throwing them away. They are sacred to her memory.

The space within the house, the air enclosed in the shell, is now void, oppressively so. That space was once animated by the presence and personality of the one now gone. The absence is all-pervading.

Even though she does not believe in ghosts, the widow's house is haunted. The bereaved mind invests the house with specters and images out of recollection, a continuing occupancy despite the gone-forever.

She is frightened to be home alone, frightened of her memories and their emotional effect upon her. When she arrives home, she comes in and turns on a light, looks around at the emptiness, and locks the door behind her.

A widow alone in her empty house, the sole resident of a home once shared. She hadn't really related directly to the house before; it was just the surroundings within which she related to her husband. But now she must confront the house directly. She has lost any interest she once had in its furnishings and decoration. It was for his sake, or theirs, really, not her own, that she had tried to make the house homey.

Her body and mind have lost their most cherished human relatedness. She feels an ache in her breast; the whole front of her body tingles with longing for the press of male muscle against it. No more warm touch, moist kiss, comforting—deeply comforting!—embrace. Her body is stripped and shivering, reverted to its virginal forlornness. And her mind too. She no longer has him to talk to, to share, to unburden upon, to confide in.

Her ears long for that baritone timbre. But there is only silence. She soliloquizes, all her thoughts futile, her mind conjuring a repeating cycle of the same memories again and again. Those memories make her weep, not because of what they are, but because they are only memories. All she now has of him is memories. She wants them to console her, but they only deepen her grief.

She feels like Eve, the only woman, as if Adam had died and left her alone in the unpeopled world. For without that relatedness to her husband, she wants no other relatedness. He was her prime contact; compared to him all others were mere appendages. Now, as never before in her life, she feels what *alone* means. Even though she knows that sharp grief passes, that mourning has its period, that time is healing, she suffers the irrevocable finality of her new aloneness.

All that she is—human, female, woman, person, member of a family and a society—suffers bereavement. What is now missing in her life, what has been taken away from her, outbalances all the riches of her living. She carries on now not in a continuation of her living, but in loss and lack and absence of the one missing.

A widow's consciousness, the one recurring thought, is of the nothingness that has happened to her. Her life has been emptied of its purpose, of its very liveliness. Every day is an ordeal of privation. She has lost interest in everything and everybody. Even her instinct for self-preservation has become feeble. She has no appetite for food or life.

How many and varied and recurring all those thoughts about the absent one! Grief is obsessive, mourning is chronic. The ache of absence strikes deep, and throbs, and persists. There can be no complete disengagement or total forgetting.

The loved one who dies takes away much of our own life. What remains of life to the widowed is a living-out of the loss. All that is left of love is the ache.

"Leavings"

He was an old friend of mine, (the words *old friend* denoting both longtime friend and a friend who has become an old person).

One day he remarked to me in a tone of regret, "Life is leavings."

"What do you mean?", I asked.

"Well," he said, "we are born into a family, and the members of that family are the closest and most dear to us.

"But, as the years pass, they leave us one by one. They die. First the grandparents, then aunts and uncles, our parents, brothers and sisters, cousins, one after another, they die, they leave us.

"In school some of your classmates become your good friends, but then they graduate and disperse. Friends made, friends lost, the same in elementary school, high school, college.

"Your neighbors may become over-the-fence friends. But we are all such transients through life. Neighbor friends move away. Left. Gone. Lost.

"A lot of people come into our lives as passing persons, acquaintances, some for a short time, some for a longer period, but, one way or another, sooner or later, they too all leave.

"At work or through some social organization you make friends. You get together for social occasions or you join them in some shared interest of sport or hobby.

"Some of those that you felt were your real close friends just drift away. Maybe you had some disagreement that you thought could be resolved but somehow led to total estrangement. Or maybe they just lost interest in you and they sought out other people as friends.

"When I look back over my life, all I see is leavings. Family members, schoolmates, neighbors, acquaintances, coworkers, and friends, even intimate friends..."

"And I didn't mention those we loved..."

He paused and swallowed.

I detected a pang of anguish.

Then, "my wife", he said softly. (He had not so long before been widowed.)

"Leavings," he finished.

There was silence, sad and awkward.

"I'm still here," I said in reassurance.

"Yes. Good. Stay," he said.

"I value your friendship," I told him.

He looked up and over to me.

"I value your friendship," he answered.

177

"The Broken Thread"

There are some whose attachment to another person is their attachment to life. They live not so much in and of themselves as through and for the other. Their loving is their living.

In their youth, they felt a powerful love-longing, which, eventually, found its fulfillment in another.

Personalized passion and concentrated loving devotion then bond them closer and closer to the living of the beloved, until their very love of life becomes indistinguishable from love of the beloved. Where love is the meaning of life, the life of the beloved is one's own living.

Love makes living transitive. As one loves the other, so one lives the other. What is *I*, the ego, except the agent of loving?: "I am less important than the one I love; no, I have no importance at all, except in as much as I enrich the life of my beloved by my love. I want to live, not for myself, but for the sake and benefit of the one I love."

It is through such love that living becomes selfless and self-effacing. Living is a daily gift, and it is as if the giver disappears with the giving of the gift. Sometimes what one may give is one's life itself.

Not in every person does love so dissolve the self. Most can give and receive love while maintaining their strong self-interest, the independence of their living, the autonomy of their love of life. Love need not be the whole of life, but, when it is, such living is exquisite... but also vulnerable.

In a longtime marriage in which both have given all their living to their loving, in which each lives only in the other, living has been transferred by the mutual gift-giving, he now in her, she now in him. The bond of marital love, the loveline, is now the lifeline.

But that lifeline is a thin thread, and a fragile one. Instead of a broad net of attachment to the world and interests and work and the many others in one's life, there is only that thin thread of attachment to the beloved. The concentrated narrowness of love is a disengagement from all worldly attachments, from the world itself. There is only the soul-to-soul thread.

What happens when that thread is broken?

The beloved dies. Whether in a prolonged anxiety preceding an expected death or in the shock of unexpected sudden death, the spouse suffers, an empathy more intense than any sympathy. And afterwards, the aloneness, a reversion to life as it was being lived before meeting the beloved, a living now lovelorn and meaningless. What is felt is not only grief and mourning over a loved one, but a bereftedness of life itself.

For those who love so much, the witnessing and experiencing of the death of the beloved is worse than the apprehension of one's own death. When the other has died, why live on? The thread, the one thread of attachment to life, has been broken. Love of life died with the love of one's life.

Love less, we might advise one another. Keep your own self-sufficiency, stabilize yourself with broad interests and involvements, love but be somewhat detached—for your own sake. Don't let your own life become so dependent upon that of another. We each have to live our own life. Love, but don't let love be your ultimate undoing.

Wise psychological advice, that. Yet, there will be those who would rather love much than live long, who will take the wreck of their own life as the inevitable consequence of the loss of the other. They longed for love, found love, gave love, and lived wholly in love.

Now, with the death of the beloved, they want to die, they want to relink the two strands of the broken thread.

178

"Outliving"

The old married couple have been together so many years that the living of each has become identical to the living of the other. Their love has been so deep that their shared living has become as one life.

The husband and wife, aging, think about approaching death, their own death, the spouse's. The death of one of them will be the death of their mutual love, and so the real end of life for the other, for what life could there be without living in the love of the other?

Single ones suffer only the apprehension of their own death. Married couples suffer a double apprehension; love's concern and responsibility worry over how the spouse will deal with one's own death.

The husband and wife look into each other's aged faces and are afraid, for themselves, but, also, for the other:

"Which one of us will die first?", the husband wonders. "If it is she, how could I go on? If it is I, how will she manage?"

"Which one of us will die first?", the wife asks herself. "If it is he, I don't want to live anymore. If it is I, how could he cope with my leaving him alone?"

The inevitable must happen; the only uncertainty is with the sequence. Which is more agonizing,—to suffer grief or to be the cause of another's grief?

Selfishness would say, "I hope I die first." Selfishness doesn't want to undergo the trial of grief, would avoid it, even if the other must undergo the necessary ordeal in one's stead.

Love would say, "I hope my spouse dies first." Love wants grief, if it is the only way to spare the beloved grief.

Strange that the more we love our spouse, the more we should wish our spouse dead before us.

Nature carries the secret timetable of our individual longevity, does not disclose that secret. Our life-cycles are predetermined; love can avail nothing against the inevitable. We are all apprehensive about our individual personal extinction. No one wants to die; we all dread it.

Love makes us ache with a doubled anxiety. My own beloved said to me, "I love you so much, I don't want anything bad happen to you."

Eternal love is a metaphysical fantasy. Deep down honestly, we know that the limit of the term of our shared love is set by the term of our individual lives. Half of us will suffer widowhood, the other half inflict that widowhood upon another.

If only the intertwining of marital love fused the life force of husband and wife together, so that life would expire for both of them at the same time. Some desperate ones who could not live without the other have effected that by double suicide. For most of us, however, one will die, the other continue to live on and linger and languish. We are born to outlive and to be outlived.

One case of near synchronicity of life and marriage that I know about was that of the historians Will and Ariel Durant, partners in vocation as well as mates for life. When, after 68 rich shared years of marriage, Ariel died, Will lingered just thirteen empty, solitary days thereafter, then followed her.

In a local instance, it was not only one funeral to follow soon upon another, as in the case of the Durants, but one death very soon upon the other, for the wife died just fifteen minutes after her husband.

A long outliving may be a fate worse than early death. Why hold on to life, when one has been torn from the embrace of love?

179

"To Whom Does the Great Man Belong?"

We have our private lives, and we have our public lives. For some the latter runs roughshod over the former. That is especially true in the case of great men and heroes and martyrs.

I remember vividly the assassination of President Kennedy and its aftermath. His violent death made him a martyr and evoked public veneration by his country and the world. 125 million people in the United States, as well as untold hundreds of other millions around the globe, were witnesses and participants in President Kennedy's lying-in-state and funeral. During all that, his family were mere bystanders.

At the time, we did not know the troubled state of President Kennedy's marriage. The family image presented to us was a combination of a brilliant and charismatic husband, a charming and elegant wife, and darling children. The idyllic marriage was a fraud, as we would later discover. Yet, even if marital bliss was absent, there was a marital life-bond.

I can still conjure the figure of Mrs. Kennedy, the distraught widow, during the ordeal of the funeral. The children, fortunately, were still too young to feel the full emotional impact of what had happened. The boy even made a flippant salute; he must have thought that all around him were just playing soldiers.

I wondered at the time, as many must have, how Mrs. Kennedy could keep her composure through it all, not only at the sudden violent death of her husband, in her presence, his very brains and blood spattered over her own body, he dying in her arms, but also at the protracted funereal ritual in the intrusive presence of the millions. I kept expecting her to collapse from the shock and grief of it all.

The President was a public personage, performing a public role not only of national, but of worldwide significance. That person, as well as the private person, had to receive due funereal rites. But how the open publicness of it must have intensified the grief of the stricken widow.

At the death of President Lincoln, Secretary Stanton proclaimed, "Now he belongs to the Ages." Mrs. Lincoln must have felt some resentment at that conferring of heroic stature upon her husband, divesting her, when his significance to her was not as President or great man or martyr, but as beloved husband. She had lost her life-partner. She had no willingness to hand him over to *the Ages*. Abraham was taken away from her, taken away to homage and heroization as Lincoln, while she herself had to suffer a solitary grief. And she did succumb to breakdown.

The masses want to participate in the deaths, as in the lives, of the great men of the world. Their insinuation is an intrusion into the private life of the family. Even at the funeral, the widow and children must stand aside, bystanders at the spectacle. And their grief is put on display. That seems to me heartless.

After President Kennedy was dead and gone, Mrs. Kennedy was still subjected to invasions of her privacy, on her own cause now, for she had become the glamorous widow, a spinoff celebrity made so by her onetime association with the martyr-hero. I would not condemn her if she may even have felt some hatred toward the faithless husband so canonized. In any case, she fled, from the country, from the devotees, from the voyeurs, from all those who tried to force her grief back upon her again and again. The death of the great man turned his widow into a frightened fugitive.

Nor is it easy for the children who are offspring of a great man. Impossible expectations are laid upon them, comparisons (usually invidious) made, further intrusions into privacy perpetrated. Greatness is not hereditary; it is a cruelty upon the children to expect it to be so. The children of the great public figure must struggle to simply live their own lives. The public memory of their parent may become a subversion of the lives of the children.

Some widows wind up making a career out of the memory of their husbands; Coretta Scott King is the most familiar instance. Doesn't the poor woman have a life and identity of her own? Must she serve out a life-sentence of homage to the hero who happened to be her husband? Must she be a vestal virgin of a cult of the dead?

When a man chooses a public life and the constant exposure, unremitting intrusions, and dogged attention that go with it, he knows that he is sacrificing his privacy; he sometimes fails to recognize that he is depriving his family too of their right to privacy. Presidential wives have seemed to me miserable, and their children harassed. The great man may be the scourge of his own family.

A woman wants a husband, children want a father, neither crave to worship a hero. The greater the public man, the lesser the private; the more prominent the public role, the more diminished the family one; the more expansive the life in the world, the more contracted the life at home.

Wife and children want to love and be loved, but the great man, wrapped in himself and his public role, has little left to devote to familial love. Love from a few is a paltry thing compared to worship from the masses. The great man gives himself almost wholly to the people; he belongs to them.

It is through death, especially assassination, as in the cases of Presidents Kennedy and Lincoln and of Martin Luther King, Jr., that the great man becomes hero and martyr. Not even death releases his family from the bondage of their association with the hero. Those who may not have known the full love of husband

and father must now pay dutiful homage to the memory of the hero.

The great man diminishes those closest to him and even after his death afflicts and bedevils them. The great man is the nemesis of those seemingly nearest and dearest.

All that belongs to the family of the deceased great one is a tiny fractional share of the memory.

180

"Sea Spew"

When I was down in Florida to arrange an interment recently, I happened to read in the local newspaper about some very disconcerting discoveries made on the beaches.

What was found in several places upon the shore was a long white plastic bag, a large perceptible bulk sealed within.

A beachfront property owner looked out her window, saw one of the bags upon her territory, and went out to dispose of it, but was drawn to look inside before she did so.

A swimmer popped his head out of the water, saw a bag bobbing alongside him, and towed it to land to examine.

A curious shell collector, eyes searching the sand for small salvage, instead stumbled across a big bag and broke into it to see what it contained.

What they and a few others discovered inside each of the bags, to their shock and disgust no doubt, was a human cadaver.

There have always been burials-at-sea. The cost of Florida real estate (including burial plots) having risen so much recently, more and more people have been resorting to the expanses of the Atlantic or Gulf of Mexico for free and open disposal.

Laws regulate burial-at-sea in such respects as packaging, distance from land, and so on. Whether the regulations were adequate or not, observed or not, what had happened in these cases of bodies returning to land was thought due to storms that raged, the turbulence and wave action disconnecting the body bags from their attached weights, the bag rising buoyant, and the winds doing the rest.

One body was in suit and tie, that curious formality we persist in, even unto death. Another was simply clad, another nude.

The authorities made an effort to identify each body, in order to notify relatives and force them to make another try at disposal. Some cadavers were identified, some not. The latter were rebundled, shipped out again, and dropped overboard,—with more secure weights and at greater depths and distance from land, I would pre-sume.

What mortification the family must have felt to receive a phone call informing them that their beloved had returned. And what deceived complacency of others, those relatives of the unidentified ones, who thought that they had committed their beloved to the sea eternally. The souls of the stranded deceased, too, must have suffered chagrin to witness from on high their mortal remains become flotsam, jetsam, and lagan, the *temple of the soul* just more damn trash and water pollution.

There may have been reasons more personal than economic for these particular burials-at-sea. The de-ceased might have requested it himself—(I think all the cadavers were male)—, he being an avid fisherman or boatman or sailor or having practiced some other avocation of sea-love. He may have felt that he belonged more to the sea than to the land, an *old salt.*

Whatever the reason for the burials-at-sea, the sea would have none of it. The sea retched at such acts of defilement and spewed the offal back ashore.

We know from the biologists that all life, including that leading eventually to our own human life, originated in the seas of the Earth. All life was in the sea, until emerging land provided new opportunities. When our primordial creature ancestors ventured onto the land, they determined our nature as terrestrial ever after. The human is not amphibian, no matter how seafaring we may be. Our life is on the land, our only sea-belonging the salt amnion of our fetal stage and the saltiness of the blood that flows through our bodies.

Amnion and blood are evolutionary souvenirs, but more significant is that we breathe through lungs, not gills, we walk on land legs for locomotion, can swim but only poorly and briefly. We are land creatures. We came from the sea, but we no longer belong there, either while alive or after we are dead.

Burial is, after all, an in*hum*ation, a digging-down into land; it is not submersion.

Now, had the bodies I read about in the newspaper been cremated, turned into calcium bone fragments, the sea might have accepted them willingly. The sea has its coral formations and relishes a richness of minerals to sustain marine life. The human bone minerals would have re-integrated into the chemistry of the sea much easier than the embalmed body in its polyester suit-and-tie and leather land-walking shoes.

If disposal at sea there is to be, it should be of the raw organic elements stripped of all artificial and technological packaging. Worldwide available land gradually becoming as expensive as Florida real estate and being pre-empted by the living of our exploding population, the most practical and economic future means of disposition after death might be bones dropped into the sea. But the sea chokes on, and vomits back plastic body bags.

As I have reported elsewhere, I myself conducted a disposition of cremated remains at sea. That form of remnant human is a small bulk for the great sea to swallow and, in all, a wholesome one.

The sea is the Mother of All Life. It is an affront and desecration of her to use the sea as a dumping pool for mortuary offal. We ought to observe an ecological hygiene in death, as a personal one in life. The sea gave us life. In return, shall we only dump our death back into her? No. Let us recycle ourselves, yes, but not be another heap onto the nonrecyclable pollution pile. Whether the human soul is immortal or not, the plastic bag is nearly so.

If it is not to be "ashes to ashes and dust to dust" of land burial, let it be bones to coral in the sea.

Our human life is not the goal of all Life; we are participants, not the Culmination of Creation. Returned hygienically to the sea, the organic remains of our lives may be the stuff out of which new life may be made. That is a task for which the sea has already proven well suited. Then the sea will not reject us. She will, rather, stir us back into the organic soup.

181

"Derelict"

The body of a black man was removed from Lower Wacker Drive, the dark street beneath the street that runs along the Chicago River.

No one knew how long he had lain there dead.

The homeless spend much of their days, as their nights, lying along the walls, lying still, huddled up. Sometimes they are in a drunken stupor, sometimes in a narcotic swoon. They may be lying wide-awake and staring at the wall, or else dozing or in a deep sleep. Whatever their state, their neighbors along the wall know not to disturb them. It is only when they are sitting upright or wandering about that the homeless are bold to address one another.

The black man had lain there dead, until the stench of his decomposition drifted and disturbed the sleep of those near him. Repugnant smells are not unusual on Lower Wacker Drive. There is the polluted river nearby, the exhaust fumes of the cars, the dank dampness of the trapped air, the urine sweating off the walls, human feces, alcohol, rancid vomit, a dead rat. But the stench from the body of the black man overcame all that and permeated a wide area around him. One of the nearby homeless made a complaint to a policeman stopped in his squad car.

The policeman walked over to the area and kicked his way through the piles of rubbish. "Hey, anybody there?", he called out.

He approached the cardboard appliance carton that had been the black man's shelter. Then he drew up his arm to cover his nose and mouth and backed off from the stench of death.

The policeman returned to his squad car and called in the report.

Some of the other homeless of the area drifted over to the scene. They stood about impassive or mumbled to themselves. There was no excitement or upset or much of any reaction at all.

The policeman asked who it was who had lived in the appliance carton. No one knew any more than the black man's nickname. He had never much communicated with anyone. He hadn't caused any trouble, had steered clear of the others when panhandling, respecting their territories, never shared what he had but didn't mooch off the others either, kept to himself, spent most of his time huddled against the wall, partly sheltered by the carton and covered by newspapers and cardboard.

The ambulance arrived to remove the body. Two young black men got out. They put on rubber gloves and surgical masks. One pulled a pallet out of the vehicle. The policeman directed them to the site.

One man from the ambulance pushed over the flimsy carton, and the body was revealed. The body was on its side, huddled and contracted. The other young man tried to turn the body on its back, prodding gently with his foot, but the body was in rigor mortis. So slight of frame was it that it fit easily on the narrow pallet, anyway. The two men unfolded a plastic sheet and draped it over the body.

They then carried the pallet back to the ambulance.

As they slid the body through the back door, one of the men got a glimpse of the face of the corpse. A black face, like his own. What if it were his father? It could be, for all he knew.

As the ambulance drove off, the other homeless of the area now converged upon the site where the black man had died. They overcame their revulsion at the lingering stench, because there might be something lying about that they could take and use. They were not aggressive; they just drew near and looked over the heaps of trash.

Was there maybe a plastic basket or a cardboard box stashed away that might have anything in it? The homeless have fantasies that the one sleeping near them might have something stashed away, maybe even money that he had hoarded for the time when, panhandling failing, he might be in desperate need.

There were no baskets or boxes of hidden hoard. There was just refuse. The appliance carton was a better shelter than some of them had, but it was now too contaminated by death. No one took even that.

The homeless withdrew back to their own sites, some rummaging among their things to be sure that nothing of theirs had been taken while they had been away, others lying back down to huddle under whatever cover they had.

An hour later, city workers arrived on a truck. They broke up the appliance carton, shoveled the refuse from the black man's area, and tossed it all into the back of the truck. As they sped off, the diesel smoke from the truck spewed over the bodies of those lying in the line of the sidewalk.

A vacancy had now been created, the place where the black man had lived and died now available to someone else. None of those already in the area moved into that space; it had no advantages over where they were... .

A few weeks later, a thin stooped black man with a grizzled beard and ragged coat came by, pushing his few possessions in a stolen supermarket cart. He had been coming to the area for several weeks now, panhandling on Michigan Avenue above; he had been getting some handouts from the office workers.

Seeing that open space, he pushed his cart into it.

He looked around on the sidewalk. All he saw were the still, huddled forms of sleeping bodies.

He pulled a dirty blanket from the cart and laid it on the pavement. Wrapping himself in another blanket, he lay down on his side huddled against the wall. Oblivious to the surge of traffic past him on Lower Wacker, he drifted off to sleep.

182

"Old Wealth"

The old woman seems to have become a part of the chair she sits in every day, her convex contour matching the concave contour of the chair. Like the chair, she is rickety and frail, her once voluptuous flesh as shriveled as the stuffing of the upholstery of the chair. Her body is musty, her surface worn, her dry skin like a dust all over her.

Under the fourteen-foot ceiling, its perimeter edged in bold molding, the long icicles of the chandelier hanging from its center, she is small and insignificant, a lone house-mouse. This is only one room of the thirty-room mansion, yet it is immense compared to her body. All of the other rooms in the mansion are empty of people; this room feels empty too, even though she knows that she is there.

The textures and colors around her are all rich and dark,—damask, velvet, mahogany, the black marble of the fireplace, the brown-black hide of some African animal, the tarnished bronze of the statuary. The lace curtains would have added brightness to the room, but they are browned and dirty. Anyway, the outside shutters are all closed, so the room is dark as night, except where a thin ray of the sun penetrates a broken louver of a shutter.

The old woman lives in darkness now, because there is nothing that she can stand to look at.

The stillness inside the mansion is absolute. She has deafened herself to any sounds outside, a passing car or children running and laughing as they return from school. What she listens to is the absolute stillness of her empty house.

There is stillness in her mind too, one broken only when she hears the mumblings of memory. Remembering, the only activity of a housebound old woman. She doesn't like what she remembers, she tries to banish the memories from her mind, so that she can just sit and listen to the stillness. She thinks that she may be able to hear her own death when it arrives.

Sometimes, in spite of herself, she is afflicted by her memories. Bright lights and happy sounds from long ago intrude:

It was on the lawn of the mansion, just outside those windows now shut, amidst a profusion of flowers and banners, the gushing fountains and Greek statues, that she married. An orchestra played, and a hundred guests danced under the late afternoon June-day sun. The bride, she herself, was very beautiful. And triumphant too, of all the days of her life the most triumphant. For she was marrying Huntington W. Dennie, the richest of the rich.

She just twenty-two years old, but sure of herself, sure of what she wanted, self-assured even with the upper class. She held her head so high that they could not look down upon her and despise her because of her common origins. The other women would have to defer to her because of her husband, and, of course, for the sake of their husbands and their currying up to Huntington Dennie. She outdid them all in contempt. She showed them what *haughty* really was. All the other women would bow and curtsy and defer to her, because she was their superior in determination and will-power. She was a woman, not a parlor ornament, as they were.

She wanted money, and she had married for it. Stalked Huntington Dennie from the first chance encounter with him. He was fifty years old, crude and rude in his manners, with a bad complexion and a potbelly. His money looked beautiful enough to her. It didn't take long for her to convince him that she was the perfect wife for him.

During their engagement, he started construction of the mansion, the new mansion that would belong to her too. At first, he wanted a design according to his own vulgar aesthetic, but she persuaded him to build what she wanted. She persuaded with female persuasiveness, but more, with that personal willfulness, her most prominent trait of character. Their abode would be built to her specifications.

Huntington Dennie indulged her every whim, because he recognized that she was a woman of will, not of whim. She would be his tough and strong ally.

The honeymoon was strictly business. He proved physically repulsive, as she had expected. (She had no naïve girlish illusions about anything.) She was willing to give him a son in exchange for his millions; that was the deal, mutually understood even if not in any written contract. One pregnancy would be enough. Nine months of indulged invalidism, a few hours of labor, and she would have earned the irrevocable right to all of Huntington Dennie's wealth. That was all it would take, the deal done. She would go through with it; there wasn't even a necessity for her to feign feelings, for neither she nor Huntington Dennie had any feelings, either for each other or for anyone else.

Three months after their wedding, the mansion completed to its smallest detail, husband and wife moved into separate bedrooms.

Over dinner, he would whisper a request to come to her that night—(a whispering not out of romance, but so that the butler or maid would not overhear)—, and she would either grant or withhold, as she wished. She was young and fertile, so it didn't take many times for her to become pregnant, in the condition to deny all further requests from him.

She gave birth to a daughter, not a son, but Huntington Dennie seemed satisfied anyway. When the girl proved willful, like her mother, he was even more satisfied. He believed that the girl took after him.

Between his worsening ill health, consequent impotence, and his wife's unwillingness, there were to be no more children.

As the girl grew, her nature expressing itself, Huntington Dennie became captured by the fanciful idea of a woman, his own daughter, taking over the business. Under his guidance and through her own nature, she would have all the men—both his employees and his competitors—hopping to her tune.

As for Mrs. Huntington Dennie, she had not bothered at all with child-rearing; functionaries had been hired for that. She herself occupied her life in consumption of the best of everything, in luxurious travel (mostly alone), and in a social display that put all the rest of them in their place. She had married wealth, and she was going to enjoy it. . . .

As the bright images of the memories of the grand parties came into the dark of her mind, the old woman winced, clutched the chair arms and dug into them with her sharp, horny fingernails. She panted in a little distress of her shallow breathing, and a pang stabbed her weak heart.

Drunk with champagne, she now remembered, she had waylaid a party guest, a young man her age in years but a boy in experience, and dragged him up to a guest bedroom, locked the two of them in, and stripped him and herself of all clothing of refinement. She did that not once, but several times, and not with the same man but with whichever one caught her eye just after she had come to that stage in her drunkenness.

Afterwards, she remade the bed herself. Her husband would have killed her, if he had found out, she thought, but he never did find out. How had he not detected her hour-long absences from the parties? Of course she made sure that he never found out about the abortion.

Just after their daughter's eighteenth birthday, the girl was stricken with meningitis. After terrible suffering, she died. Huntington Dennie, whether out of grief or out of the frustration of his ambition for his daughter, soon followed.

Mrs. Huntington Dennie then had it all to herself,— the company, the villa in Italy, the mansion, and the tens of millions. Now she had no need for willfulness. She had achieved her goal.

She sold off the company—had no interest in business, didn't want the responsibility—, and she got rid of the villa too. She decided to stay where she was, in the mansion.

When she became a widow, she was soon besieged by charities trying to siphon off some portion of the estate, but she rebuffed them all. Thinking that she might be vulnerable in her grief, they proposed establishing a charitable trust in memory of her husband. Grief, what grief? Memorial, hah! She had no intention of memorializing Huntington Dennie; the sooner he was forgotten, the better. She had married him for his money, had earned that money with her very life, and she meant to keep it all, not to spend now, but to hold on to for spite.

She broke out of the business and social circle she had had to endure because of her tie with her husband. They all hated her, really, and she hated them. She had become disgusted with other people. She would stay alone in the mansion. After a few years, she dismissed even the servants.

She lived poor now, in a spite against her wealth as against those who wanted some part of it. Her money was hers to keep. And after she was dead? Let them fight over it, let them tear one another to pieces to get what they could of it. No children or grandchildren, no near relatives even, there was not one with a strong claim that would override all the others. What a clutching and grabbing and catfight there would be! She shivered in a little delight at the prospect of it. Too bad she wouldn't be around to see it.

Her shiver of delight was a body shiver too. She felt a little cold and clammy. As she reached over and pulled her shawl from the side table to drape over her shoulders, she thought she could see motes of dust in the thin ray of sun coming through the broken louver of the shutter.

She coughed a feeble cough. The room was dusty and musty, but that was just the way she liked it. The room as it was, she as she was, everything as it was, without any changes. Her parlor, her mansion, herself.

And so, she sat out another day, in the darkness and stillness of her life. The only intrusions into her solitude were the thin ray of sun panning slowly across the room and the dim flitting images of her memories.

183

"Wants and Wanting"

"When I was young, I used to want so many things," an old lady remarked to me. "I took pleasure in so many things, too. Now that I am old I don't want anything…"

She didn't continue, "I don't take pleasure in anything, either," as I expected her to say. Perhaps she did find pleasure in some things; she expressed content- ment in what she called her frugal—(she pronounced it *frujal*)—life. She had disengaged herself from her wants, from much of wanting itself.

What she wanted when she was a young woman, she told me, was mostly clothes and fashionable finery. She was a bit vain about her appearance; the adorn- ment of her body was the adornment of her life. When she was depressed, she said, all it took to cheer her up was a new hat. Now, in her old age, she laughed at her girlish silliness. And she laughed away depression as easily as she laughed away its onetime cure.

In our youth, we go about our lives aggrandizing. What we crave to obtain may be materialistic,—the brand-new fashion-of-the-day hat and dress. Or it may be some intangible but nonetheless real goal, as achievement, success, recognition, status, power, pres- tige, fame. We can't always get our hands on what it is we want most; what we want most is not always grasp- able.

As we go through life, we accumulate things at a faster rate than we can dispose of them. The old lady had in her closet dresses she had worn only a few times and would never wear again. Her frayed housecoat was good enough for her now, she said. She had sloughed off her former acquisitiveness and vanity.

A Buddhist monk may arrive at the wisdom of dis- engagement in youth, but, for most of us, we consume away unto geriatric surfeit. Only late in life might we gradually free ourselves from our material attachments, divest ourselves of our frippery. We do so not out of philosophical or spiritual enlightenment, but out of sheer sick-and-tiredness of insatiable craving. All wants and wanting itself are cloying.

One way or another, old age is the period of life of diminishing wants. Much of what was wanted and obtained has lost its allure, become common, tiresome, burdensome. Intangible acquisition too seems suddenly empty. What do success and even fame matter, when the old body and mind ache every minute?

Like the lady I mentioned, many old people look back upon the acquisitiveness or ambition of their youth as both vain and in vain. We think the old are wise about values, but, really, they are just worn out with themselves and their wants. They have exhausted and used up their wanting.

If a life has been a life of wanting, what then is left of living when the wanting ceases? And so, the lives of many old people seem so empty to them. When they want nothing, the only thing left for them to want is to want to die. Death is the ultimate divestiture.

One irony of human life is this: Just when we may have obtained what we want, we find ourselves wanting nothing at all. The craving to consume ultimately consumes itself and us along with it.

Aging is a losing-of-interest, not only in material things and ambitions, but also in experiences. After a long life of activity, the old are plum worn out. When one has done most of what one wanted to do, or recognized that what one wanted to do is utterly impossible, what is there left to be done? Nothing, except to die. One last experience, then done with it all.

Old age is a stripping-away of what one has spent a lifetime accumulating. The contents of the overstuffed closet are disposed of. The mind becomes as naked as the body was at birth. Nakedness is, indeed, the appropriate attire for death, but how few can die naked. The disrobing is seldom complete; we cling to a scrap or two pressed against our skin, so that we make a modest and presentable appearance at the wake.

At the time of death itself, there may be some wanting left, if only the contrary wanting *not* to die. That last want, more than all the others, will be frustrated of satisfaction.

In the final ambivalence, that of old age, one may want to die one moment and want not to die at the next. Wanting becomes all muddled up, as the hand, so used to grasping, grasps one last time, even as the mind is directing it to let go.

"I want to live... No, I want to die... I want, I want, I want...What? Nothing. And nothingness."

The terminal stage of human will is reached when wanting doesn't want itself anymore.

184

"The Ebbing of *Eros*"

Sexuality is the energetic of life. It urges on not only the generation of new life but also the living of the body itself. The flow of sexual hormones within the body of the male, within the body of the female, disturbing and disrupting as it often is, is the fuel that burns and powers our vitality.

In youth, there is sexual energy to squander. No matter how much used and abused, the flow seems inexhaustible. Unlike the ephemeral insects, whose sexual act is the bringing-on of death, we humans enjoy a long life of repeated sexual expression. Through decade after decade our sexual energy enlivens us. Every act of sex may be an affirmation of life and of one's own living.

But then *eros* gradually ebbs.

In men, intensity and gratification diminish, the power to show the usual stamina is lost, along with reactivity to stimuli, leading ultimately to an impotent end to most of the sexual energetic itself.

For women, menopause is an ordeal, the hormones once so seasonal and predictable now become disturbing and disorienting. She may feel some relief that the bother of menstruation and the risk of pregnancy are past, but that relief is only through a forced sterility, an irreversible loss of female fecundity. The sterility of old women may be as demoralizing as the impotence of old men.

The ebbing of *eros* in the male is an impotence psychical as well as physical. Since adolescence, a man's sense of himself has been so intertwined with his sexuality that the two seem inextricable. He can remember himself as a boy; yes, he found his life exciting in those days before his full sexuality emerged; but the wonder a boy finds in life cannot be recaptured by one who has lost the most wonderful of all wonders,—the male's own potency and generative energy. It is difficult for a man to disengage himself from a half-century of sexual self-identity. He continues male, of course, as the boy before was male, but, to him, what is maleness without the capacity to act as the male acts? Few men can endure with equanimity the impotence that Nature imposes upon them in their old age. The sense of male incapacity is the most dreaded of masculine afflictions.

A woman's being may be more in her feelings of love than in her sexual acts, but sex is a means by which she expresses love. Love may deepen rather than wane over time, but that does not mean that she escapes the consequences of the ebbing of *eros*. She has come to appreciate sex with the one she loves so much. She enjoys her own, as well as her husband's gratification; she desires the desirability he has found in her; she is the willing means to enhancement of his sense of self with her. Now, in the menopause, she may be more out-of-sorts than ever she was in the cycle of her periods. She also becomes self-conscious about her diminished allure, her loss of voluptuousness, the drying-out that frustrates the communion that needs flow of fluids. Her man's frustration at his impotence may frustrate her too.

Then husband and wife carry on in a marriage without sex; only love remains. Of course, love is more important, is higher than sex, both have long since recognized and agree. Still, a feeble hand-holding is no compensation for the loss of the delectation of passionate fusion. Happiness is not bliss; comfortableness is not ecstasy. Something in their marriage has been lost along with sexual capability and responsiveness, they must admit.

Along with erotic nostalgia for their lost past, the couple feel apprehension for their future. The loss of sexual power and feelings is a sign that Nature has given the organism its chance and is now just about done with it. As sex recedes, death approaches.

Widows and widowers know the same compensation as old married couples, that is, they have experienced love. Even if the love of their lives is deceased, at least they can be consoled in the memories of their onetime fulfillment. The grief for another mitigates the feeling of pity for oneself. The widowed can endure the loss of *eros* in the knowledge that it was once well used. Given as a gift to the beloved, it need not be clung to now that the beloved is gone.

For those who never found a mate, the ebbing of *eros* is especially bitter. They have repressed or ill-used the very energetic of Life-Itself. Sex did not lead to love for them, so they do not have the married couple's or widow's consolation. The worst failure an old person can accuse oneself of is the failure to live life fully and drink deep of its human—and, yes, sensual—joys. The old bachelor and old maid face death with the self-accusatory haunting ache of lack of fulfillment.

Do the old celibate Catholic clergy or Buddhist monks and nuns feel a pang at their willful self-denial because of ideology? How they so struggled against sex, beat it back, beat it down, for the sake of their vocation and dedication. Now, aging, they need struggle no longer; the corrosive fire within is nearly extinguished. They have made their sacrifice, they have, more or less, triumphed over all the temptations. But was the sacrifice worth it, the sacrifice of body for the sake of soul? Was self-denial life-denial?, they must wonder. Was their only victory one over their own vitality?

Most of us let the sexual instinct run amok in us from time to time; we lack the disciplinary throttling of the celibates. We deeply regret our sins, even when, in old age, we look back upon them with yearning and nostalgia. Yes, we sinned in our life, but wasn't there a zest and aliveness in our sinning, an aliveness now withered with the capacity to sin again? Sex causes regrets, but the geriatric loss of sex is an even deeper regret. *Eros* was a problem for us. If only we had to deal with that problem again.

The mind may take to the library and find solace in books, but the organic body and its memories cannot do so. Our real living is not the life of the mind, but the life of the body, one energetic of which is the erotic flow. Old-age impotence and sterility are curses upon us as individuals, even though we recognize that Nature, when depriving us of our sexual powers, has no personal malice against us. Flows must ebb; that is the natural way of the scheme-of-things.

What we miss in the ebbing of *eros* is not the gratification, but the satisfaction. And, yes, the fulfillment.

Sexuality atrophies in the body, the only remnant of it the memories in the mind. Much of the life of the old is the memory of what life was, including the sex and love experiences of former years.

And then, at last, as death approaches, *eros* ebbs even in the mind. Forgetting *eros* is the prelude to death.

185

"The World or Yourself?"

As death is about to happen, which is the loss that you will most regret,—the world or yourself?

The orb of the Earth is the sparkling ornament of the universe. What a world there is around us! What limitless experiences it offers! The varieties of scenes of lands and waters are inexhaustible. Who has had a lifetime long enough, rich enough, to have traveled all the jungles and forests, deserts and gardens, islands and mountaintops, seas and lakes and rivers? Some of the vitality of life is in the exploratory impulse. As long as we live, we want to go places, experience the many possibilities of environment. The world is a wonder to us.

The world contains not only the Nature of it, but the cultures in it. Culture offers its own fascinating experiences. There is Rome, my Rome, and Athens and Paris and London and St. Petersburg and Istanbul and Casablanca and Kyoto and Hong Kong and Sydney and Buenos Aires and Mexico City and New York, and, yes, even Chicago. Within the great cities are colossi of architecture, great temples, historical sites and monuments, museums and shrines. Little villages too have their cultural charms. What the human has wrought upon the Earth provides experiences to well fill up a single lifetime.

Culture is superimposed upon Nature and that context is stimulating: Rome on its seven hills astride the Tiber, Luxor on the Nile, Rio de Janeiro in the Bay of

Guanabara, Machu Picchu in the Andes, Lhasa in the Himalayas, and other such civic constructions in splendid evocative settings.

Life is a journey, in reality as well as in metaphor. We are all nomadic still; to live we must move. Only the dead are stationary.

Interesting as it all is—Nature and culture, I mean—we do have to keep up our interest in those times when we are not going anywhere. Even if we are not free to wander our entire life, the body moving, the mind can wander,—into art and music and literature and crafts and all the other expressions and experiences of indoors culture. Those are available to all, not just to rich travelers. As Nature stimulates the vitality of the senses, so indoors culture stimulates the vitality of the mind. In the human, it is necessary for both the body and the mind to want to go on living.

How insatiable is the craving to appreciate, to learn, or, for the few of us, to create! We want to see more beautiful artworks, hear more music—(whether new or our lifelong favorites)—, read more books, the classics or some new masterpiece just written. We are all, in one way or another, aesthetes and scholars. Our aesthetics and our intellect make life so much more interesting for the human than it can ever be for the animals. Because there is so much to appreciate and learn, it is fitting that God created man as one of the most long-lived of the animals.

Then, too, there are all those other people. We are social animals, so a lot of our vitality is in our human relatedness. As well as to travel and experience and appreciate and learn, we live to love. Our personal individual living is within a broad network of the lives of others. I have my family—parents, spouse, children—and a wider circle of good friends, colleagues, and acquaintances. It is through those many strands of relatedness to others that I am linked to the humanness of my living; it is because of my ties to others that I want to go on living. Others are part of the environment within which I carry on my life, but they are also part of myself and my own living. I live among others, with others, and I may even live for others. The alone are moribund. But I am not alone. I enjoy the vitality of my relatedness.

I know that when I die I will lose the world and all in it,—Nature, culture, and fellow humanity. What an immense loss that will be! It will all go on without me, of course; most of it won't miss me at all, but how much I will miss the world!

The longer we live, the more we understand how much we shall lose when we die. We feel the inadequacy of our lived lives, no matter so seeming rich and full. Why didn't I travel more, seek out more experiences, learn more, love more, or, for the creative ones, produce more?

The world is not "too much with us". Really, as long as we live, we cannot get enough of the world, because we realize that the time will come when we will be deprived of the world. It is death that takes the world away from us.

There is the world, but there is also the self. What is the balance of world and self in the life and mind of each of us?

I am important to myself; indeed, to whom could I be more important? My self-interest is a self-preservation. I am a living self, so I must devote much of my living to maintaining myself, meeting the needs of my individual body and soul.

I am precious to myself. I love and pamper my body, I enjoy my animal senses and sensuality, I relish pleasing emotionality and try to avoid emotional upset, I strive for equanimity of mind. No matter how much I may live for the world and for others, I must perforce live for myself. Without self-interest, I would not live very long.

I live to please myself, don't I? But how much of my living is in that pleasing of myself? Do I float receptive and open to becoming absorbed in the world and others, or do I just try to siphon off as much as I can of the world into myself? Not many love Life-in-the-abstract; what most people love is their own personal living.

There are some in whom the self looms larger than the world. It is an aggrandizing self, and it must be indulged. The living of such a one is beyond self-preservation and self-interest; it is a self-indulgence, a gorging of the body, gratification of the senses, ego-obsession, acquisition of material things, personal ambition, in short, a hoarding unto oneself of all that can be extracted and filched from the world.

How much of my living is the experience of the world, and how much of it is the experience of myself? At death, both the world and my self will be lost; which is the loss that arouses more anticipatory regret?

I have delved into the lore of *last words*, those terminal utterances of brink-of-death regrets. The last words of the dying may not be characteristic of their living, but they do reveal what will be missed, what is the deprivation inflicted by death, whether loss of Nature or culture or others or self.

There are very few whose death-gasp is an exclamation of wonder at Nature. Yet, there may be a deathbed nature aesthetic, as in General Tojo's, "Oh, look, see how the cherry blossoms fall mutely!", or Czar Alexander I's appreciation, "What a beautiful day!", or the solar idolatry of the painter J. M. W. Turner's, "The sun is God!". Goethe resisted the closing of his eyes upon the world with his famous yearning cry, "More light! More light!".

There are more who will miss culture, even to the extent of denying that death is the end of culture, as in the painter Corot's, "I hope with all my heart there will be painting in heaven." Another painter, Hokusai, lamented the death of his creativity in the death of his body: "If heaven would give me five more years of life, I might become a truly great painter." On his deathbed, Pushkin addressed his books with, "Farewell, my friends," and Daniel Webster's last word was "poetry". The dying Abelard expressed the exasperation of his unquenchable thirst for knowledge with the admission, "I don't know. I don't know."

Francis Marion Crawford, author of a cherished book of mine, *Ave, Roma Immortalis*, left as his last words a double appreciation, of both Nature and culture: "I love to see the reflection of the sun in the bookcase."

Beloved others hold us to life in a stronger embrace than either Nature or culture. A dying Maurice Maeterlinck told his wife, "For me this is quite natural. It is for you that I am concerned." Ferruccio Busoni the composer told his wife, "Dear Gerda, I thank you for every day we have been together." The love-longing of Heloise was, "In death at last let me rest with Abelard."

The name of the loved one has been the last word of many who have loved, as Frank Harris: "Nellie, my Nellie—I'm going!" and Victor Hugo: "Goodbye, Jeanne, goodbye" and President James K. Polk to his wife: "I love you, Sarah—I—love—you" and Queen Victoria's last breath: "Bertie". Even W. C. Fields: "God damn everything and everybody. Except you, my dear Carlotta."

Regarding the loss of oneself, of one's self, in death, I have earlier quoted William Saroyan. To which I may add Nero's egotistic megalomania: "Alas, what a great artist the world is losing!" and Caligula's willful contradiction of death: "I am still alive"; but then he wasn't. The boxer Max Baer resisted release with, "Oh, God, here I go!", while Winston Churchill was impatient to die, because he had lost interest: "Oh, I am so bored with it all." The world-weary British find even death boring.

Regarding the attitude of the ego at death, there are some who desperately try to hold on, others who accept ego-extinction, even if with reluctance, and some few who are impatient to make the leap into personal non-existence.

At death, what is lost of Nature, culture, and others is only awareness of them; but what is lost of the self is the self itself, so it is understandable that the self should loom large at the threatening imminence of death. All my life I have become more and more attached to myself; the detachment at death won't be easy.

As death is about to happen, which is the loss that *you* will most regret,—the world or yourself?

186

"The Futility of Flight"

"O, George, it is idle to run from Death. I shrank down behind the sugar canes of Santa Cruz, Death was there, too; then I sneaked into a Swiss valley, there he was; and here he is at Rome. I shall come home and meet him on my own dunghill."

It was not upon his dunghill that Theodore Parker died, but in Florence, where he could gaze upon the art of living before he himself had to master the art of dying.

We may live wandering around, but we cannot die that way.

I myself have been somewhat of a wanderer, seeking a stimulating variety in this place, that place, and another place. The accumulation of novel sights and experiences would culminate in ultimate living, I thought. Hungry for life, I pursued it in peripatetic polyglot cosmopolitanism. My living, for a long span of it, was a moving-on.

Travel was also my attempt to get away from myself and my inadequacies, to banish unhappiness by means of distractions. I had been stewing in my own juices too much. Casting myself adrift would be the flushing cure. And so, I made myself into vagrant and vagabond, always chasing after my own becoming by drawing the culturally extraneous into the psychologically intrinsic.

I used to measure my life not in time but in mileage. I was one who "got someplace in the world", at least in my version of that expression.

I can't say that I found life by getting myself lost, except in that life was already within myself, unlosable, inescapable, irrespective of whether I stayed home—(or even had a home)—or went off somewhere. We describe life with the *journey* metaphor, but, really, where are we going in life? What destination is there?

Life has no destination, but it does have an end. An end that will come to us in some place,—Santa Cruz, Switzerland, Rome, Florence, or the dunghill. How few die in the same room in the house where they were born. No, death overtakes us far from where we started, at some random stop in a long series of dislocations.

Oh, the places we have been along the way, the sights we've seen, the interesting life we have led! But then death imposes a fixity upon us. In that we must die somewhere, dying is the final experience that happens in a particular place. But death makes the place seem irrelevant to the essential reality of what happens.

In life we may go places but get nowhere. Then, where do we go after death? When we think about after-death, we persist in the journey metaphor. We're off! But where to?

There are guidebooks, metaphysical ones, describing destinations, yes, ultimate terminal destinations, where we will have to stay for eternity. Some primitives may think that their afterdeath afterlives will be nomadic, but the theologically sophisticates are dead certain that we will take up a sedentary abode forever fixed, householders in Heaven or inmates of Hell.

At the end of our lives, we know where we have been, each and every place, our memories supported by stamped passports, here's-me-at photographs, or other proofs. Life was a tourism. We went where we wanted to go. Whether we traveled to acquire experiences or to escape ourselves, we wrote our own ticket.

Death takes away our freedom of movement. Death grounds us. Death stops us in our tracks.

During our lives, we could not accept the simplicity of belonging-here. We had to be off somewhere else. Ever restless, we sought our destiny in destinations.

For us, death is another departure. We cannot be so sure of where we are going as where we have been, the proofs of the metaphysical itinerary not so convincing as our photographic record, the travelers' reports having been written by those who have never been there.

In our lives, we may run toward or run away, only to be seized and held at last. Death puts a stop to all our frantic, confused aimlessness.

It takes the allure of Heaven to cure our restlessness and make us want to stay put at last.

"The Uselessness of Culture, and the One Exception"

We undergo our education in preparation for the life before us, and all through our lives we further our enculturation by literature, music, art, and all the other cultural adornments.

By the time we are old, we have accumulated a heap of culture, our own contemporary one, necessarily, and, to a greater or lesser extent in each individual, some parts of other cultures distant in place and time. Language, knowledge, aesthetic experiences, values, ideas and ideologies—all the various aspects of human culture—have been assimilated by the mind and applied to the living of a life.

But what is all that culture at the time of death?

Thomas De Quincy, a literary man, lamented that you have to read a thousand books, only to discover that you needn't have read a single one of them. In all of those books, what one sentence from any of them is any consolation at the moment of death? All the learned facts and information, the fictions, fantasies, and fancies, of prose and poetry are as dust at the time of death. Reading was a time-killing, a life-killing. The last thing—I mean, the least thing—a dying man wants is to take up a book and read another page. At death, we revert to illiteracy. It is not that we regret having read so much; it is only that we now find the culture of literacy irrelevant to the reality of dying. A *Book of the Dead* or *Matters of Death* may be read only by the living. Some last words may precede death, but death itself is wordlessness.

And all that music we have heard,—what was it but noises to divert us during our days? A sensory stimulation to keep us from falling asleep. We hummed a tune to banish boredom, danced a jig to burn off excess energy. Yes, there was an exquisite pleasure in music, pleasure to ear and heart. We hear many melodies during the course of our lifetime, but not even the most cheering sprightly ditty is a distraction from the impending reality of death. A Requiem may be heard only by the living. Death is soundlessness.

During our lifetimes, our eyes too seek their sensory delights. Lascivious art, alluring and seductive, all that visual eroticism. As long as we can see, let us look and delight in looking. Whether high art or Hollywood, we are entranced by visual imagery. Like music, art is rooted in animal senses and sensuality. But death, we know, snuffs out the senses. Does any dying one want something novel to look upon as a last sight? No, the dying close their eyes. The art and architecture of mortuary monuments are to be seen only by the living, not by those to whom they are dedicated. Death is sightlessness.

Culture is enrichment of our lives, but it means little on the occasion of our death. We neither regret having had too little of it, nor do we crave extension of life in order to acquire more. A thousand books, a million melodies, museums of art images:—All vanish like wisps at death. Death reduces us, from civilization to essential animality. It is not the cultured human that dies; it is the animal body.

A dying Chinese, a dying Tahitian, a dying Pawnee, a dying Czech, a dying Bolivian or Bantu or Eskimo;—yes, there will be different cultural rites surrounding each death, but the deaths themselves will be the same in their organic reality. Culture may be very long lived, but its carriers are not. Culture is only for the living.

A person of high culture may have lived a richer life compared to an uncultured or poorly cultured one, but in death all are equalized. Culture is a garment of the mind that is stripped off at death. We die as simple naked animals.

But just when I would conclude that culture has no relevance to death, I think of an exception. For there is one aspect of culture that is, indeed, directed to the time of death. That is religion. (I exclude philosophy, because those who can find any consolation in it at death are even fewer than those who can find consolation in philosophy during life.)

Religion claims a relevance to death, to the investing of higher meaning to death, to the coping with witnessed death, and to undergoing the personal experience of dying.

Some die clutching a crucifix or rosary or other cultic talisman. Some think as their last thought a promise from scripture. (We need not die thoughtless.) Others try to visualize a metaphysical realm to which they believe they are headed, an inner vision overcoming the sightlessness of death. In some form or other, religion draws near the bedside of the dying.

Of all of culture, religion is the only aspect applicable to death,—that is, for those who believe in it. Some who have not much believed during their lives come to desperate belief at the time of death, having lost the vitality of philosophical skepticism. Religion may be the last grasp at the last gasp.

Religion purports to tell what death really is and prescribes how to die. The human search for spiritual meaning persists to the very last minute. And so, unlike literature and music and art and other aspects of culture, religion is not sloughed off at the end. Religion culminates and triumphs at death; necrotherapeutic, it is the sole cultural necessity at that time.

Religion is the only cultural baggage we carry with us into eternity. Isn't religion the culture of God Himself? Anyway, it is the only cultural credentials we need when we present ourselves to God.

188

"Disengagement"

The most difficult trial in the ordeal of dying or of watching imminent death is the disengagement of person from person.

Love is much of the value of our living, as we realize, sometimes belatedly, on the occasion of death. We cling to love, as we cling to life; we struggle against letting go of either. Human relatedness may be the strongest tie to continuing life.

The dying one is in an anguish, from both a feeling of dependence and a feeling of responsibility. He needs others, depends on them, now in the death crisis as through all the crises of his life. He looks to them desperately for help, even though he knows that they are as helpless as he is in dealing with inevitable death. At the same time, he may feel dereliction of his own responsibility for them, especially if there is wife and small children. In death he is abandoning them, failing in his responsibility. Death is the breakdown of human mutual assistance.

If he lingers long, the dying one may review in his mind all the important relationships of his life, from parents and family to friends and lovers to spouse and children, and to all those others who passed through his life, whose lives he himself impacted. Some of his recollections may be of adversaries and enemies he now would forgive. During those recollections, he may feel satisfied or regretful, or he may accuse himself.

The dying are more likely to think of their human relationships, whether past or present, than they are to think of their career or successes or achievements, all of which now seem so empty and insignificant. Our ultimate realization, if we are to have one, is that it was only the relationships that mattered.

The dying one wants to keep open the book of his relatedness. As long as he is still living, he belongs to those who belong to him. It is not the loss of his wasting organic form that he resists; it is the severing of his lifelines of human ties; not his own death that he dreads, but the effect of his death on those others. He resists by reaching out.

The bystanders to the imminent death suffer their own pangs of disengagement. They don't want to be abandoned, forsaken, left behind by one they love and depend on. Human love makes the witnessing of the death of a beloved a more wrenching and tragic experience than undergoing one's own death.

As the dying one reviews the many relationships of his life and passes judgment on himself regarding them, so, too, the bystanders review their relatedness to the dying one. They wish they had loved more, helped more, been kinder toward. In the last remaining days or hours they attempt, in some way, to make up for the deficiencies of what they have given in love. There is something of a too-late in deathbed relatedness, but we do not accept that. Loving relatedness is never too late.

When, at last, the loved one dies, the survivors grieve and mourn, not only for the dead one, who no longer needs compassion or love, but for themselves, the bereft ones, whose thread of relatedness has been broken. We are distressed and thrown into a panic of helplessness by any rending of our web of relatedness. Even in the midst of many mutually supporting fellow-mourners, we feel alone. The survivors cling to one another, each feeling their own personal loss more than the in-common one.

It is difficult to conceive of a human being facing death without undergoing the agony of disengagement from relatedness. No one can be so isolated as to face death in utter aloneness. Even the loneliest must conjure a ghost of love out of the past.

Death severs ongoing interactions, but a relatedness continues, in our memories. The dead still belong to us, remain tied to us all our lives. There is no "out of sight, out of mind" when love has been interrupted by death. As long as we remember, we are related. The dead had to let go, but the living do not let go.

And so, we tell our children about grandparents they never knew, and, as they listen, they too acquire an extended relatedness. We communicate the richness of human belonging, those many and far-flung ties to loved others, those lifelines of love and support and sustenance. Death may cut some of those lifelines, but in the human heart and mind there is no total disengagement. Living and dead are linked to one another by bonds that, after death, are tenuous but indissoluble.

189

"Unfulfilled"

To arrive at the end of life, to look back upon it, to look within, and to see an utter emptiness!

The life lived may have been a small and selfish one. Engrossed in oneself, always looking out for oneself, plotting and manipulating to one's own advantage. The sole subject of consciousness was oneself; I-and-I-alone was the all of life. Years and years of egoistic aggrandizement, the living all the while shriveling as the ego swelled. Others hardly existed at all, except as means or obstacles. Any relationships had to produce a net gain; if others seemingly had little to offer, they were rejected and abandoned. Life was a taking, a series of acquisitions. Why, now, after all that taking, is there nothing left? How has the miser become destitute? What happened to all that accumulation? The selfish one has hoarded…nothing.

Another one refused to become what he was. In his youth he recognized his nature, saw clearly what he was destined for. Yet, he did not pursue his own becoming. Others wanted different from him, or the world seemed to require a different type. He was persuaded by others to forsake his authentic self. He followed the recommendations of others, answered the recruitment call of the world, turned himself into what was wanted, rather than into what he was destined to be. Self-suppression, seemingly noble, actually a perfidious self-betrayal. Now that he has spent all his life being what they wanted him to be, he confronts his estranged authentic self at his side by the deathbed. What a treachery he has committed, he now realizes. Why did he listen to them? What has been his reward? He faces death in the bitterness of self-recognition. He never really was, his life never really was.

Another may have lived for an ideology, an ideology that he now perceives as fraud. He devoted his life to an idea or construct of ideas,—others' ideas, not his own. The ideology now appears false, and he, devotee of a false ideology, has been a dupe. To commit oneself to a cause seemed a higher life. What went wrong? He understands now that he was drawn to the cause, committed himself to it, only to fill the void of his personal living. He craved a life of meaning; he mistook an ideology for meaning. He gave up his own life to others' ideas, became a propagandist of values actually alien to his own basic nature. What irony! At death the true believer has lost his faith, because he realizes, at last, that values that are not out of one's own insights are valueless.

The ideology may have been one of disciplinary self-denial. A moral judgment being rendered against the selfishness and self-indulgence of others' lives, something higher was desired, a more spiritual way of living. The body indicted as the coarse component of life, the soul was nurtured, by self-denial in all its forms, asceticism, mortification of the flesh, sexual self-suppression, plainness and poverty. A fullness of life would come out of such privation, it was thought. Paradox! But now that the body, the despised body, is about to die, what is the state of the soul? Not enriched, not spiritual, not even wholesome. Instead, there is a feeling of cumulative withering, of a perverse repudiation of living itself. So much was given up, for a higher purpose. The body was throttled, yes, but wasn't living thereby throttled too?

Yet another victim of privation, an isolated one. Estranged from all others, the ultimate consequence of a lifetime of battling against all others. And now alone. None to come to one, to comfort, to reassure, to look upon with eyes of love and compassion. How had it come about that he has wound up so alone, that there are none in the whole world who care for him? To die alone! How could an entire life finish in such friendlessness?

In another, a life postponed, living itself put off. There were those opportunities, but they were too risky to be ventured upon. Better to be prudent, wait until later. Education, travel, love, and all other sorts of enrichment offered themselves, but were turned down. Not now, not quite ready for it, maybe later. There was too much risk of failure. Why didn't she ever become ready to take the chance? Postponement had been such a habit as to become engrained, its exercise automatic. The years passed, the opportunities all flitted away. Now no opportunities, no prospects present themselves. Death is not an opportunity; it is an imposition, a venture forced upon one. Death brooks no postponement.

Or, a contrary type, the one whose life was a series of impulsive wrong choices, of wrongheadedness itself. Why couldn't he ever get it right? All those deathbed second guesses: "If only I hadn't done that...If only I had done something else instead..." A rewriting of one's life at the end of it, all regrets and futile what-ifs. A real life could have been lived, if only one had been smart enough to make the correct choices. And so, he looks back upon the life he never lived, the life he should have lived, life as it should have been for him. And then all his actual life seems a blunder, wrong from start to finish. But even as he rewrites, he knows that he cannot relive.

To have wound up alienated from oneself and others, to have thought wrong, to have done wrong or not done what should have been done, to have made a botch of one's life,—what a terrible realization! Enlightenment at last is bitter, because nothing can be done to correct or remedy any of it.

Imminent death presents us with the task of evaluation of oneself and of one's lived life. Cursed are those who look back, who look within, only to stare into a stark emptiness!

190

"Death Sudden, Dying Gradual"

When I was in elementary school, the nuns used to tell the class that we should live each day as if it were our last, because God might snatch us away to Judgment at any moment. Now, there's a prescription for anxious living.

Of course, we might die at any moment, but whether daily meditation on that fact insures a moral life I doubt. The fear of death is not an adequate conscience, nor is it by any means a tonic to vitality.

Whether or not there is to be a postmortem Judgment, a sudden death, that snatching-away, is a blessing to be prayed for. If death is sudden, one is spared any suffering of body or mind, the physical pains and agony of lingering illness, and the accompanying anxieties and apprehensions about death. Going quickly is the best way to go.

Sudden death is the best way for the deceased, but not for bystanders or those related to the deceased. A sudden death causes dismay and upset among those who witness it; the sudden irruption of death into everyday routine is discomposing. Then, too, those widowed or orphaned by a sudden death suffer a terrible shock. An unprepared mind deals poorly with crisis and tragedy. The mind suffers its sharp grief and self-accusatory second thoughts too: "If only I had made him take better care of himself, made him stop smoking, taken better care of him, loved him better, and why did I provoke that fight with him on what would be his last day on Earth?", and so on.

Embarrassments may follow a sudden death. We go along in the assumption of our life continuing, and we may be careless in leaving evidence of wrongdoing,—an adultery, an embezzlement, a secret vice. We made attempts to conceal our guilt, hide it away, but now that death has left everything exposed, vulnerable to discovery and ransacking, something might be discovered to the detriment of the reputation of the deceased and to the shame of his survivors. We live untidy, and a sudden death is an untidy one. When the survivors go through the task of picking up the pieces, they may find some pieces that they do not like. Grief may be adulterated by unpleasant discoveries.

Still, whatever the postmortem evidence against, a balanced judgment of the deceased will be made in time, and loved ones will feel a gratitude that he died without enduring protracted suffering. Yes, they will feel abandoned and blame him for his abrupt departure, in all, going through the ambivalent process of coming to terms with the loss. Acceptance comes, the shock and grief of the sudden death eased away by happier memories of times lived together.

If sudden death is best for the deceased but bad for the survivors, a gradual dying is somewhat the reverse.

To waste away and endure pain and lie abed hopeless is a torture to the one who must undergo it. That a human life, even one that had much bad with the good, should finish up in ignominious extended agony arouses an obsession with the pathology of one's own deterioration, a frantic impatience for it all to end, despair, and even thoughts of, or attempts at, suicide. Nature and God himself seem to have turned cruel. Counseling and consolation may be offered to the terminal one, but he finds little real comfort in them. He wants only to die and to die soon, to get life over with. Bitterness may be his ultimate human emotion.

The loved ones who must witness the wasting-away of a beloved suffer, too, from the frightfulness of what they must witness and, of course, from sympathy with the beloved. And they dread that a like fate may await them; how would *they* endure it? Sometimes, compassion and pity for the long-suffering one impel to desperate acts and interventions,—an unauthorized surreptitious disconnection of life-supporting equipment or even a violent attack upon the one most loved in all the world. In such cases, those related to the gradually dying one suffer in their minds an agony comparable to that suffered in the body of the terminally ill.

Usually, however, a gradual dying enables the family to prepare themselves for the inevitability, to come to terms with the approaching death, and forestall some of the impact of the grief that must be endured.

Then, too, communication is still possible with the dying one. Love may still be extended. The family that may have drifted apart in life may be drawn together by impending death. There is possibility for reconciliation of estrangement, for expressing gratitude, for re-affirming the bonds that had been taken for granted previously. Deathbed scenes are seldom pretty, but they may be beneficial to those who participate in them. Even the terminal one, despite the agonies, might come to a peaceful resolution, forced as he is to think over and extract the meaning and value of what has been his life.

We plan and schedule so much of our lives, but we cannot do so for our deaths. No one, except a suicide, can predetermine the exact nature and manner of one's death. The nuns' counsel to be prepared is sound, provided it does not become a morbid preoccupation. But we cannot be fully prepared, really. Death always catches us unawares, whether it is a taking-away abrupt or a lingering, suspenseful departure. We die with an uncompleted thought in our minds or in the midst of a dream never to be finished.

We want dying to be quick-and-easy, and for some lucky ones it is. Which of us will be that lucky we do not know. Nature is not considerate in her processes. One way or another, she will process us out, whether in her haste or at her leisure.

191

"Death of Body and Mind"

There is an attrition of the body, and there is an attrition of the mind.

In the beginning is the germ of life. From its first vital instant, that germ takes nourishment into itself, to grow, to develop, to become what it is innately patterned to be. So the human body, from the zygote, takes its nourishment, grows and develops, from within the womb to life outside the womb, then from infancy to maturity to middle age.

There is a lifelong wear-and-tear upon our bodies, a daily attrition. At a certain time in the processes of the body, there occurs a pivot point, at which the stresses upon the body, relentless stresses from the environment, begin to overcome the vital processes. The coming-to-be, growth, development, and full maturation are to be followed by the decline toward death.

Not only the external stresses from the environment, but also the failings of the operations within the body cause the decline. The very complexity of the body, its efficiency, breaks down, autonomic controls fall lax, cell biology commits errors. The body then begins to deteriorate, the aging process gradual for most bodies, but, for all, inevitably, the decline toward death.

How we regret the ebbing of our bodily powers, so much did we love, and glory in, the physiological vitality of our youth! We regard that ebbing, especially the ebbing of *eros*, with nostalgia and dismay. Yes, we recognize the inevitability of the course of natural processes, but we resent that we, being made in *the image of God,* should be, like all other organic creatures, subject to them.

Our minds too follow a similar course of coming-to-be, growth in powers, a pivot point, then decline and deterioration. Attrition upon our minds may come from such experiences as disillusionment with ideals and heroes, disappointment in love, or lifelong frustration of our ambitions.

That bright, curious insatiable mind of our youth! Very few are those who keep the curiosity and eagerness to learn from their youth into their old age. Most of us become as mentally tired as we are physically tired. As we read in Ecclesiastes, learning becomes stale. Curiosity ages into senescence, or, worse, senility.

And so, we fall into a world-weariness and even a weariness with our own selves. (There was one who said upon his deathbed, "I've had just about as much of myself as I can stand.") The aged become sick and tired of it all.

So, the aging of our bodies and our minds, that inevitable succumbing to the attritive wear-and-tear upon both.

The attrition on the body and the attrition upon the mind do not proceed at the same pace.

For some, the body takes an early wear-and-tear that enfeebles it for life;—a poisoning while still in the womb, a developmental slip-up, a severe disease or accident of childhood. Then, emotional stresses and behavioral practices like smoking, narcotics, or alcohol abuse may impair the vitality of the body and impel it toward a premature sinking toward dissolution.

Nonetheless, there may be vital minds in sickly bodies,—Alexander Pope, Nietzsche, Kierkegaard, and Stephen Hawking. Intellectual vitality may compensate for physiological weakness, so that, one way or another, one may feel fully alive, no matter what harms have befallen the body.

Conversely, the body may thrive while the mind languishes. There are some shocks to the mind that may subvert its vitality,—some terrible disillusionment suffered in impressionable youth with a consequent onset of cynicism, or a paralyzing confusion of values that collapses into nihilism, a *nothing to live for*. In such cases, the person has a mind world-weary but a body possibly still brimming with vitality. That person's mind wants to lie down and die, even as the body is eager to vault fences.

Now, if only the attrition of our bodies and that upon our minds were dealt out in equal portions, so that we could proceed toward death in a balanced decline; but that is rare, I think.

Instead, most approach death with the body yielding but the mind resisting, or with a mind yielding but a body resisting. How difficult it is to die as a whole undivided human being, how unusual the synchronous decline and death of body and mind.

No, we exit agitated, either the body resisting or the mind resisting, one or the other clinging to life and hating the other for its succumbing.

Does the body ever will itself to die, as the mind sometimes does? Can the body too feel a world-weariness after having become spent by gorging self-nourishment, self-spending sex, and the exhaustion of having run hither-and-thither and being knocked about for decades?

To die divided in oneself. Is there no other way?

"I have lived all that I am capable of living. I have learned all that I was capable of learning. And now, worn out but fulfilled, I lie down to die. My body and mind are at peace with each other, and I—my self or whatever I am—am at peace with both of them. I yield to the inevitable. Better, I embrace the inevitable. Farewell, friends, and do not regret my passing, for I have achieved a great success. I have come to terms with the necessary."

A remarkable deathbed speech that, one that has never been heard.

Contrary to that exemplar, we struggle on, we resent the winding-down. Is it in our nature to resist, to try to persist? Healthy body, unhealthy mind; or unhealthy body, healthy mind. Anyway, attrition upon both unto a consequent deterioration and inevitable dissolution.

If only our bodies and minds could tap into the Process. If only we could understand and, with integrity intact, accept and let go!

192

"Kicking and Screaming"

It is said that he was even born reluctantly. From the very first, his most primitive consciousness expressed itself in resistance and willfulness.

His mother had been in labor for sixteen hours. She pushed and pushed, her womb contracted and contracted. But still he would not come out.

"Come out, little baby, come out!", the doctor urged, peering down at the orifice.

But he would not come out. When, at last, the contractions got the better of him, he tried to rip out his mother's innards with him. The doctor was astounded; he had never seen such a thing before. The baby had to be thrust into the world kicking and screaming.

When the time came for weaning, the infant would not give up the nipple. He clung and sucked, even when he was not hungry. He refused to let go, despite his mother's best strong efforts to push him away. No, he would hold on and suck on that nipple forever. His grandmother had to wrench him from the nipple kicking and screaming.

Time came for him to attend school, but he refused to. On the scheduled first day of school, he hid himself under his bed. His mother discovered him there and towed him off to school kicking and screaming.

He had to go to the dentist, his mother told him. "No, it will hurt," he objected; he wouldn't go. On the way to the dentist, he ran away down the street. His mother couldn't catch him. The next week, she tied him to herself and took him to the dentist kicking and screaming.

"Get a part-time job," his father urged him. No, he wouldn't. He was just a little boy. He didn't want to work; he wanted to play. But his father knew somebody, a boss whom he persuaded to hire his son. So his father brought his son to the job kicking and screaming.

She loved him so much, the girl said. Why didn't he marry her? No, he was not ready for marriage, he told her. He claimed that he loved her, but he wanted no commitments. The girl stayed steadfast in her devotion. Eventually, she drew him to the altar kicking and screaming.

Then things weren't going well in the marriage. She wanted to work it out. He did too, he said, but it was obvious to her that he didn't want to make any effort at it. Despite the fact that he fought her every step of the way, she wouldn't give up, until, at last, she was able to lead him to the marriage counselor kicking and screaming.

Many years passed. The time came for his retirement. No, he was too young to retire, he protested. He had a lot of timeserving left in him. But rules were rules. He was put out the door kicking and screaming.

He became old and ill. "It's very serious," the doctor told him. "You have to go into the hospital." "No, no," he answered. "I'm not that sick. I won't go into the hospital." Against his will, he was checked into the hospital. He lay in the bed kicking and screaming.

Then, in the deepest dark of a night shortly thereafter, Death walked into his hospital room and approached his bed.

"Let's go," Death said.

"No! No! No! I won't go!", the man protested.

Death had no patience with resistance or willfulness. Grabbing hold of him roughly, Death dragged him out of the world kicking and screaming.

193

"Death Resisted, Death Accepted"

There is a much quoted verse by Dylan Thomas that reads:

"Do not go gentle into that good night,/Old age should burn and rave at close of day;/Rage, rage against the dying of the light."

Those lines are taken as inspirational, as a model of courage and defiance of death. A Buddhist, however, would shake his head in sadness at the foolishness and futility of all that raving and raging. A Buddhist always "goes gentle", whether through life or through the passageway to death. Death can no more be fended off than life can. The above verse is a self-abusive, malicious counsel, redolent of drunken violence and desperation.

We often read of someone who died "after a long, valiant struggle against cancer" or "after a courageous fight" against some other fatal disease. They fought, and then they succumbed. That they so struggled against their disease is considered heroic, laudable, and exemplary. Death must be resisted.

Disease and accident come to us all many times through our life. The body wants to go on living, so it struggles to beat back the infection or heal the injury. The body rallies to its own preservation, spontaneously and autonomically, until all its resources are used up and it is overwhelmed by some pathological process.

We do not need inspirational poetry to urge the body to its own defense. Should the mind be goaded to resistance?

Of course, we can never know which one of the many mishaps of the body might be the fatal one, the particular end destined for us. Every doctor will tell you that a wholesome attitude and a will to recover aid the body in its effort, because the human is an organic-spiritual compound of body-and-mind, each of which must rally to the other. The disease must be fought back by the mind as well as by the body. Some even assert that the power of the mind can heal the body on its own, without medical intervention; the mind has power over life. That belief, however, cannot be extended into the hope of overcoming death by means of the mind. The mind has no mastery over death.

Ecclesiastes recognized "a time for dying", the antithesis to "a time for giving birth", but that is little more than saying that what starts must someday finish. In the same book, "a time for healing" follows "a time for killing", which, even as it sets compassion against violence, seems to accept what Yahweh forbade. Some lines should be added to Ecclesiastes to the effect that, "There is a time for resisting, a time for letting go."

Death is daunting, but the way to deal with fear is not by working oneself into a frenzy of resistance; it is to recognize the danger for what it is and respond appropriately. Raving-and-raging is never an appropriate response, not only because it does not avail against any danger, but because it wreaks havoc upon the mind of the one facing the danger. "It is not what happens to us," said a certain Eastern sage, "but how we react to what happens to us that determines our fate."

The mind should befriend itself, at the time of death as during life. Getting all worked up—even over death—has no therapeutic value. Throttling the mind no more restores health than throttling the body would do so. Nor is hatred of death an expression of the loving of life.

We want to live, yes, and, if ill, we want to recover. I am not urging a premature despair, or any despair at all. Yet, if we recognize death as natural outcome and inevitability, it is self-induced frustration and plain futility to resist it to the (then bitter) end. We should "go gentle" into death as through life.

"Easy to say, not so easy to do," you might object. Few face death with equanimity, but those who do so are the ones who have already succeeded in living life with equanimity. An entire life spent in compulsive craving will not be cured of its vice on the deathbed. The grasping hand and its spasmodic clutching will be incapable of letting go.

We don't know exactly when we are about to die; we enjoy no epiphany of angel to sound the clarion call. That puts us in a suspense as to whether we are on the road to recovery or sliding down the inexorable descent to death. How can we be accepting, if we just don't know which outcome is facing us?

I wonder how many people have recognized the onset of their own death and embraced death with go-gentle acceptance. That is the ideal I would propose, but I am unsure of its feasibility. Even so, the raving-and-raging is no alternative. At death, the body is wreckage, necessarily, but it is not necessary that the mind finish itself off in such same condition.

Our human will may be as much our undoing at the time of death as it is the means of our prevailing and thriving during life. Willfulness against the inevitable is the worst of all follies, and the most harmful. Death cannot be willed away; it comes when it itself wants.

If a wholesome will to live goes to the fanatic extreme of live-at-any-cost, the fight against death is nothing but a self-battering of the mind.

It is wisdom and compassion for oneself to recognize, accept, and "go gentle".

194

"Little Child within the Man"

The old man has just been told that his life is coming to an end. His illness is incurable, even untreatable. His situation is hopeless. Soon he will be dead.

How many years of life he has had. With those years, hasn't he acquired the strength to deal with every adversity? Hasn't life with its difficulties toughened him? Yet, against all his acquired strength, he is afraid now, afraid to die.

As a young man, he used to comfort his small children, dispel their fears by the muscular strength of his embrace. Afraid of the dark, afraid of monsters under the bed, afraid of a medical procedure, his children would run to him, find refuge in his physical strength. Nothing could hurt, if daddy was near. Daddy was stronger than everything that was feared.

Then, when his children were grown and facing adult fears, he had continued as their backup strength. Not physical strength, for that was declining, but moral strength and an example of courage. He had taught his children to stand up to adversity, but even as he did that, he did not leave them on their own to triumph or succumb. No, he stood just off to the side, watching in concern, ready to step in and bolster a son or daughter who needed him.

To his children, as to his wife, he was a strong man and a courageous one. He was their model of strength.

In his recent years, he would take his grandchildren into his arms, and they too found strength and comfort

in him. Grandpa wasn't afraid of anything. If you're a-
fraid, run to grandpa!

He must have had fears of his own during his life. As
a child, certainly, he must have been afraid. He doesn't
remember whether a parent came to him when he was
afraid or whether he was left to deal with his fears
alone. Anyway, he had made himself fearless by his own
strength of will.

What has now become of his fearlessness? He has
just heard his death sentence. Fear creeps through him
as it has never done before. His body is clammy, cold,
trembling.

A lifetime of fearlessness seems now as nothing. A
man, he has reverted to being a child again. A child
afraid of the dark and of monsters under the bed.
Death, imminent death, is the dark and the monster
under the bed.

All throughout his life, he has dispelled the fears felt
by others, but now he is in a panic of helplessness in
dealing with his own fear.

He is terrified in body and mind and soul. Whom
can he run to for comfort against death? Who will take
him in their strong arms?

195

"Last Words"

"The beaten dog lies down in the corner and dies."

The nurse turned her head when she heard those
words.

The old man squirmed in his bed a little, pressed his
bald head against the headboard, shuddered, and was
still.

The nurse, holding the bottle of medication, looked across the room at the old man. His words echoed in her mind. Terrible words, words of utter defeat.

"Now, now, Mr. Cragin," she said as she walked over to him, intent upon rebuking his despair and bolstering his will to live with the medication she would administer.

The nurse put down the medication on the bed stand, in order to straighten out the contorted body, rouse the patient, and force the medication on him.

The body of the old man was limp, as she pulled the legs down from their contraction into the fetal position. The nurse grasped the shoulders to turn the old man onto his back. She did so, but the old man's head, pulled away from its press against the headboard, fell between the two pillows. The jaw dropped open, the eyes stared wide straight at the nurse. But those eyes had become as inert as glass.

The nurse felt the pulse, held the wrist for a while, then backed away from the bed. She stood there looking at the horrid sight of the wasted body of the old man, now become a corpse. She glanced over at the opened bottle of medication. Then she left the room to summon the doctor.

The nurse was about to telephone Mrs. Cragin, but, looking up at the clock on the wall, she saw that visitors' hour was twenty minutes away, and Mrs. Cragin would probably show up just as it began, as she did every day.

The nurse would look out for Mrs. Cragin and inform her of her husband's death as soon as she arrived.

After the doctor certified the death, the nurse closed the door to the room, and, informing the other on-duty nurses of what had happened, stood watch.

Sure enough, just as visitors' hour began, Mrs. Cragin came shuffling down the corridor. She was an obese old woman, very polite and appreciative of the attention her husband received from the nursing staff. The nurse liked her, because Mrs. Cragin never complained or tried to tell the nurses their duties or interfered with any of the routine of the hospital.

Mrs. Cragin was devoted in her daily visits to her husband. She usually stayed the entire time of the visitors' hour, sitting with her husband, talking to him quietly, even if he seemed not to listen or even care that she was there. She was the only one who ever visited the old man.

As the nurse saw Mrs. Cragin approach, she greeted her and intercepted her progress down the corridor. As soon as Mrs. Cragin looked into the nurse's face, a look of alarm came over her own.

The nurse led her to a pair of chairs against the wall of the corridor, sat her down, sat down herself, and told her the news, simply and straightforward.

Mrs. Cragin was impassive at first. Then scant tears, barely discernible, formed in the corners of her aged eyes.

"May I see him?", she asked.

"Yes, of course," the nurse answered. "He passed away peacefully."

The nurse silently accused herself of a lie.

The nurse led Mrs. Cragin to the room, opened the door, and stood back, so that Mrs. Cragin could go in.

The corpse was on its back, the eyes now closed, the jaw shut tight.

"Would you like to be left alone awhile?", the nurse asked.

"Yes, please," Mrs. Cragin said.

The nurse withdrew from the room but remained just outside the door. She waited there until Mrs. Cragin came out.

After some brief conversation about the removal of the body, Mrs. Cragin asked, "Did he say anything at the end, maybe about my visit today?"

The nurse repeated in her mind the last words the old man had said: "The beaten dog lies down in the corner and dies." She wondered what it meant, but her curiosity did not extend so far as to report the words to the widow.

"No, he didn't say anything," the nurse lied again.

Mrs. Cragin looked at the nurse blankly.

"Well, there was one thing...," the nurse corrected herself, as if suddenly remembering, "but, you know, the medication kept him asleep most of the time..."

That was why her husband had been so nonreactive to her recent visits, Mrs. Cragin thought to herself.

"He may have said your name," the nurse continued, not sounding very convincing to herself. 'Amy', yes, 'Amy'. I believe I heard him call your name...not at the very end, but earlier this morning."

Mrs. Cragin nodded. "Thank you," she said. "Thank you and the other nurses for all that you did for him. I know that you did your best for him."

As Mrs. Cragin shuffled away, she said to the nurse, "Well, he's at peace now."

196

"Two Faces of Despair"

The disintegration has already begun, a disintegration of body, mind, and morale. The doctor has told him that all medical measures have been tried and have failed, that the latest tests reveal the worst, that it is hopeless, the prognosis a virtual death sentence. He himself already came to his own conclusion that he is malignant, worn out, on a downward spiral, a done-for specimen.

The recurrent pains have become insupportable, and he is driven to desperate impatience by his creeping feebleness. His body has become repugnant to him; he repudiates his association with it. He has no prospects, and he is too sick even for regrets.

In the lucid intervals between his coma-like sleep induced by the painkillers, he reflects upon his situation. As he reflects, he comes to a realization. He knows that his death is imminent.

Contradicting both the doctor's prognosis and his own realization is a wish, the most powerful wish he has ever felt. He wishes *not* to die, in spite of it all. He rejects the facts, he refutes his own realization. More than anything, he wants to recover and live again. A miracle should happen. He wants to live, he is determined to live, he wills it with all his remaining strength. He tries to rouse himself, fight back, force life to reclaim him.

Despite his wish and will, he is getting worse each day, sinking toward death, as the doctor said and as he himself realizes. The truth, the truth as undeniable as his pain and feebleness, compels an acknowledgment that overrides his resistance.

He must accept what he knows. Now he falls into despair, despair at the imminent, irresistible, inexorable loss of his life. He had wanted to go on living, but he knows that his wishing is futile. And so, he abandons wishing for other than what must be. He tries to accept, if not embrace, the coming death. He accepts, he despairs, he is resigned.

But then, despite his critical physical state, he does not die. He does not improve, either. He lingers on, days and days of prolonged pain in the body and agony in the mind. He has despaired of life and accepted death. Why, then, does Death not come and take him?

Now he struggles and wrestles with a new impatience.

He is teetering on a pivot point, that pivot point between life and death. Just when he thought that he had given up wishing, exerting his will against the inevitable, a new wish arises. He wants to die. Before, when he refused to face facts, he wanted to live. Now that he accepts facts, he wants to die. . . .

In frustration of that new wish, the reversal of the old wish, he does not die. As if God himself had turned perverse and cruel, the dying one does not die, but instead lingers on in a life not worth continuing, a life devoid of hope, a life already let go of.

He wants to die, but he cannot, his will to die as stymied as his earlier will to live.

As he continues in his helplessness, he plunges into a new despair, a despair of death. Where before he wanted rescue, now he wants release; but that release is being denied and withheld from him. Death,—he has accepted it. Why, oh why, does Death not come? Why is he tortured by living on? He suffers an agony of impatience and impotence and hopelessness.

It is terrible to despair of life, but it is worse, much worse, to despair of death.

197

"Human Living and Dying"

The last wholly natural thing that we do is being born.

Well, that might be stating it in too extreme a manner. During our infancy and early childhood, we do live as little animals, but upbringing soon drives the nature right out of us. We learn language, we get educated, we integrate into society, we bond with technology, we gradually get turned into, and turn ourselves into, unnatural beings, that is, thinkers.

What lives is the animal, but what we perceive as our living is the mental.

The essence and substance of human life is the continuum of thinking, (we think). We don't so much sense and feel our way through life, as we think our way through it.

The organic would atrophy, if it weren't so indispensable. We must nourish and protect the body, if the thinking is to go on. We do take pleasure in the body, but we often do so willfully; we exploit pleasurableness, *exploit*, I say, because the mind is the master. The mind, expressing itself as ego and exercising itself as will.

The mind is ambivalent toward the body. Bodily pleasure is fine, yes, but what about the frailties and afflictions of the body, the pains against the pleasures? If it could, the mind would dispense with pleasures and pains, with the body itself. The body is a nuisance, a pesty tag-along.

We objectify, hold at a distance, our bodies. In our infancy there was a period of both delightful and painful bodily self-discovery, in adolescence and young adulthood some decades of available gratification in the sensuality and sexuality of the body, then, in middle age, impatience with the body's decreasing powers, and, at last, in old age, utter exasperation with a body broken down. Damn nuisance of a body!

As we find in religion and philosophy—(the body as ashes and dust, the body as cage of the soul)—, the mind passes negative valuation upon the body. The mind as ego and will even conceives of itself as that *soul*, immortal spirit. The mind would like to be pure spirit, but, because it cannot be, the body is the necessary container.

Real living, organic living, must go on parallel to, but subservient to, the operation of the mind.

The human being is the only animal that has convinced itself that its living is elsewhere than where it really is, in despite of the reality, the natural reality, that it is the body that lives, not the mind. Intellection is just a more sophisticated consciousness, and consciousness is a function of a living organism. We've got it all backwards. Nature hasn't given us a body so that the mind may be housed; Nature has given us a mind so that the body may preserve itself against threats to survival. Intelligence was not the goal; intelligence was the means;—that is the way we naturalists understand it.

It is not only the educated who think that their living is in their mind; the primitives and peasants harbor the same illusion. Intellectuality is not a rare attainment of higher education; it is a common psychological trait. Mythologizing is as cerebral as science. Look as hard and far as you can, you will never discover a *natural man*. The human is, through-and-through, unnaturally intellectual.

There is the natural within us, of course, the tenacious remnant natural. Gnawing hunger, desiccating thirst, and shivering skin mock our intellectuality. We think about and objectify the organic, try to master it, put it in its place, virtually repudiate it. Even so, we must eat and drink and clothe our skin.

The pressing sexual energetic, too, challenges control by the mind. We drive ourselves into one another in sexual compulsion. The moment of orgasm blots out intellectuality, strips the mind of control, but only momentarily. We soon recover our composure and return to our wonted ways and attitudes toward our bodies.

Birth is a raw experience of the natural, although what our personal consciousness of that experience was none can remember. The sexual climax is a reversion to that raw natural, but orgasm is momentary and episodic, a kind of animal fit we fall into. We should be better and higher than such lack-of-control behavior. Even when we eat and drink, we pretend that what we are doing is cultural and social, rather than simply animal.

Like religion and philosophy, science too promotes a devaluation and denigration of the body. Our most prominent contemporary cultural trait is the technologization of the body, first by devices that draw in the senses, then by devices that mimic human faculties, and finally by robotic substitutes for the body. The body has been detached from the natural world, the biosphere, and plugged into the technosphere.

Strangely enough, the scientific mind also strives to create a technological replacement for the human mind itself. The computer! Now, there's a mental aberration, if ever there was one.

This pitiful animal, this human, with its *life of the mind!* Trying to live somewhere else than where life really is, with the consequence of no life at all.

Look at the content of our lives and try to determine what its relevance is to real living. We need survival information, yes, but what good is the accumulation of all those other facts, knowledge, fantasies, notions, and dogmas? Well, we are learning about life, (we think). What we are actually doing is constructing an imposing edifice of anti-Life. Every single thought is a further departure from elemental living. The sum total of our acquired knowledge is a huge debit against our vitality.

What we live is not life, is not even reality. What we live is a megalomaniacal fantasy: "We are not just organic; we are intellectual, we are spiritual. We are not just a body; we are a transcendent mind and an immortal soul."

Our megalomaniacal fantasy is detached from real life and hostile to it. It is life-denying, life-suppressing. The totalitarianism of the mind is what makes the human the most pitiful animal.

Oh, this human body, this subversion of our self-estimate. Besides being born and submitting to sex, the other wholly natural aspect of human life is dying. What, you don't believe that death is just an event of raw organic nature? You think that death is an intellectual terminus, or, more hopefully, a spiritual transition to some *real* life?

It should not be surprising that we consider death in the same denaturalized terms as the other events of the organic body. We'll intellectualize death, spiritualize it. But in so far as we do so, we will deprive ourselves of the experience of it.

Our consciousness at birth was too inchoate to enable us to intellectualize the experience of birth, (although the mind might later pass judgment, "I wish I had never been born," or conjure scenarios of having been born in another place and time or to other parents). As for sex, it is too powerful, it overmasters us during the performance, but, there too, the mind will later criticize, regret, and then employ the will to reassert some control over future behavior. But death, we earnestly believe, will be fully subject to our intellectualizing during the event. We'll die with a last thought, perhaps the thought of becoming a bodiless pure spirit at last.

Might death, like sex, be an orgasmic gratification for the organism undergoing it? Might there be such satisfaction and fulfillment in death, the raw bodily experience of death, that the mind cannot imagine? "To die is different from what any one supposed, and luckier," surmised Walt Whitman.

Birth was a natural organic pushing-through a resistance. Sex is a natural organic yielding against resistance...And death? Who is capable of leaping over the brink without any thought of resistance? Death is no time for thinking. Yet, the human will try to get a last thought in...Well, death is the one experience we won't be able to analyze after-the-fact.

What's on your mind now, pitiful animal? Death, is it? Do you hope to subdue dying in yourself, as you subdued living in yourself, to flex and exert the same mastery of mind over death as you have had over life? A last thought, at the last moment. Any second thoughts in your last thought? Any belated realization of the privation of living by your intellectualizing of it all?

No, we won't *really* die, the mind tells itself. The mind remains hostile to all simple direct animal experience. The mind is the master of life, death, and everything else in the world.

The human is the only animal that thinks itself out of existence. And the last thought is...resistance against thoughtlessness.

198

"Flames of Consciousness"

The surface of the Earth dances with the flames of consciousness.

It was the sun that ignited the spark of Life upon the Earth; ignited, then sustained a small glow that burst out into scattered flames. The little fire of Life replicated itself all over the seas and lands of the Earth. And that Life evolved into consciousness.

And now a flame of consciousness, set sparking by the sexual dynamic, approaches an oppositely charged flame. The two briefly fuse into each other, then give off a new flame, itself charged with inherent polarity. That replicative process is an energetic of continuing Life.

The flame of individual consciousness burns for its time, then burns itself out. But general consciousness continues on. The evolution of consciousness has acquired a powerful momentum. There will be more and more consciousness, and it will become more sophisticated and complex.

We are aware of the consciousness of others—of all living beings and of others of our own kind—through our own personal consciousness, *ego*-consciousness. Generally distributed consciousness does not really matter to us; what matters is our own, the one sustained by the living of our organic body.

We know, however, that our organic body is mortal, and so, if our consciousness lives only as long as our body lives, then it must die with the body. But our minds repudiate the natural way-it-is. We fantasize an eternal continuation of our ego-consciousness somewhere else than on Earth. Metaphysics contradicts Nature.

We have spiritualized our animal consciousness. What we treasure is our *soul,* a metaphysical entity identified with personal living. The soul is the unperceived organ of our ego-consciousness. Metaphysical as it is, we say, it is also immortal. We deny that the individual flame really goes out.

The sun, progenitor of all the flames, is itself a mortal flame, although its lifespan is aeons. With the eventual extinguishing of the sun, Nature knows, Life on

Earth too must be extinguished. Nature would tell us that the extinction of organic Life will be the extinction of consciousness. Earthly life and mind both die with the death of the sun.

We have taken consciousness away from its dependence on a mere sun. The human mind has taken custody of consciousness. The sun, the believers say, was only God's ignition tool. God is the Cosmic Consciousness, and we ourselves are sparks of God, not sparks of sunfire. When the sun is extinguished, we will be drawn up (soul and body too) to sustaining closeness to the light and heat of God Himself. And then our consciousness, so sustained, will continue immortal, immortal like God.

We consider human ego-consciousness not a mere accidental epiphenomenon of the operation of the sun, but as the ultimate goal of God's creativity. What God really was about at the Creation, we say, was not a haphazard assemblage of myriad proliferating forms of Life, but a culminating perfection, the human soul, a consciousness derivative of that of the divine,—an *image of God.* The sun may die, the Earth become lifeless, but all that is insignificant. What is significant is that God has destined us to live forever.

We deny death away. Denial of personal extinction is the most significant *truth* our consciousness and mind have led us to.

We repudiate the sun and argue on behalf of God and his teleological Creation. The sun doesn't matter, nor does the Earth, nor the Nature on the Earth, nor the organic, nor the animal, despite the undeniable reality of all that. The ultimate reality, we insist, is God, the metaphysical realm, and the destiny of sharing immortality with God in His realm.

Our most fervently held article of creed is the cosmic importance of our soul, an importance that requires immortality. God the Creator will sustain us. Our personal individual flame of consciousness will never really be extinguished.

Human consciousness, fascinated with itself, wants immortality. Immortality-as-destiny is our ultimate ambition.

But our consciousness suffers its anxieties,—anxieties of total eclipse, of agnosticism, of extinction.

199

"On the Brink of Oblivion"

The periods of wakefulness are getting shorter now. There is a fading in and out of consciousness. The sleep is the blackest it has ever been, a dreamless sleep almost absolute. The wakefulness is not so satisfying; it is a half-awakeness.

During the wakefulness there aren't really any more thoughts. A fragmentary phrase, a few random unrelated words, or a name. It is not that the capacity to think has been lost. It is just that there is no motivation to think about anything. It seems that there is nothing left to think about. No energy left, either. Strange that thinking, a psychological process, requires animal energy.

Any thoughts under these circumstances must be demoralizing. It is hard enough to go through it, without suffering the analyzing of it, too. No thought is any help in the dealing with it. A lot of thought is planning, but now there is no planning to be done, for there are no prospects. Thinking, a spent faculty at last, now obsolete and irrelevant. He doesn't think anything about what is happening to him. He doesn't want to think anything about it.

Still, there is consciousness, those brief periods of wakefulness. How can there be any consciousness that is completely thoughtless? Thoughts arise on their own, but they are mostly incoherent, those fragmentary phrases, unrelated words, and a name. They are disturbing intrusions, but, fortunately, sleep intervenes to dispel them.

There had been pain, yes, but the sensations of pain, like the thoughts, are becoming fragmented and feeble. The body is doping itself against pain, perhaps more effectively than the narcotic painkillers. The numbness of feeling is like the drowsiness of the mind. There is little feeling now, nor is there any desire to feel. Pleasure is as indifferent as pain; neither seems real anymore.

Now and then a little glimpse of memory, a dim image, arises in the mind. The past makes its appearance in the present. But what does any memory of the lifetime have to do with this dying? The memories mock. And they cause pain. There is no stopping their arising, but now their appearances have been rarer, weaker, less disturbing. The memories are fading along with the thoughts and feelings.

The only thing left seems to be awareness of the body and of its pathological processes. The deteriorating, deteriorated wreck of a body now. There is an impatience with it, what had been an exasperation. The medical ministrations have all been futile. The inevitable approaches. Any impatience now is not with the body, but with the tardiness of the arrival of the inevitable.

Exhaustion has become almost total. If only there were enough energy for one last consoling thought, one gratifying feeling, one heartening memory.

But life does not have such a fine punctuation. Instead there is this lingering-on and wasting-away, not a torture by any means, but an ordeal of mind and body, and, worse, an ordeal of morale.

The only thought or feeling that avails anything is endurance and patience. Release will arrive, sooner or later. Anyway, it is getting easier by the moment. The letting-go seems natural.

The very last moment of consciousness. A blink of awareness.

Then, oblivion.

200

"Life Synopsis"

"Well loved, well lived," I gasped on my deathbed.

(*"Well loved"* meaning both *have loved* and *was loved.*)

END

Matters of Death

(Volume Two of ***Matters of Life and Death***)

Footnote:

Matters of Death has been about interpretations, ideas and ideologies, literary morbidity, and death incidents. What about personal experiences? Those may be found in the second part of my *Autobioscenes & Necrographies.*

Norman Weeks is an autobiographical and experiential writer.

An Autobiographical Letter is the straight-through narrative of a half-century of the author's life, relating the experiences that fed into the writings. Its companion volume, *Autobioscenes & Necrographies,* extracts and expands some episodes from that life. The first book is the panorama, the second some snapshots.

Also derived from personal experiences are several books of travel narratives: *Nature Norm's North Woods,* excursions into the natural world. *Tropical Ecstasy,* a nostalgia trip back to Brazil, to the town where the author lived as a Peace Corps Volunteer. And *Two Weeks in Eternal Egypt,* as a member of a tour group exploring the antiquity and sociology of that country.

Out of the author's deep experience of Rome came the trilogy, *Roman Ruminations,* "The Psychology of the Human as Enculturated Animal". Its three volumes are: *Loneliness, Instinct,* and *Love.* (The three volumes of the series also available separately.)

Matters of Life and Death (two volumes) contains further excursions into human psychology.

Culture-versus-Nature is the principal theme of *Walden Contemporaneous,* bringing the various values of Thoreau's book from 1845 Concord, Massachusetts to 2020s United States.

The author's one major work of fiction, *Symphony of Stories* presents its characters in the cultural contexts of art, music, literature, and our technoculture.

Throughout his varied writings, Norman Weeks expresses a cosmopolitan appreciation of our world and the wide range of experiences possible in one human life.

www.ingramcontent.com/pod-product-compliance
Lightning Source LLC
Chambersburg PA
CBHW070820250726
48662CB00003B/1021